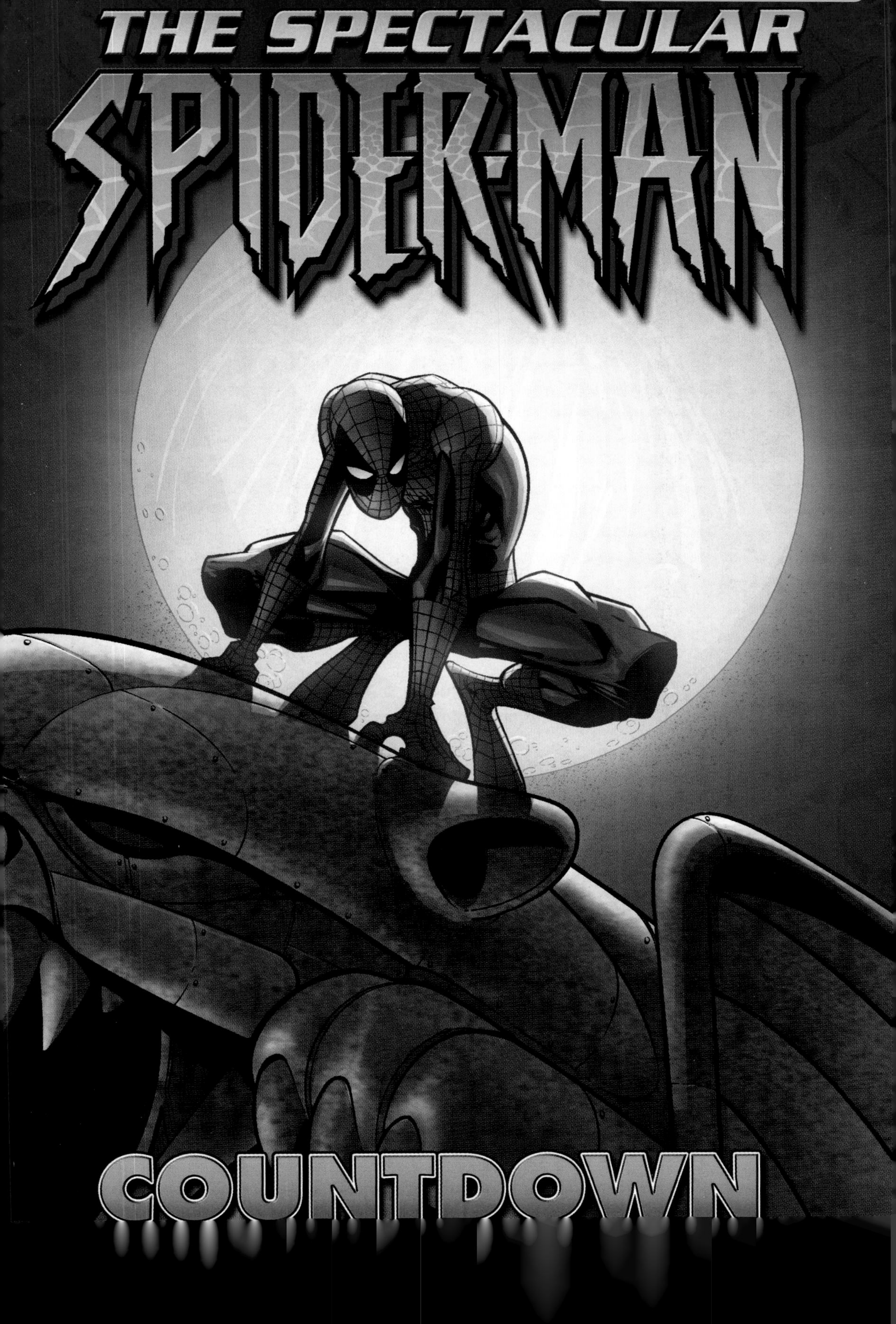
THE SPECTACULAR
SPIDER-MAN
COUNTDOWN

THE SPECTACULAR
SPIDER-MAN

COUNTDOWN

WRITER:
Paul Jenkins
PENCILS:
Humberto Ramos
INKS:
Wayne Faucher

COLORS:
Studio F
LETTERS:
Virtual Calligraphy's Randy Gentile & Cory Petit
ASSISTANT EDITORS:
Andy Schmidt, Marc Sumerak & Nicole Wiley
EDITORS:
John Miesegaes & Tom Brevoort

COLLECTIONS EDITOR:
Jeff Youngquist
ASSISTANT EDITOR:
Jennifer Grünwald
BOOK DESIGNER:
Patrick McGrath

EDITOR IN CHIEF:
Joe Quesada
PUBLISHER
Dan Buckley

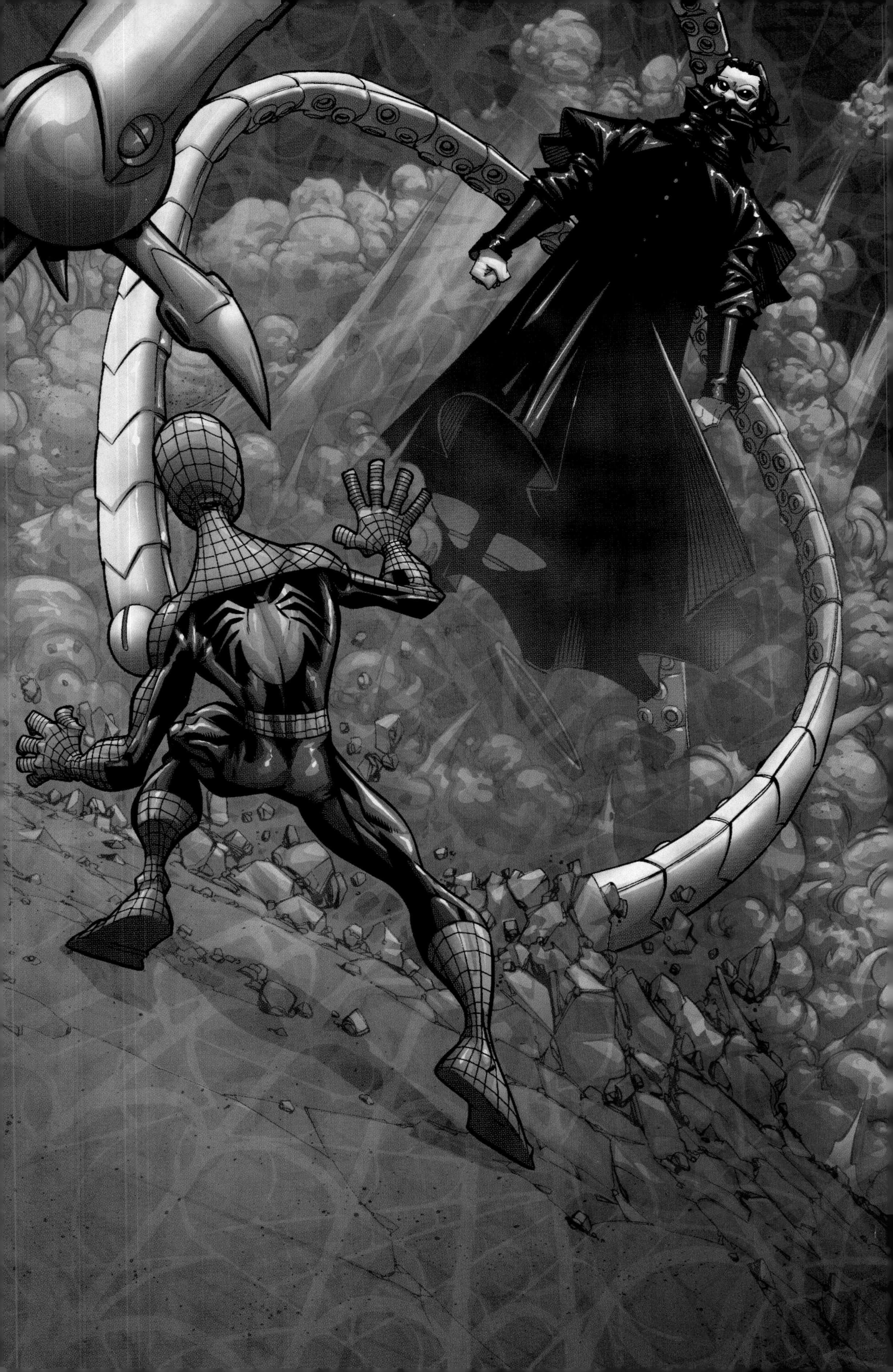

PREVIOUSLY...

Peter Parker

Mary Jane Watson

Aunt May

Flash Thompson

Doctor Octopus

Peter Parker's life returns to normal following his harrowing encounter with the creature known as Venom—a synthesis of alien and human who is torn between its need for Spider-Man and its hatred of him.

Venom has now disappeared, having revealed that its alien half is pregnant. Presumably, the creature has gone to produce its offspring, taking its hapless human half along for the experience.

Peter now returns to his daily routine: teaching at a high school in the daytime, spending time in his apartment building, and patrolling the streets at night in the guise of his alter ego, Spider-Man. Even so, his life remains troubled.

During a previous encounter with the Green Goblin, Peter's long-time friend, Flash Thompson, suffered an injury that rendered him brain-dead to all intents and purposes. Even though Spider-Man knows he could have done nothing to prevent Flash's injuries, he blames himself.

Flash has now moved into the apartment below Peter—his presence is a constant reminder to our hero that his life becomes a challenge every time he dons the suit and becomes Spider-Man.

For with great power there must also come great responsibility.

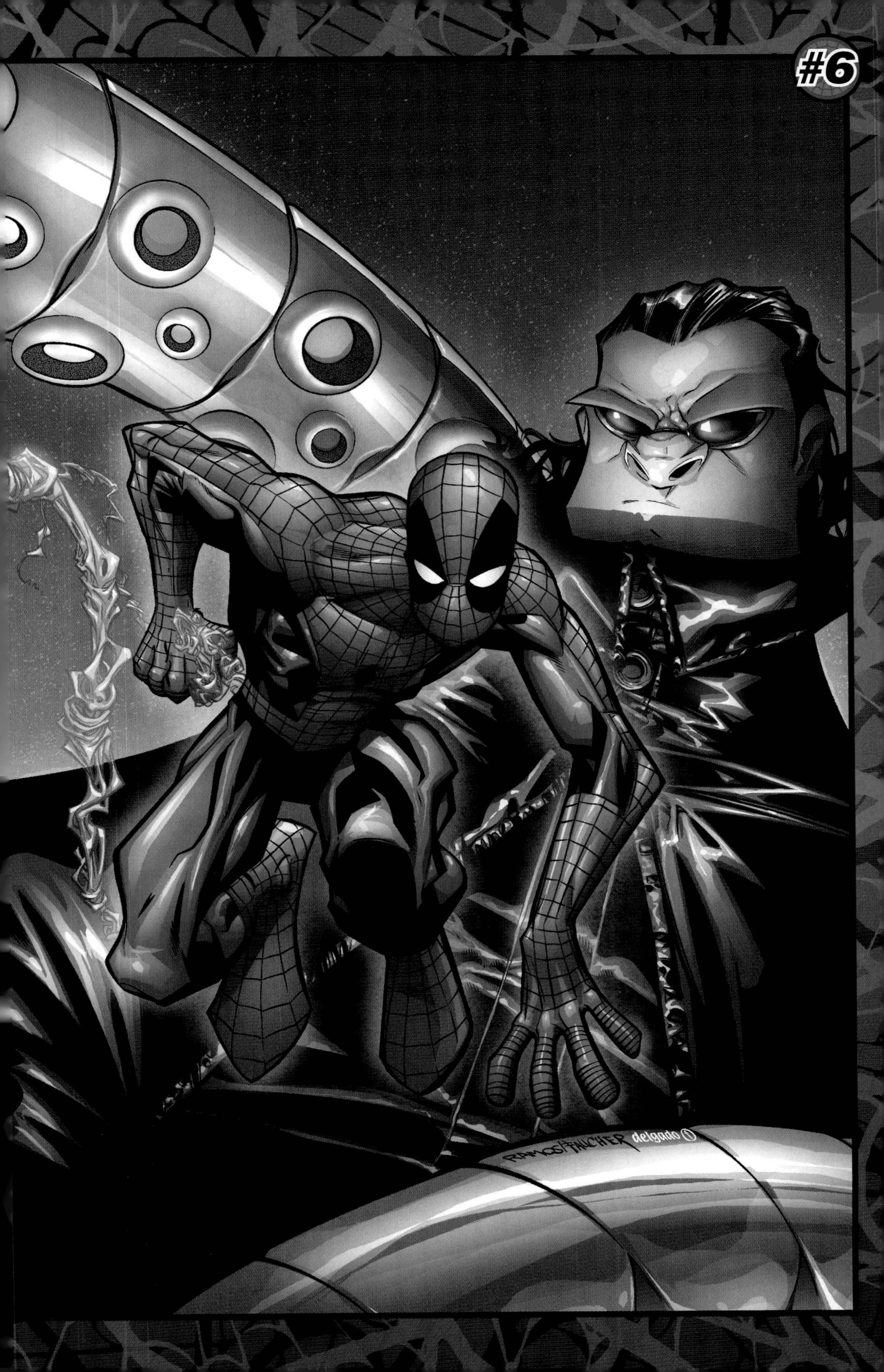
#6
RAMOS/FAUCHER delgado

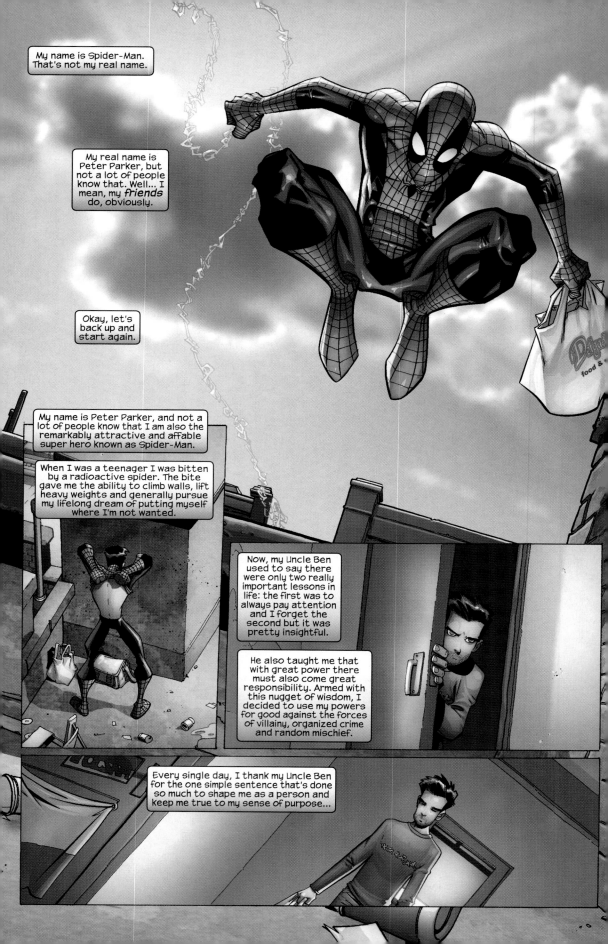

My name is Spider-Man. That's not my real name.

My real name is Peter Parker, but not a lot of people know that. Well... I mean, my *friends* do, obviously.

Okay, let's back up and start again.

My name is Peter Parker, and not a lot of people know that I am also the remarkably attractive and affable super hero known as Spider-Man.

When I was a teenager I was bitten by a radioactive spider. The bite gave me the ability to climb walls, lift heavy weights and generally pursue my lifelong dream of putting myself where I'm not wanted.

Now, my Uncle Ben used to say there were only two really important lessons in life: the first was to always pay attention and I forget the second but it was pretty insightful.

He also taught me that with great power there must also come great responsibility. Armed with this nugget of wisdom, I decided to use my powers for good against the forces of villainy, organized crime and random mischief.

Every single day, I thank my Uncle Ben for the one simple sentence that's done so much to shape me as a person and keep me true to my sense of purpose...

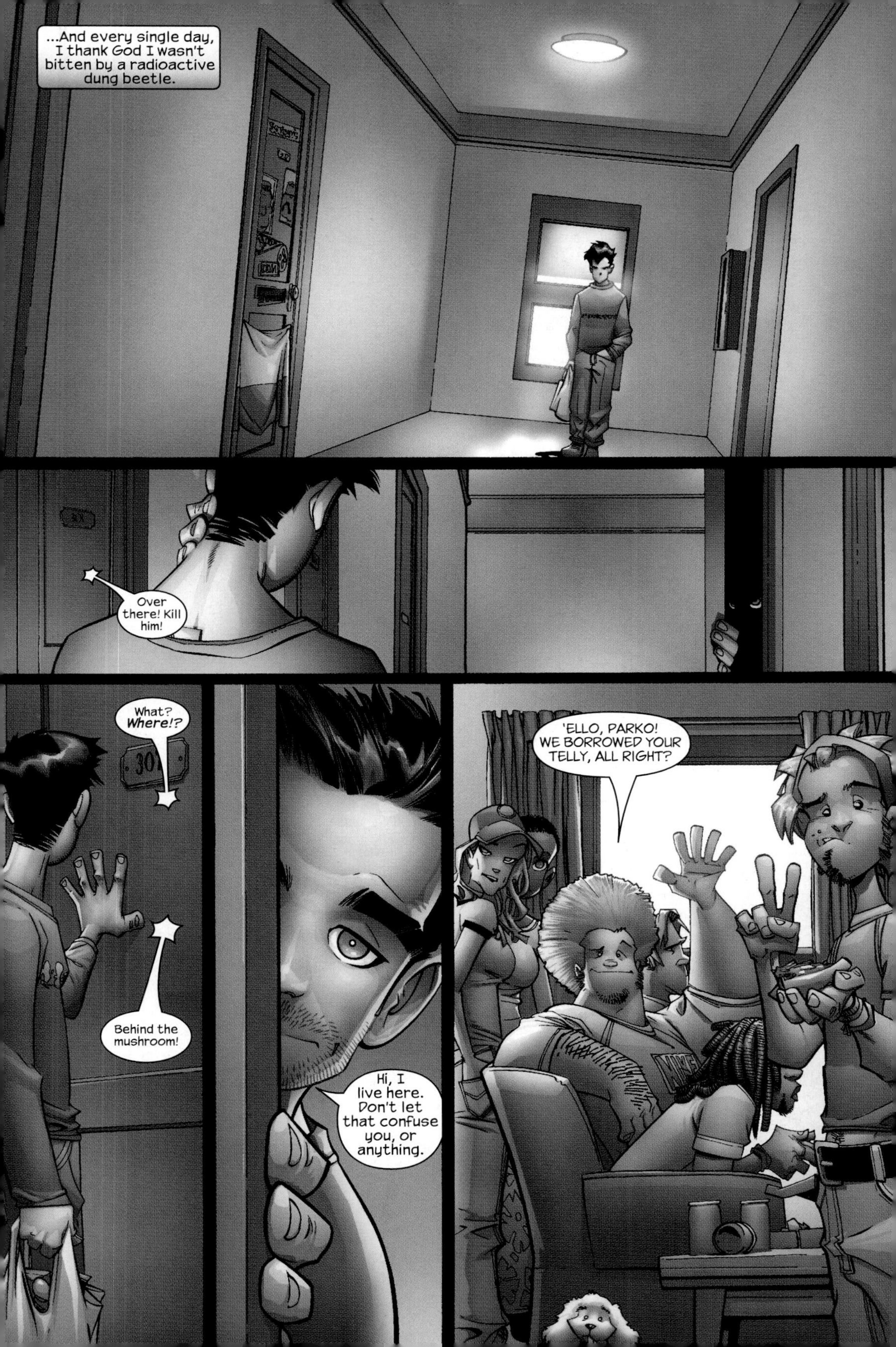
...And every single day, I thank God I wasn't bitten by a radioactive dung beetle.
Over there! Kill him!
What? Where!?
Behind the mushroom!
Hi, I live here. Don't let that confuse you, or anything.
'ELLO, PARKO! WE BORROWED YOUR TELLY, ALL RIGHT?

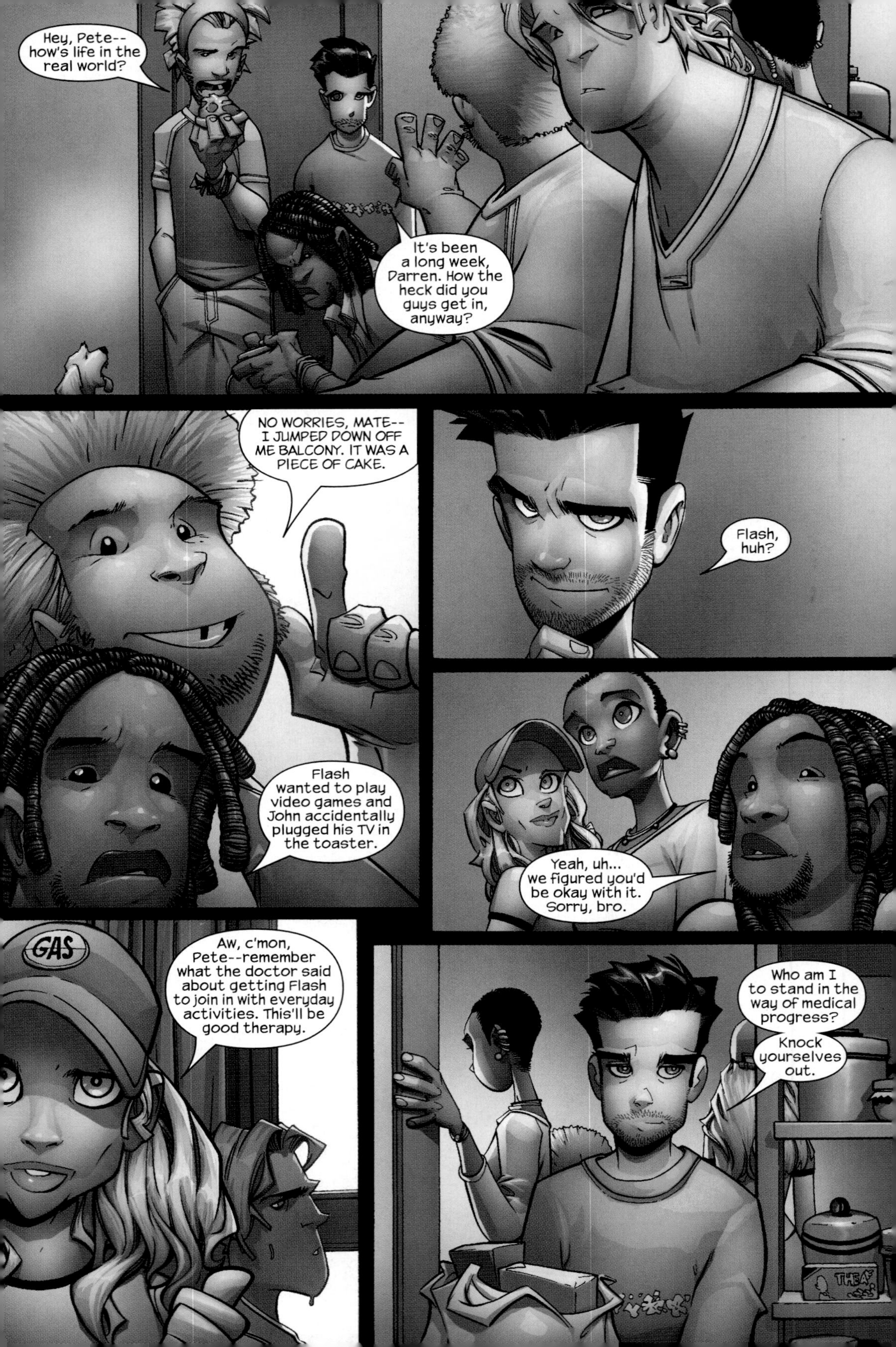
Hey, Pete-- how's life in the real world?
It's been a long week, Darren. How the heck did you guys get in, anyway?
NO WORRIES, MATE-- I JUMPED DOWN OFF ME BALCONY. IT WAS A PIECE OF CAKE.
Flash wanted to play video games and John accidentally plugged his TV in the toaster.
Flash, huh?
Yeah, uh... we figured you'd be okay with it. Sorry, bro.
GAS
Aw, c'mon, Pete--remember what the doctor said about getting Flash to join in with everyday activities. This'll be good therapy.
Who am I to stand in the way of medical progress?
Knock yourselves out.

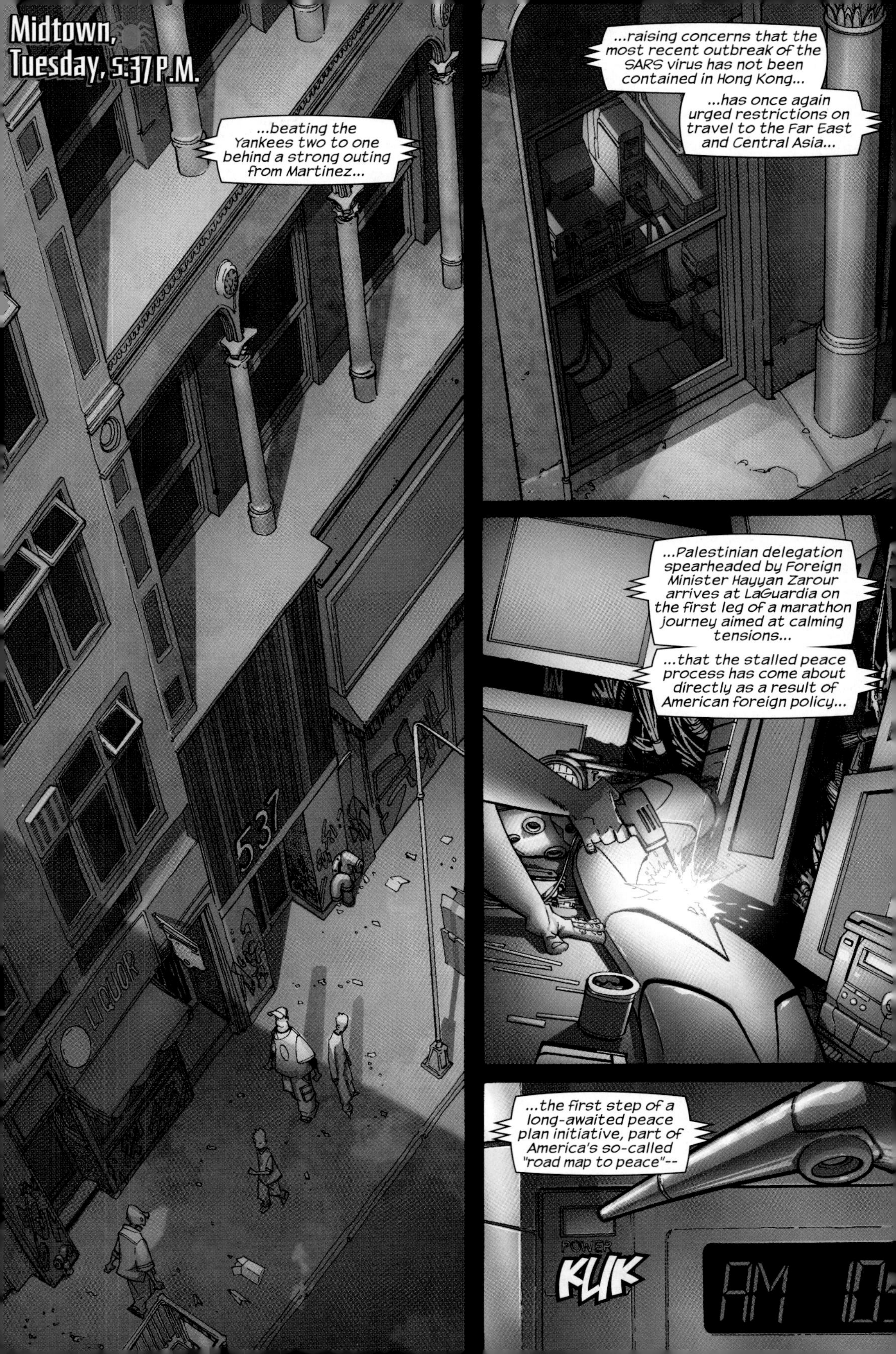
Midtown, Tuesday, 5:37 P.M.
...beating the Yankees two to one behind a strong outing from Martinez...
537
LIQUOR
...raising concerns that the most recent outbreak of the SARS virus has not been contained in Hong Kong...
...has once again urged restrictions on travel to the Far East and Central Asia...
...Palestinian delegation spearheaded by Foreign Minister Hayyan Zarour arrives at LaGuardia on the first leg of a marathon journey aimed at calming tensions...
...that the stalled peace process has come about directly as a result of American foreign policy...
...the first step of a long-awaited peace plan initiative, part of America's so-called "road map to peace"--
POWER
KLIK
AM

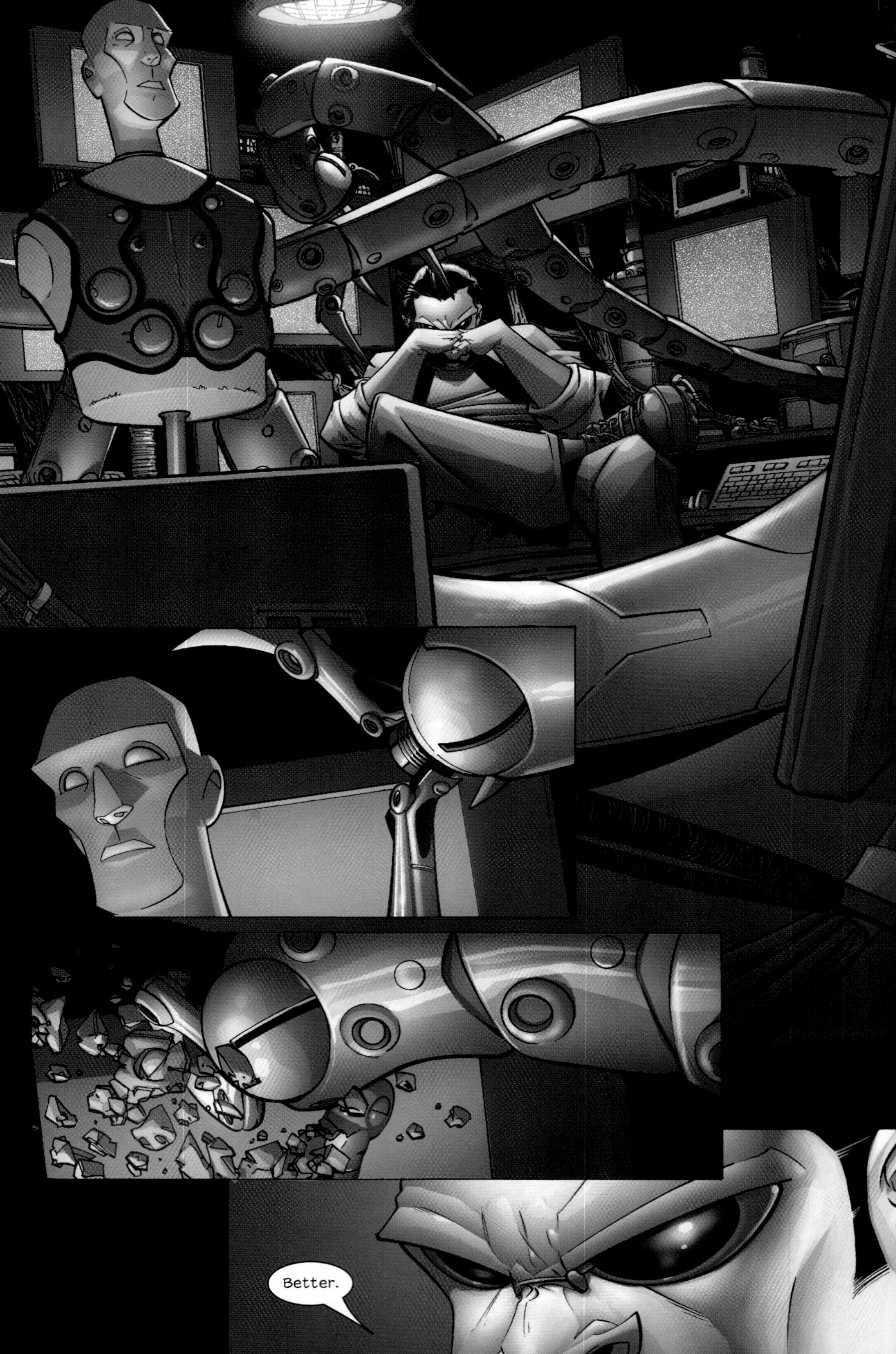
Better.

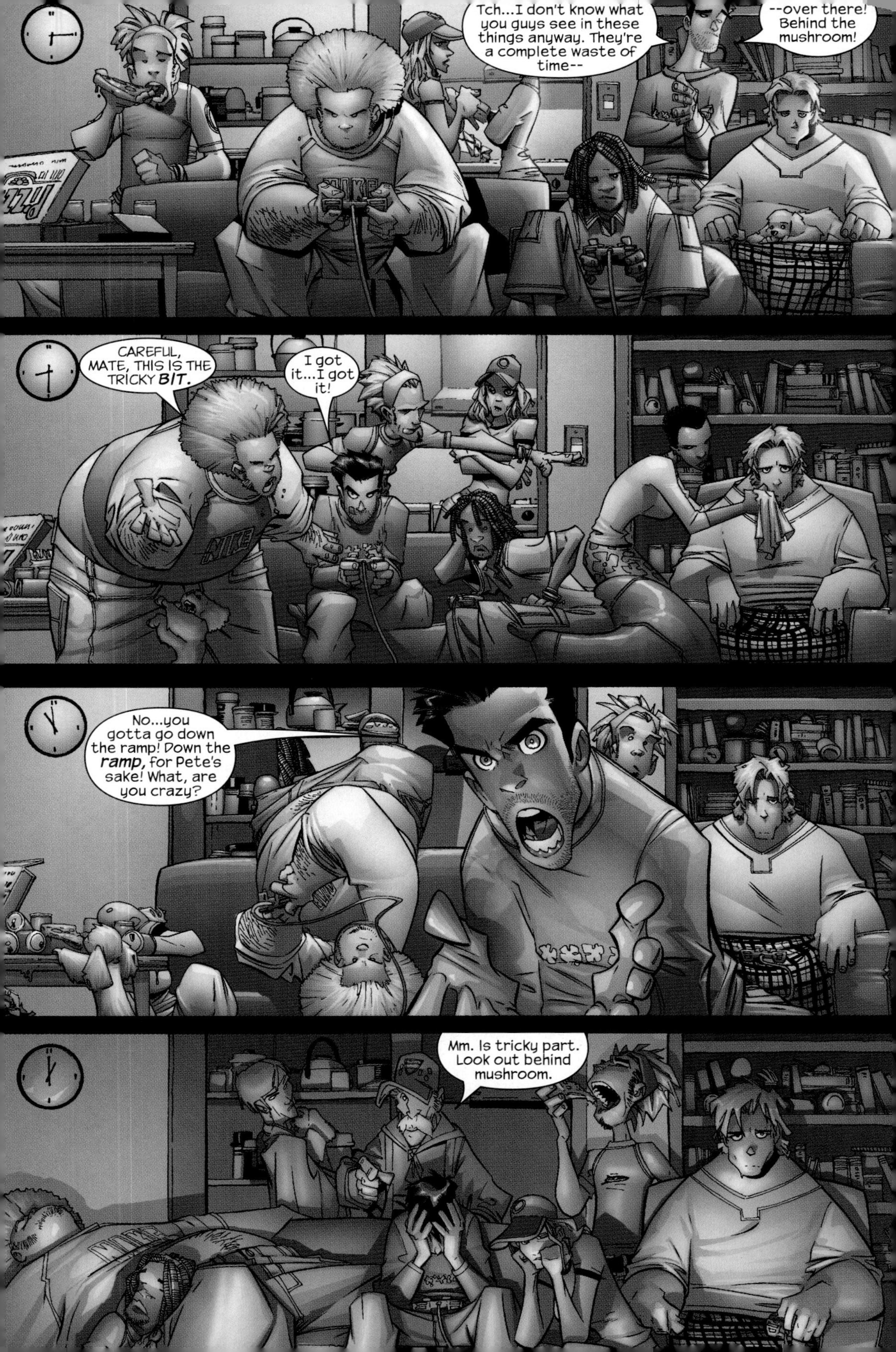
Tch...I don't know what you guys see in these things anyway. They're a complete waste of time--
--over there! Behind the mushroom!
CAREFUL, MATE, THIS IS THE TRICKY BIT.
I got it...I got it!
No...you gotta go down the ramp! Down the ramp, for Pete's sake! What, are you crazy?
Mm. Is tricky part. Look out behind mushroom.

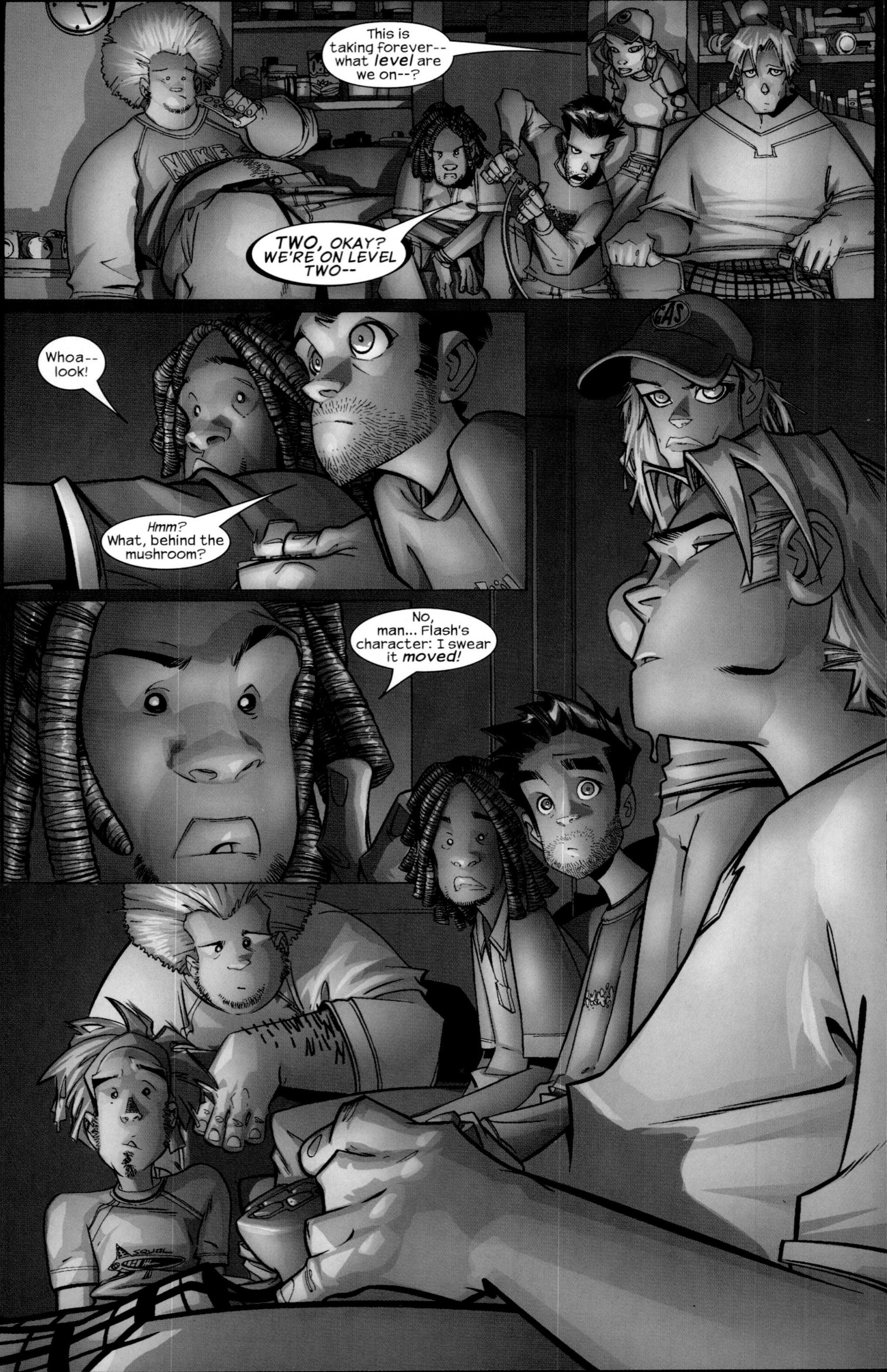
This is taking forever-- what *level* are we on--?
TWO, OKAY? WE'RE ON LEVEL TWO--
Whoa-- look!
Hmm? What, behind the mushroom?
No, man... Flash's character: I swear it *moved!*

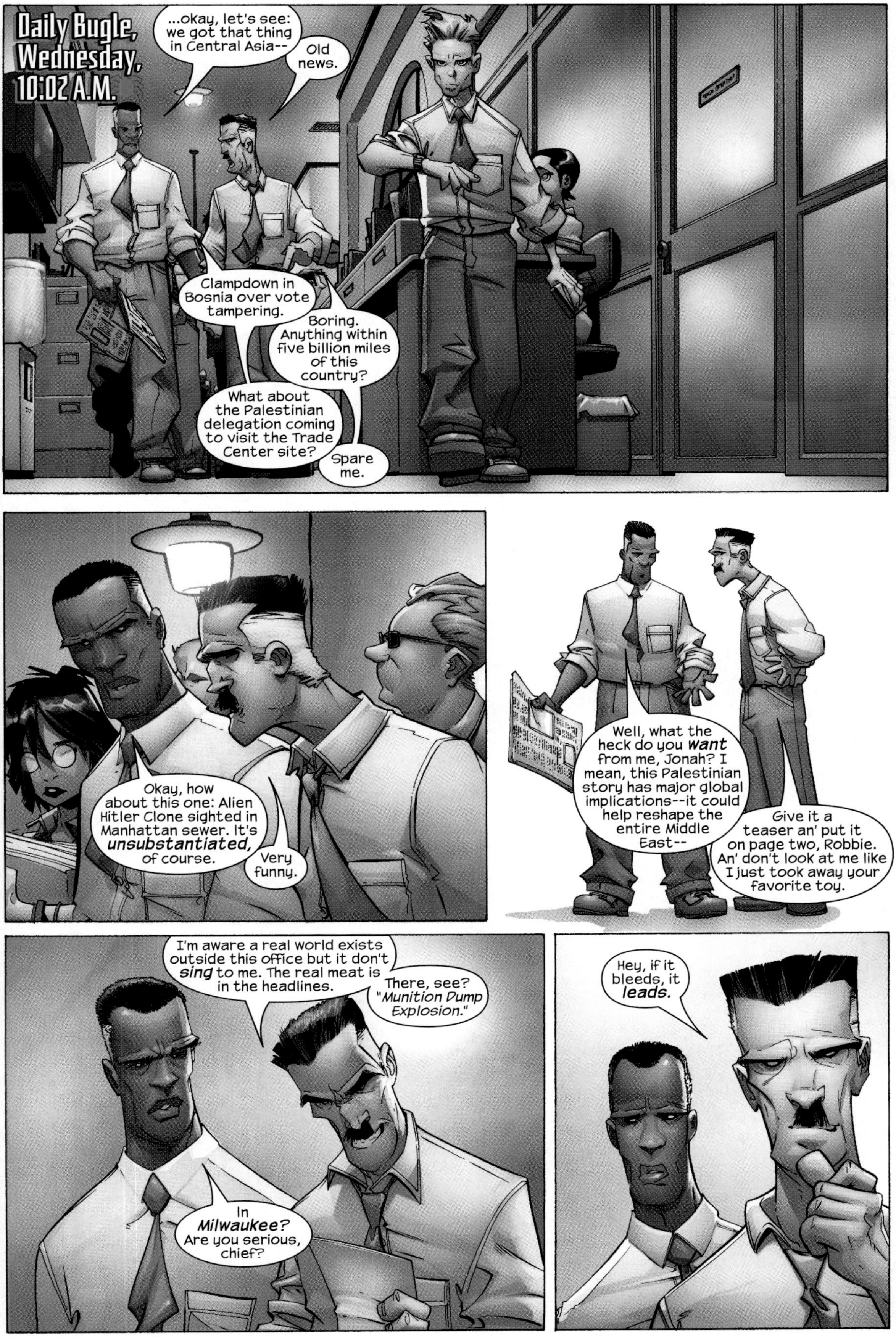
Daily Bugle, Wednesday, 10:02 A.M.
...okay, let's see: we got that thing in Central Asia--
Old news.
Clampdown in Bosnia over vote tampering.
Boring. Anything within five billion miles of this country?
What about the Palestinian delegation coming to visit the Trade Center site?
Spare me.
Okay, how about this one: Alien Hitler Clone sighted in Manhattan sewer. It's *unsubstantiated,* of course.
Very funny.
Well, what the heck do you *want* from me, Jonah? I mean, this Palestinian story has major global implications--it could help reshape the entire Middle East--
Give it a teaser an' put it on page two, Robbie. An' don't look at me like I just took away your favorite toy.
I'm aware a real world exists outside this office but it don't *sing* to me. The real meat is in the headlines.
There, see? "*Munition Dump Explosion.*"
In *Milwaukee?* Are you serious, chief?
Hey, if it bleeds, it *leads.*

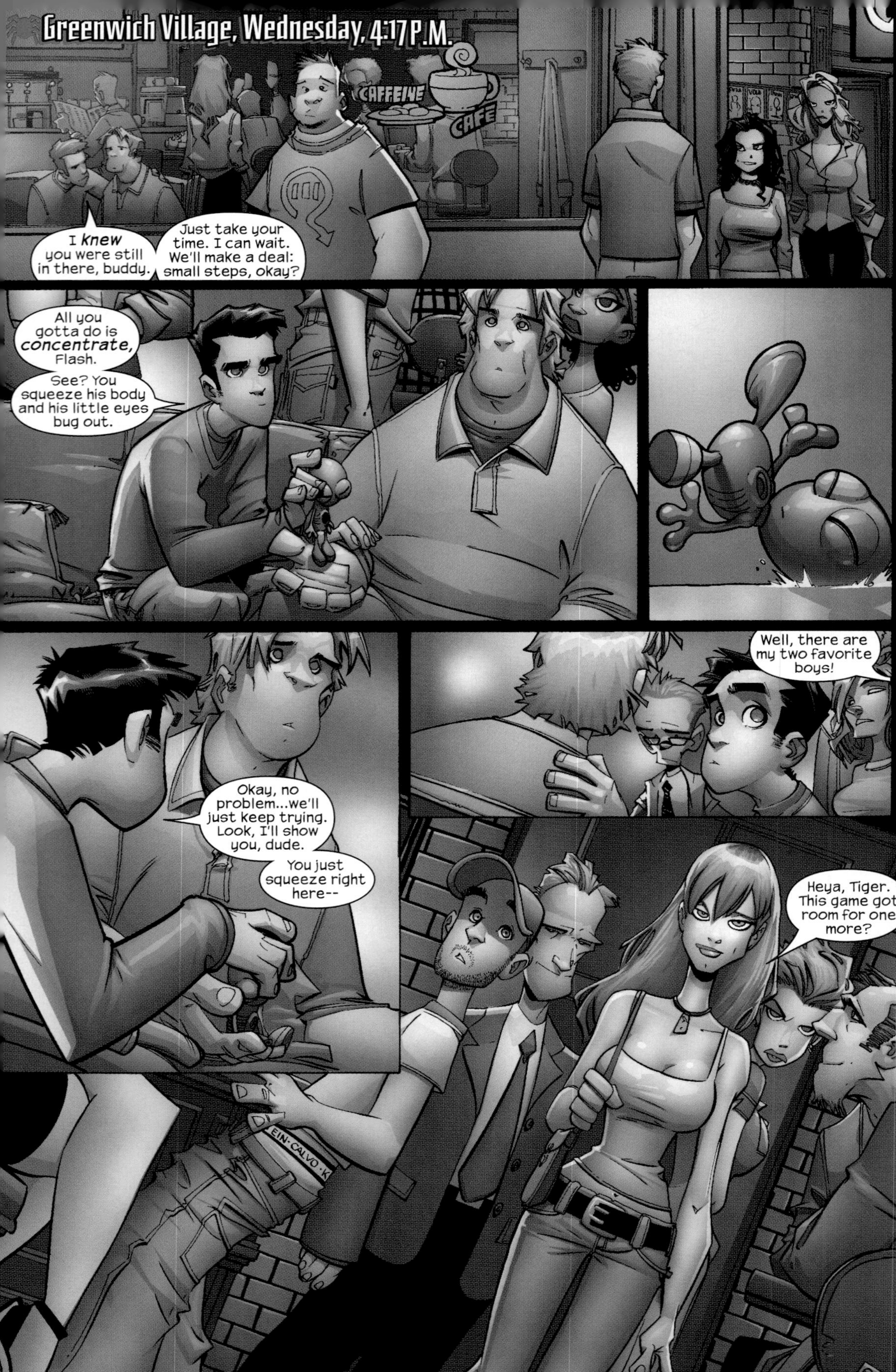

Greenwich Village, Wednesday, 4:17 P.M.
CAFFEINE
CAFE
I *knew* you were still in there, buddy.
Just take your time. I can wait. We'll make a deal: small steps, okay?
All you gotta do is *concentrate,* Flash.
See? You squeeze his body and his little eyes bug out.
Okay, no problem...we'll just keep trying. Look, I'll show you, dude.
You just squeeze right here--
Well, there are my two favorite boys!
Heya, Tiger. This game got room for one more?

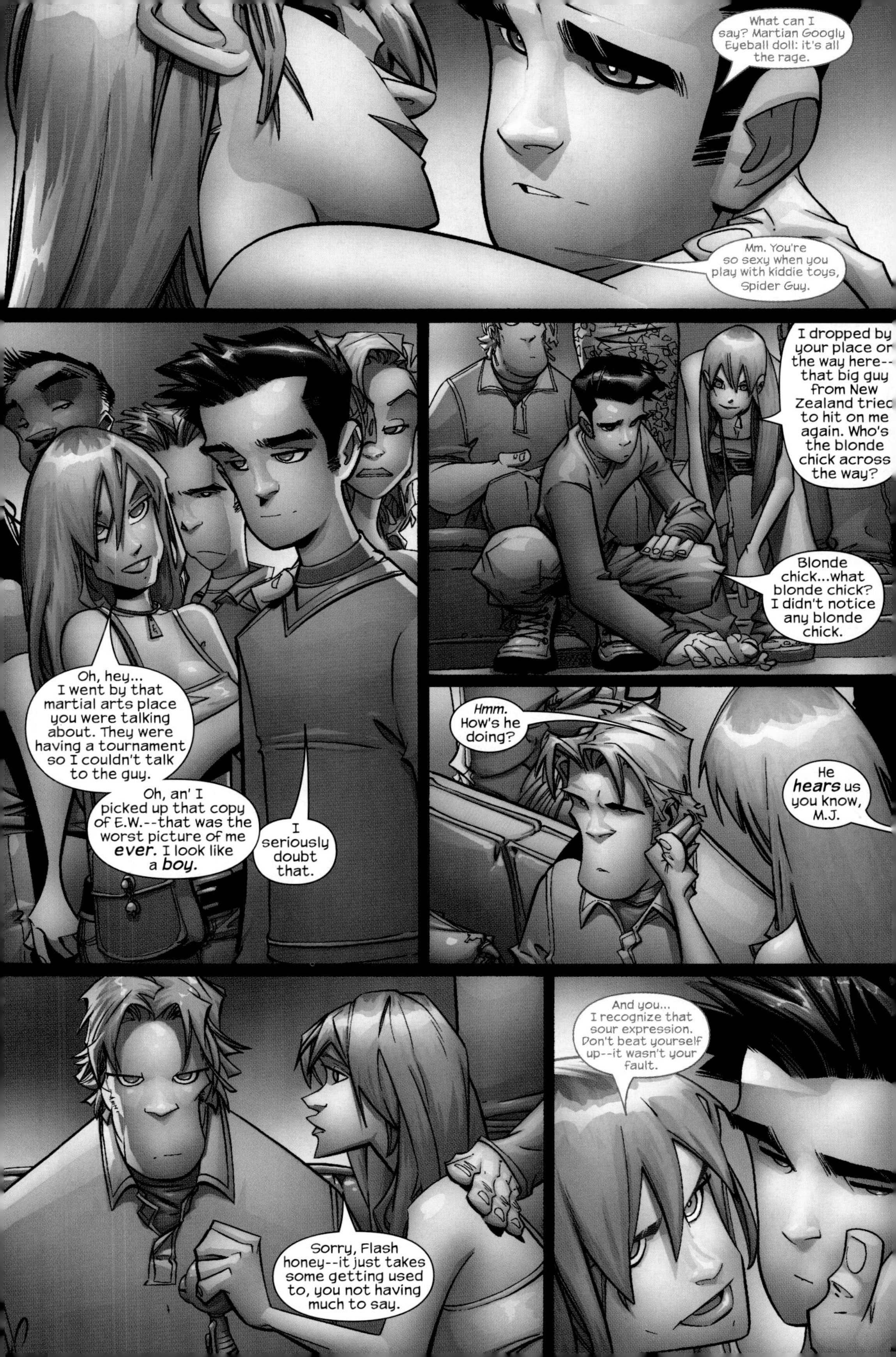
What can I say? Martian Googly Eyeball doll: it's all the rage.
Mm. You're so sexy when you play with kiddie toys, Spider Guy.
Oh, hey... I went by that martial arts place you were talking about. They were having a tournament so I couldn't talk to the guy.
Oh, an' I picked up that copy of E.W.--that was the worst picture of me *ever*. I look like a *boy*.
I seriously doubt that.
I dropped by your place on the way here--that big guy from New Zealand tried to hit on me again. Who's the blonde chick across the way?
Blonde chick...what blonde chick? I didn't notice any blonde chick.
Hmm. How's he doing?
He *hears* us you know, M.J.
Sorry, Flash honey--it just takes some getting used to, you not having much to say.
And you... I recognize that sour expression. Don't beat yourself up--it wasn't your fault.

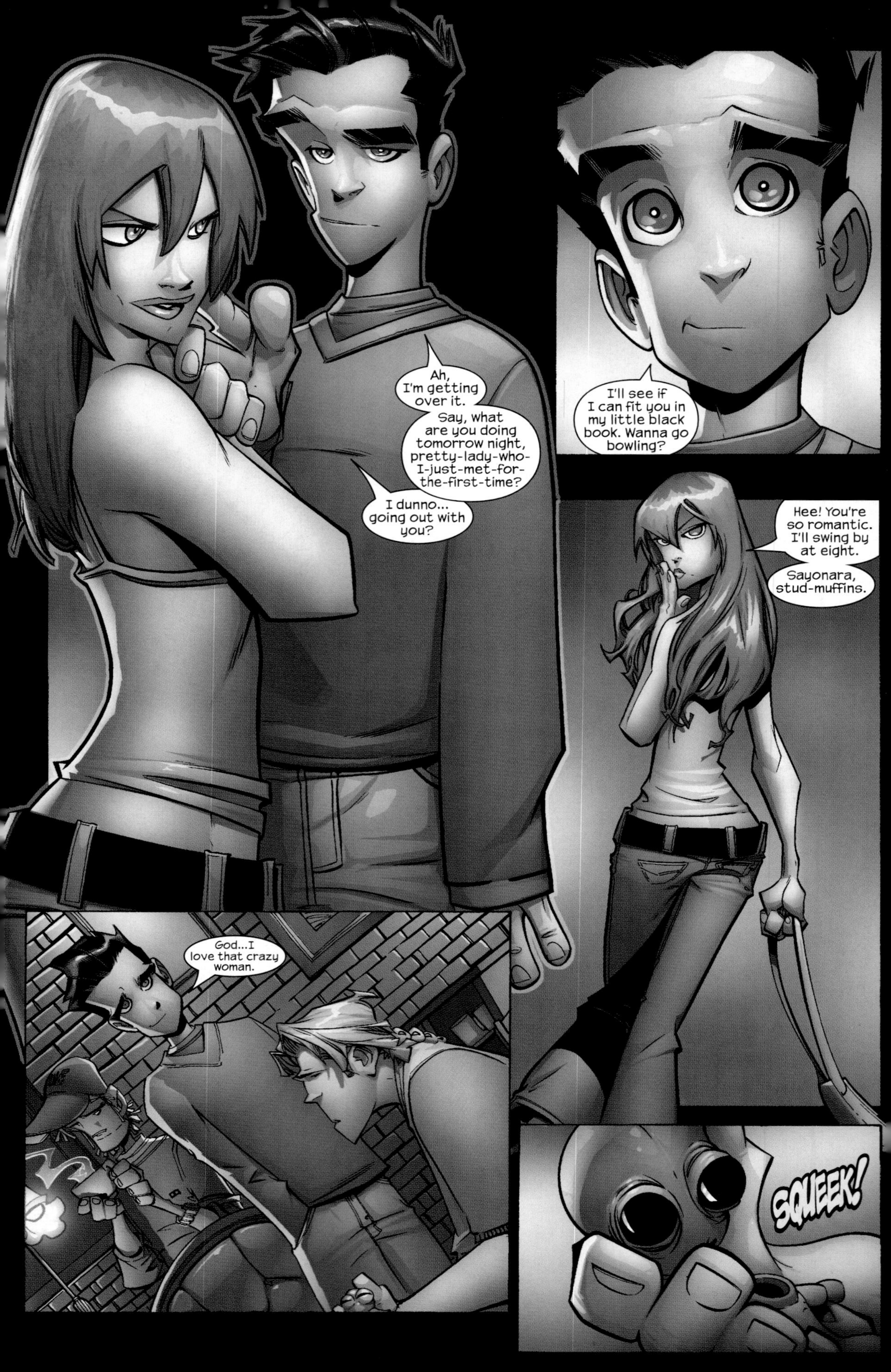

Ah, I'm getting over it.
Say, what are you doing tomorrow night, pretty-lady-who-I-just-met-for-the-first-time?
I dunno... going out with you?
I'll see if I can fit you in my little black book. Wanna go bowling?
Hee! You're so romantic. I'll swing by at eight.
Sayonara, stud-muffins.
God...I love that crazy woman.
SQUEEK!

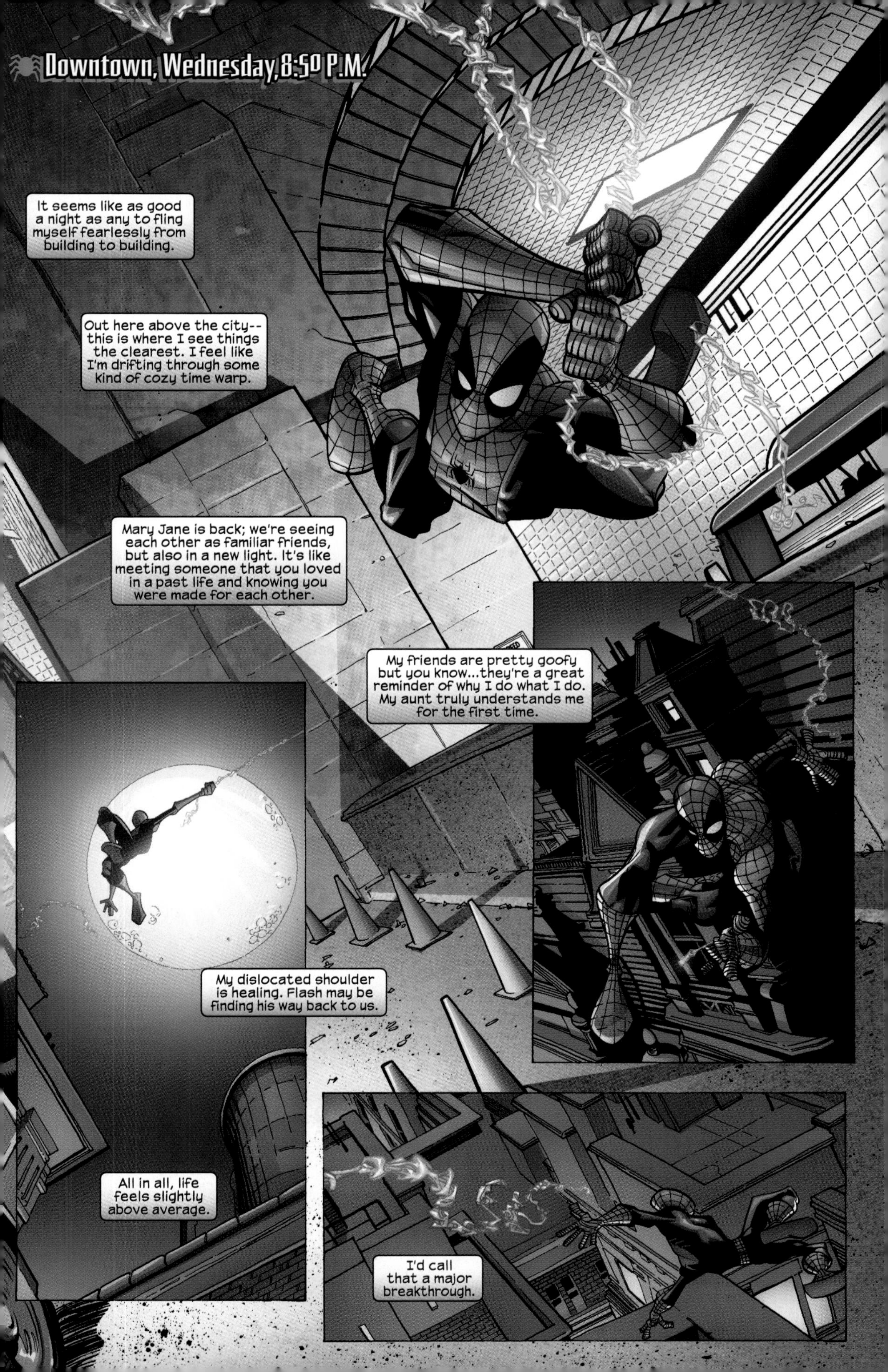
Downtown, Wednesday, 8:50 P.M.
It seems like as good a night as any to fling myself fearlessly from building to building.
Out here above the city-- this is where I see things the clearest. I feel like I'm drifting through some kind of cozy time warp.
Mary Jane is back; we're seeing each other as familiar friends, but also in a new light. It's like meeting someone that you loved in a past life and knowing you were made for each other.
My friends are pretty goofy but you know...they're a great reminder of why I do what I do. My aunt truly understands me for the first time.
My dislocated shoulder is healing. Flash may be finding his way back to us.
All in all, life feels slightly above average.
I'd call that a major breakthrough.

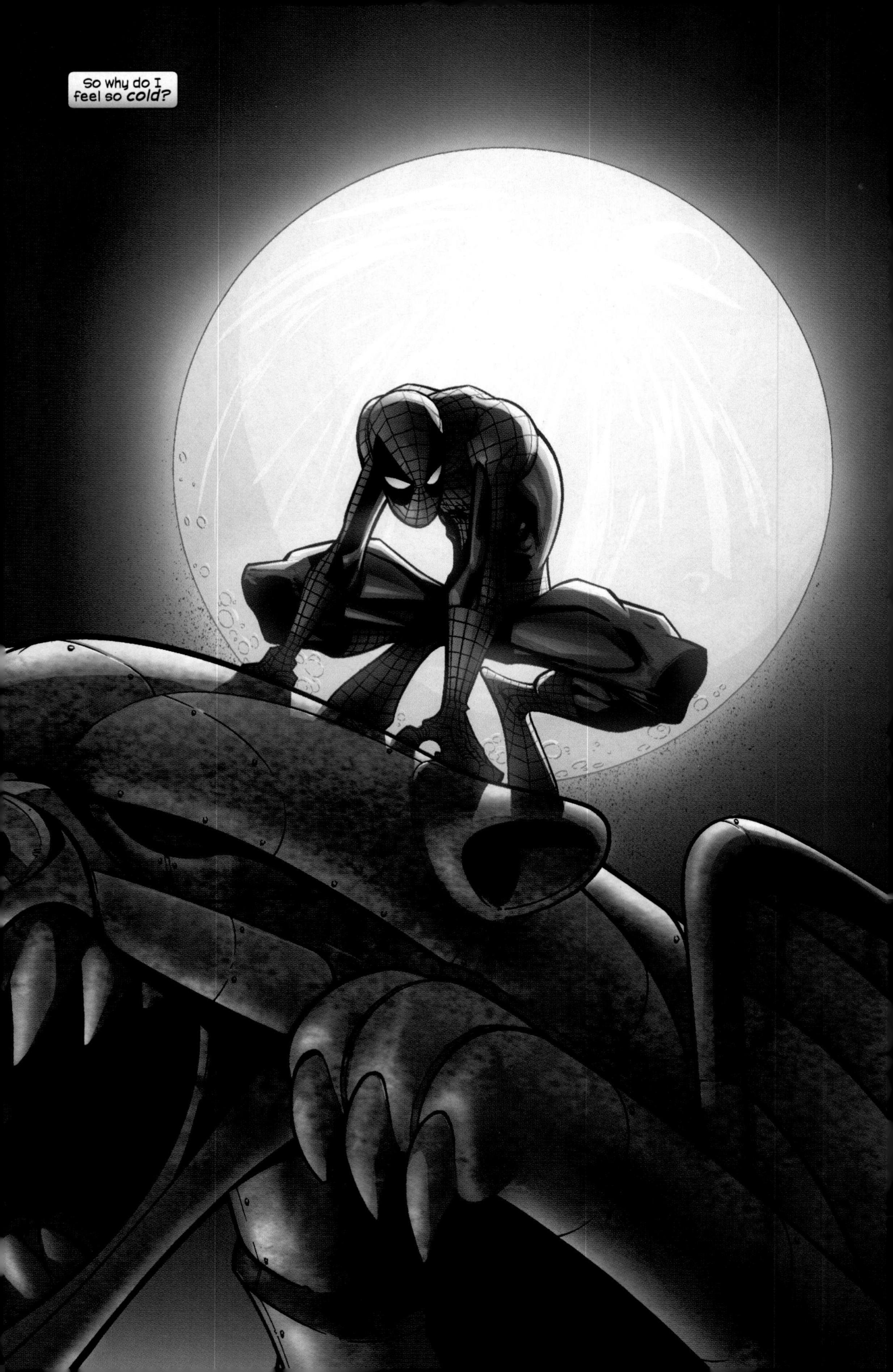
So why do I
feel so cold?

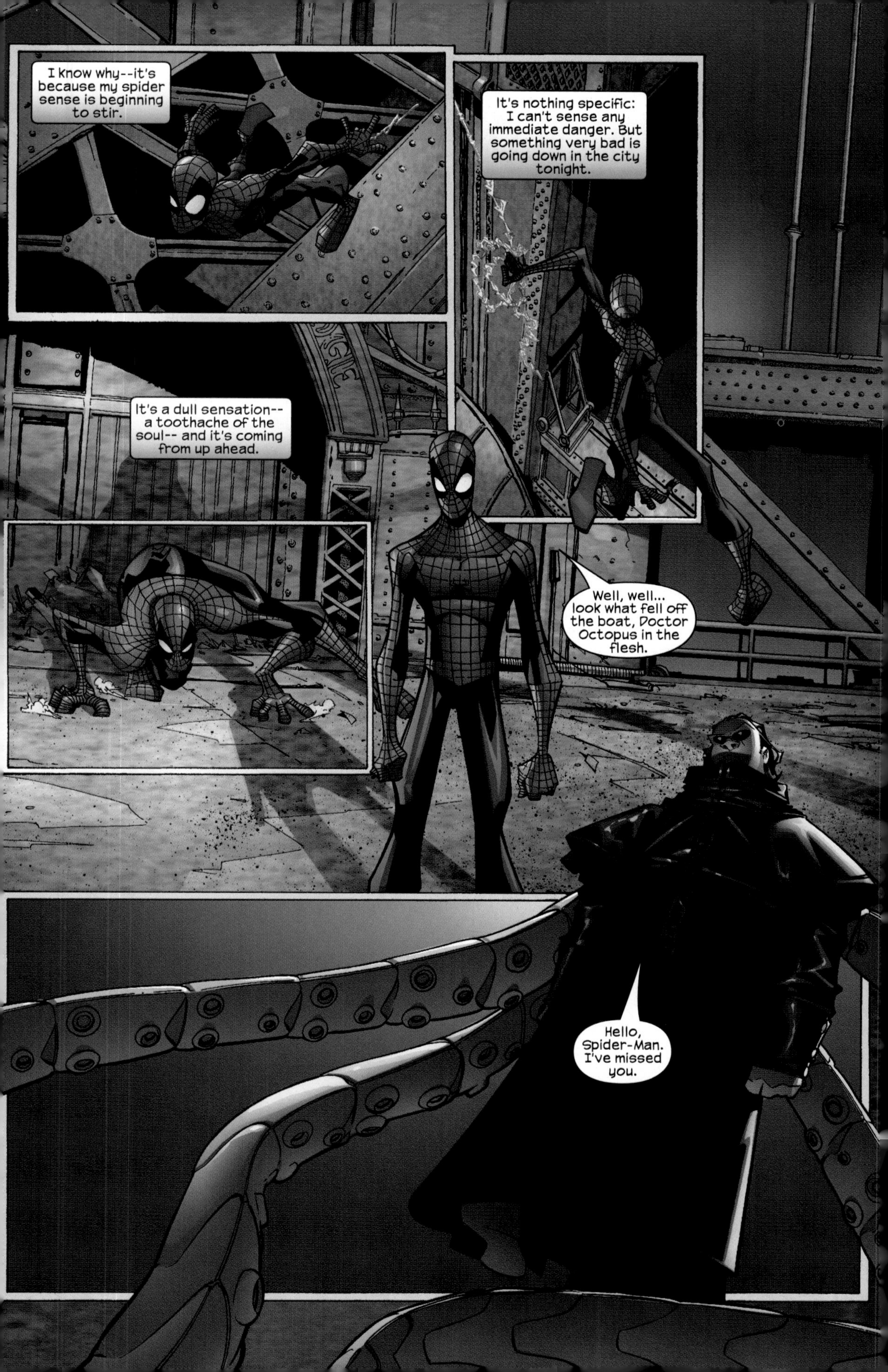
I know why--it's because my spider sense is beginning to stir.
It's nothing specific: I can't sense any immediate danger. But something very bad is going down in the city tonight.
It's a dull sensation-- a toothache of the soul-- and it's coming from up ahead.
Well, well... look what fell off the boat, Doctor Octopus in the flesh.
Hello, Spider-Man. I've missed you.

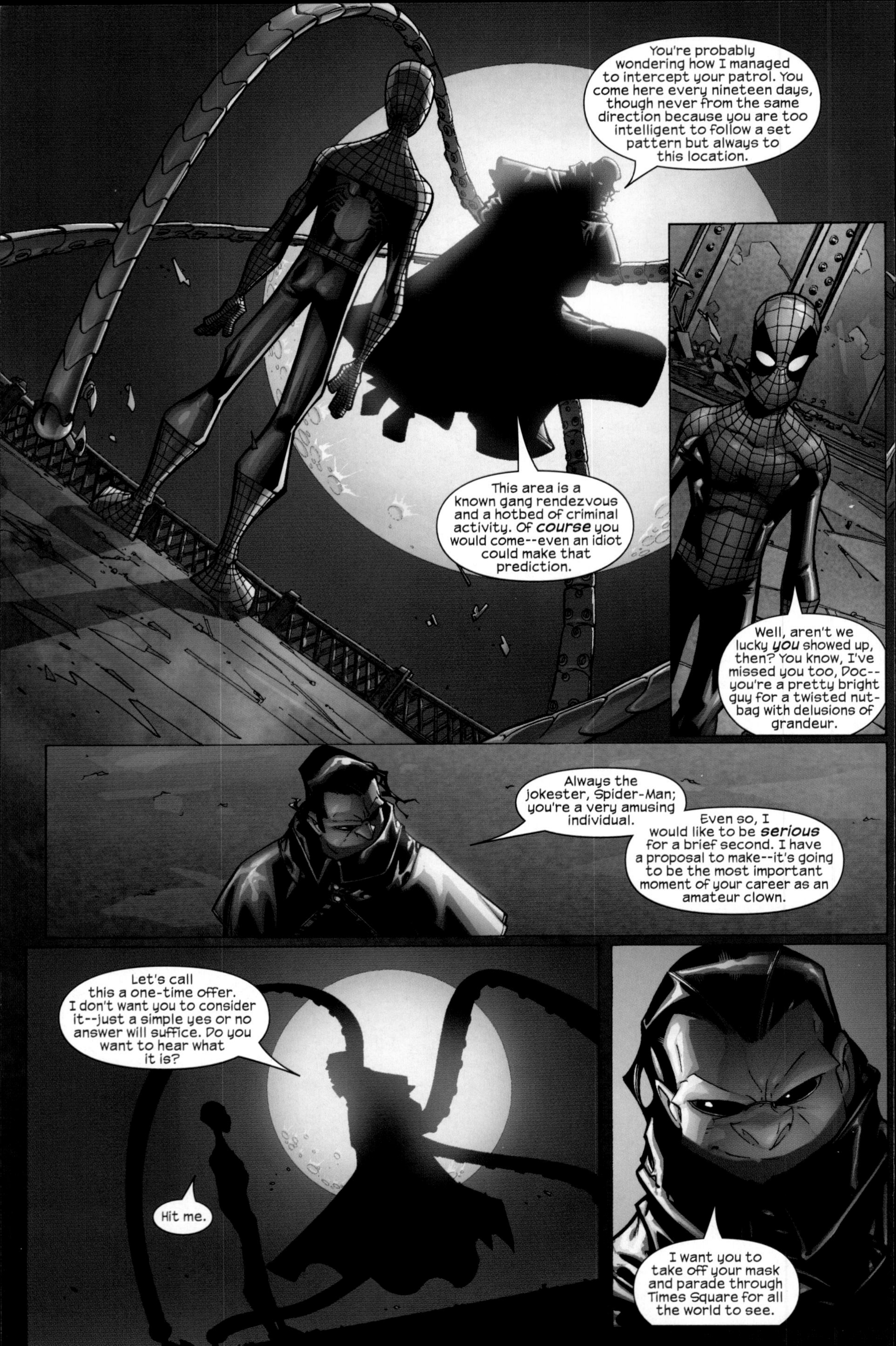
You're probably wondering how I managed to intercept your patrol. You come here every nineteen days, though never from the same direction because you are too intelligent to follow a set pattern but always to this location.
This area is a known gang rendezvous and a hotbed of criminal activity. Of *course* you would come--even an idiot could make that prediction.
Well, aren't we lucky *you* showed up, then? You know, I've missed you too, Doc--you're a pretty bright guy for a twisted nut-bag with delusions of grandeur.
Always the jokester, Spider-Man; you're a very amusing individual.
Even so, I would like to be *serious* for a brief second. I have a proposal to make--it's going to be the most important moment of your career as an amateur clown.
Let's call this a one-time offer. I don't want you to consider it--just a simple yes or no answer will suffice. Do you want to hear what it is?
Hit me.
I want you to take off your mask and parade through Times Square for all the world to see.

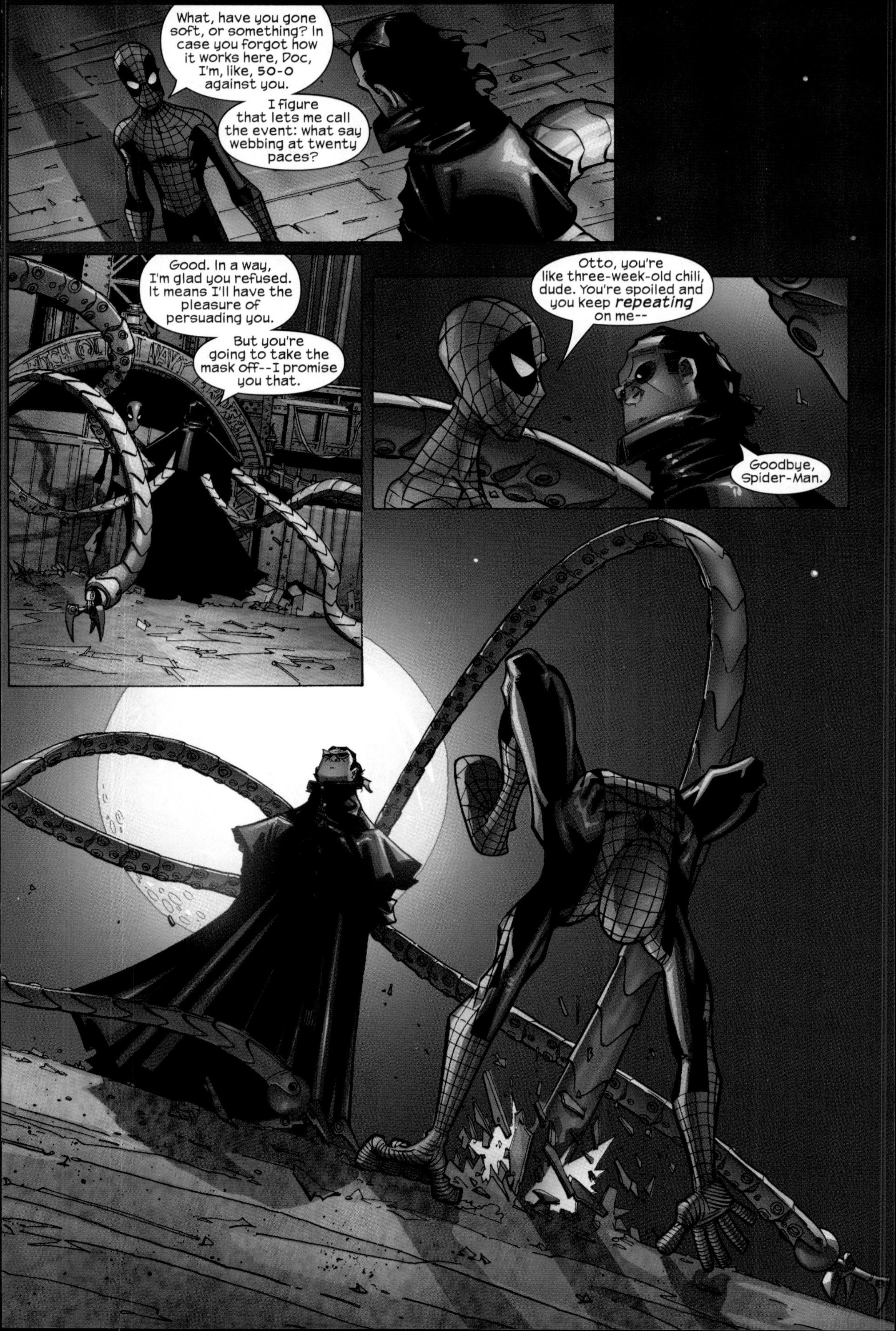
What, have you gone soft, or something? In case you forgot how it works here, Doc, I'm, like, 50-0 against you.
I figure that lets me call the event: what say webbing at twenty paces?
Good. In a way, I'm glad you refused. It means I'll have the pleasure of persuading you.
But you're going to take the mask off--I promise you that.
Otto, you're like three-week-old chili, dude. You're spoiled and you keep *repeating* on me--
Goodbye, Spider-Man.

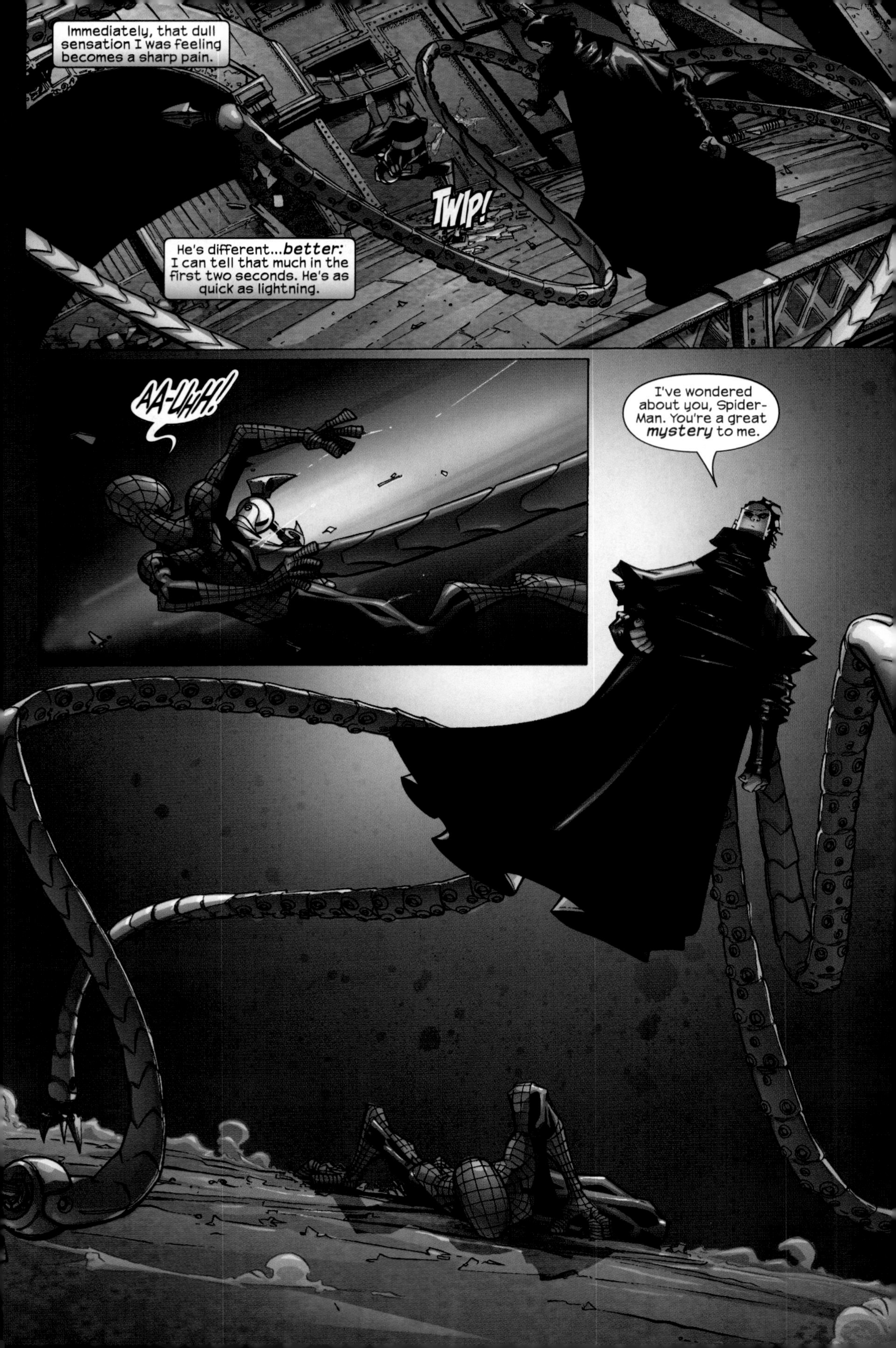

Immediately, that dull sensation I was feeling becomes a sharp pain.
TWIP!
He's different...*better:* I can tell that much in the first two seconds. He's as quick as lightning.
AA-UHH!
I've wondered about you, Spider-Man. You're a great *mystery* to me.

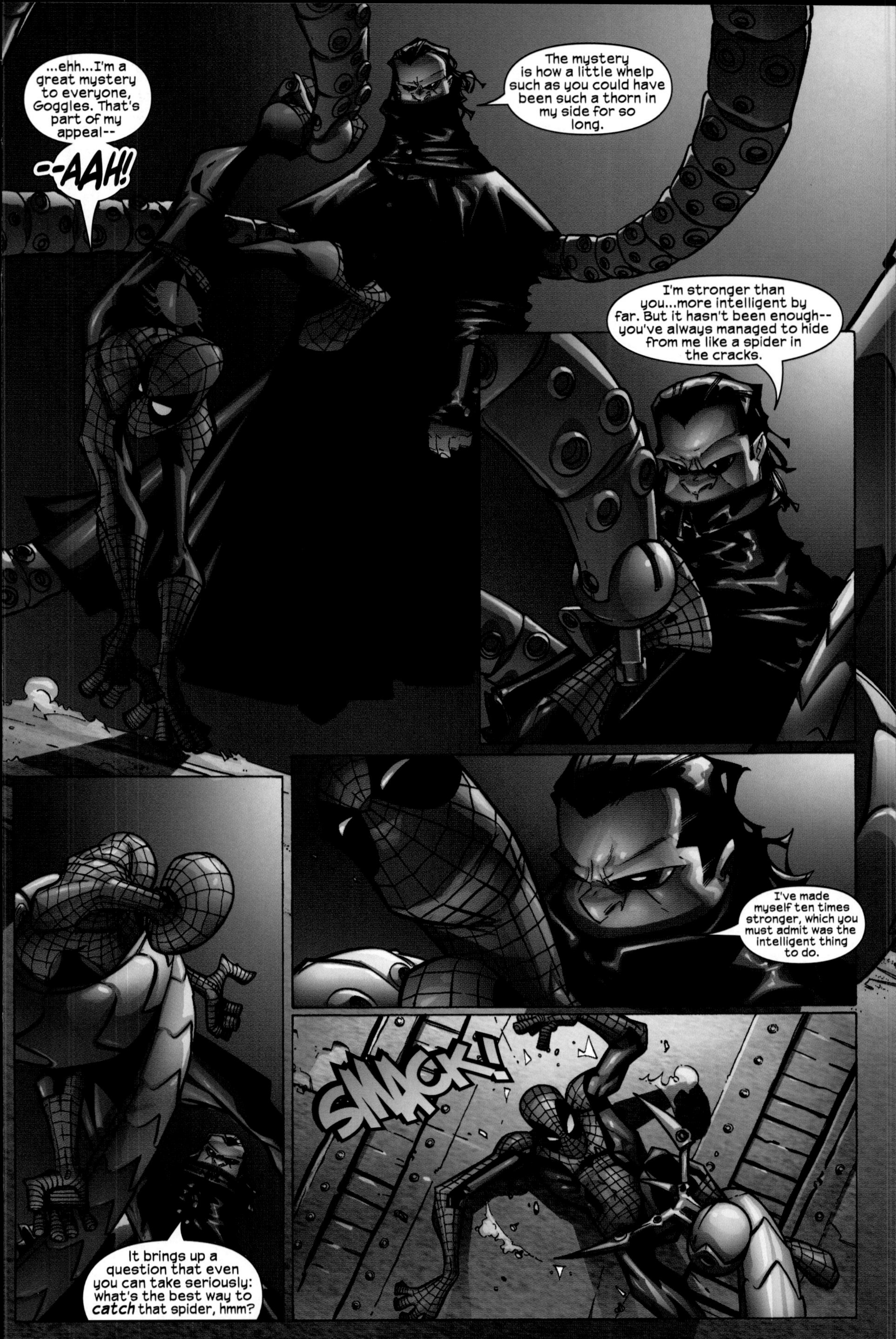
...ehh...I'm a great mystery to everyone, Goggles. That's part of my appeal--
--AAH!
The mystery is how a little whelp such as you could have been such a thorn in my side for so long.
I'm stronger than you...more intelligent by far. But it hasn't been enough--you've always managed to hide from me like a spider in the cracks.
I've made myself ten times stronger, which you must admit was the intelligent thing to do.
It brings up a question that even you can take seriously: what's the best way to catch that spider, hmm?
SMACK!

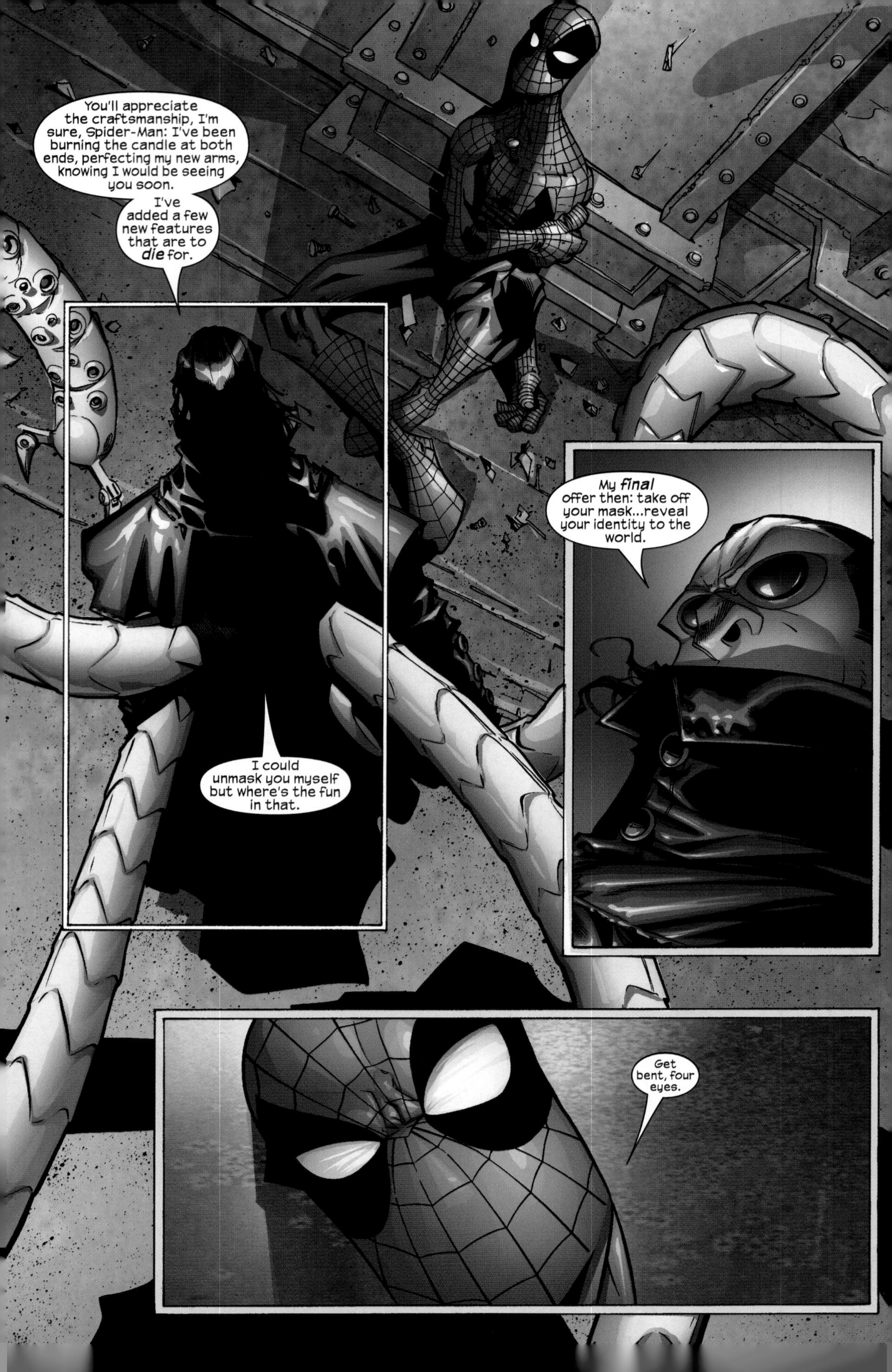
You'll appreciate the craftsmanship, I'm sure, Spider-Man: I've been burning the candle at both ends, perfecting my new arms, knowing I would be seeing you soon.
I've added a few new features that are to *die* for.
I could unmask you myself but where's the fun in that.
My *final* offer then: take off your mask...reveal your identity to the world.
Get bent, four eyes.

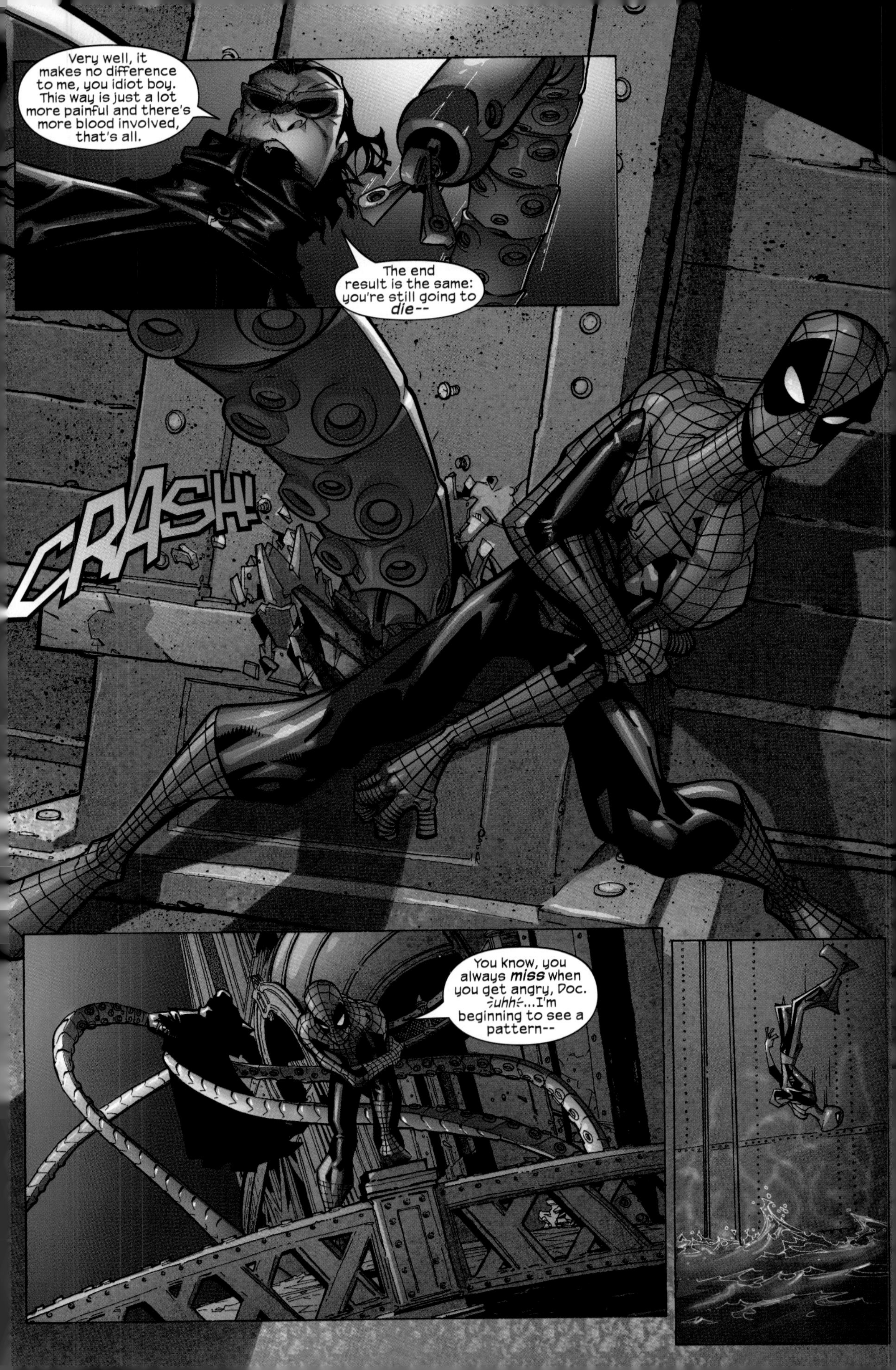

Very well, it makes no difference to me, you idiot boy. This way is just a lot more painful and there's more blood involved, that's all.
The end result is the same: you're still going to *die*--
CRASH!
You know, you always ***miss*** when you get angry, Doc. *uhh*...I'm beginning to see a pattern--

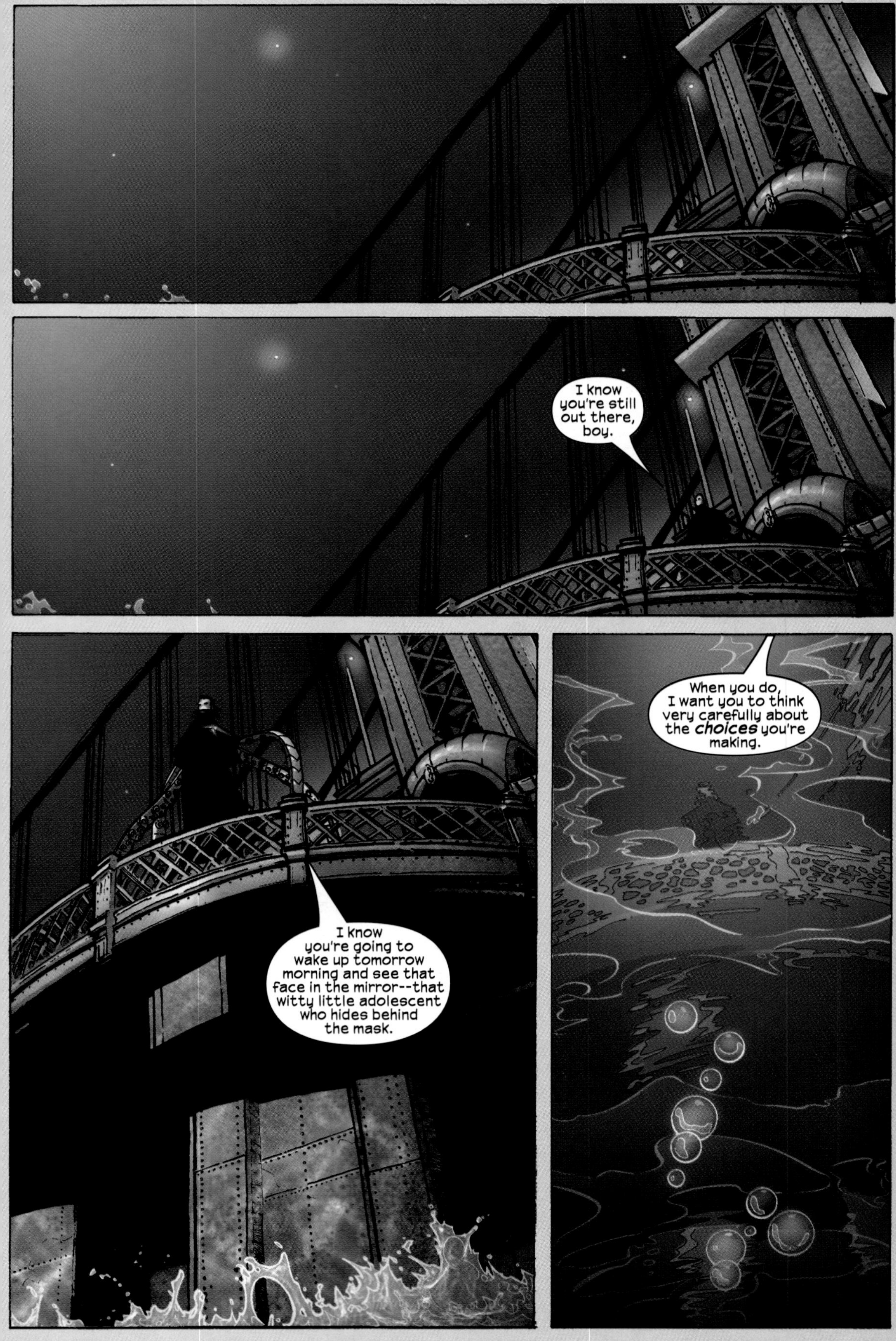
I know you're still out there, boy.
I know you're going to wake up tomorrow morning and see that face in the mirror--that witty little adolescent who hides behind the mask.
When you do, I want you to think very carefully about the *choices* you're making.

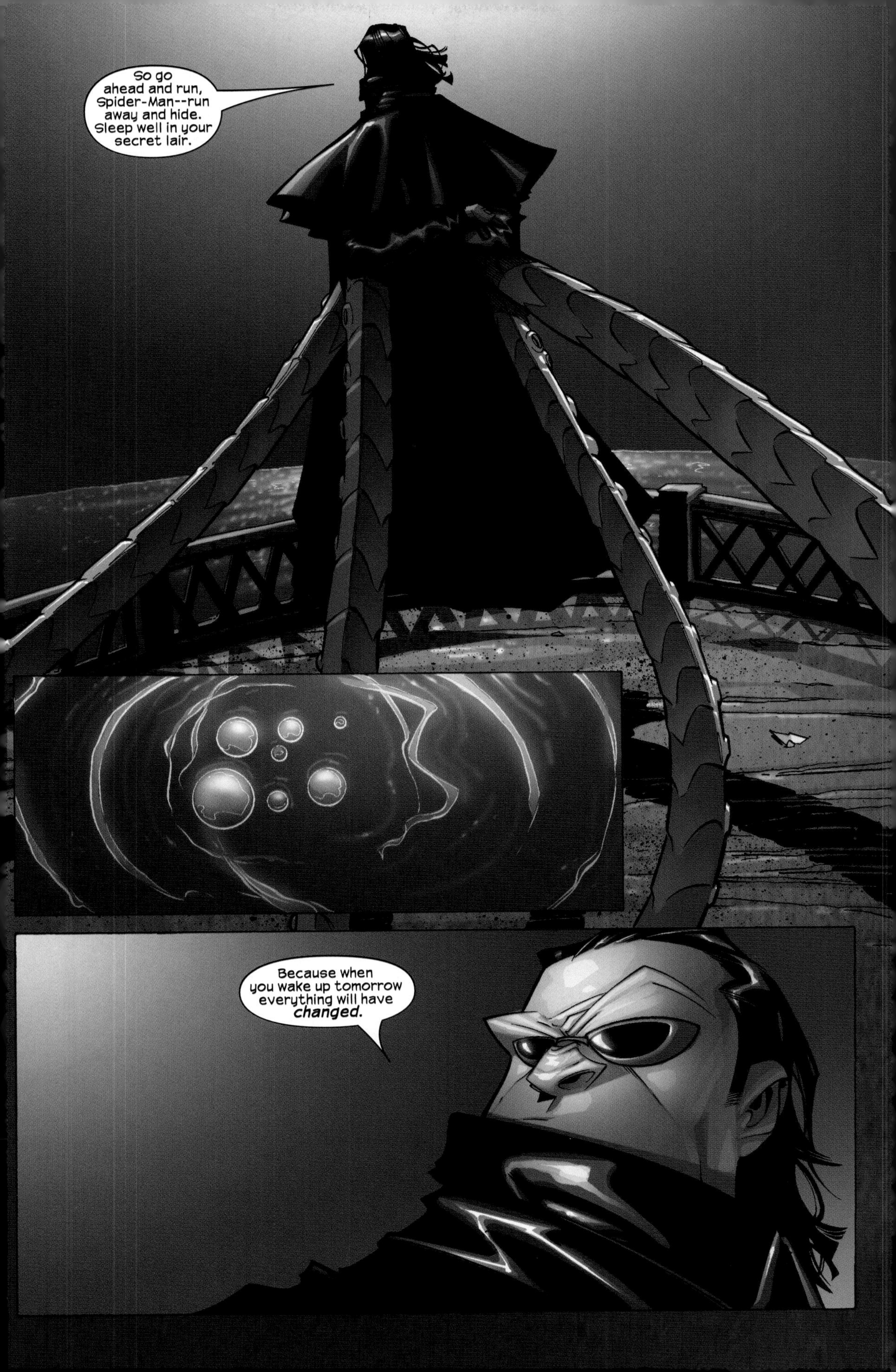
So go ahead and run, Spider-Man--run away and hide. Sleep well in your secret lair.
Because when you wake up tomorrow everything will have *changed*.

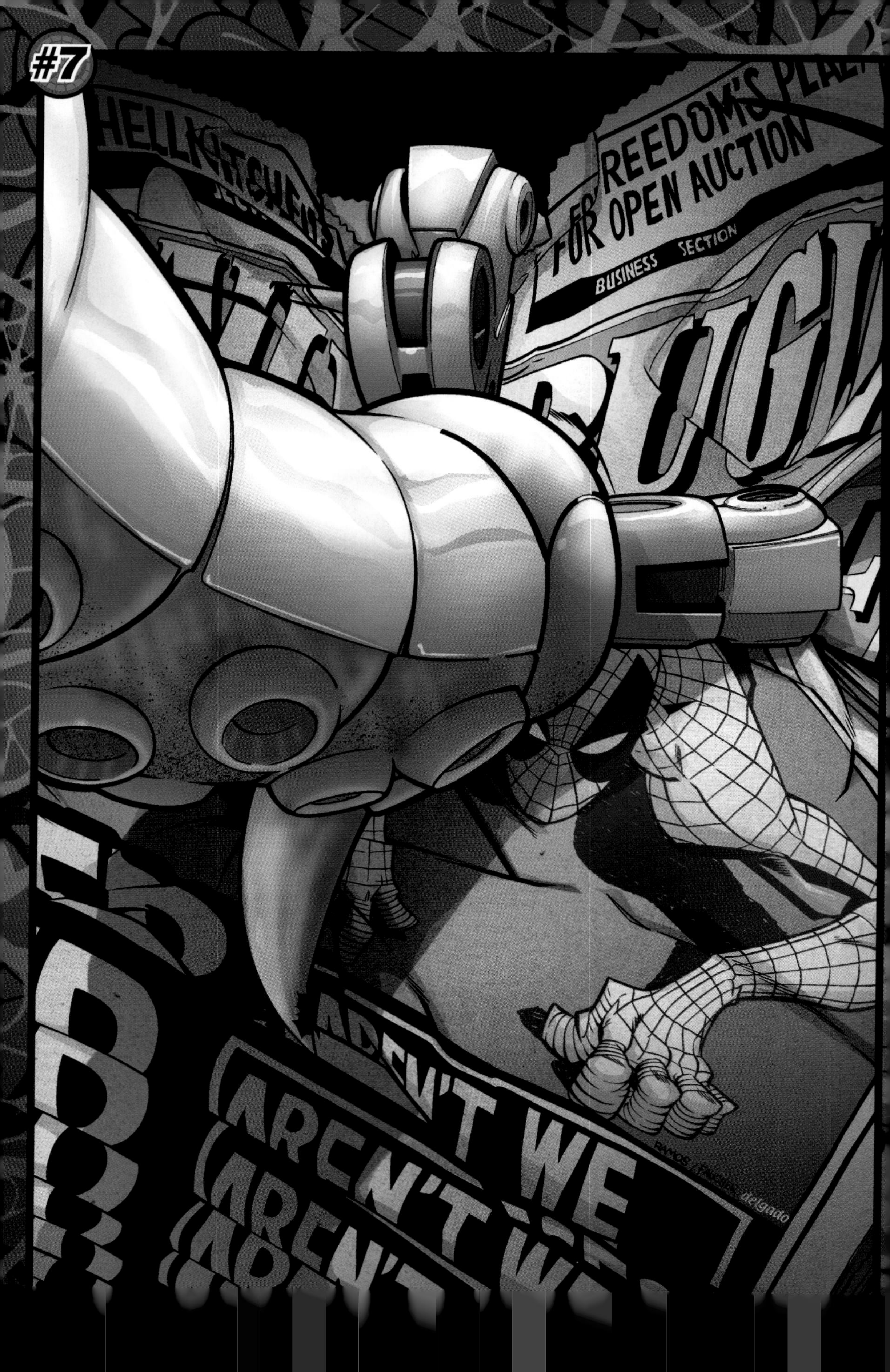
#7
FOR OPEN AUCTION
BUSINESS SECTION
AREN'T WE
RAMOS/FAUCHER delgado

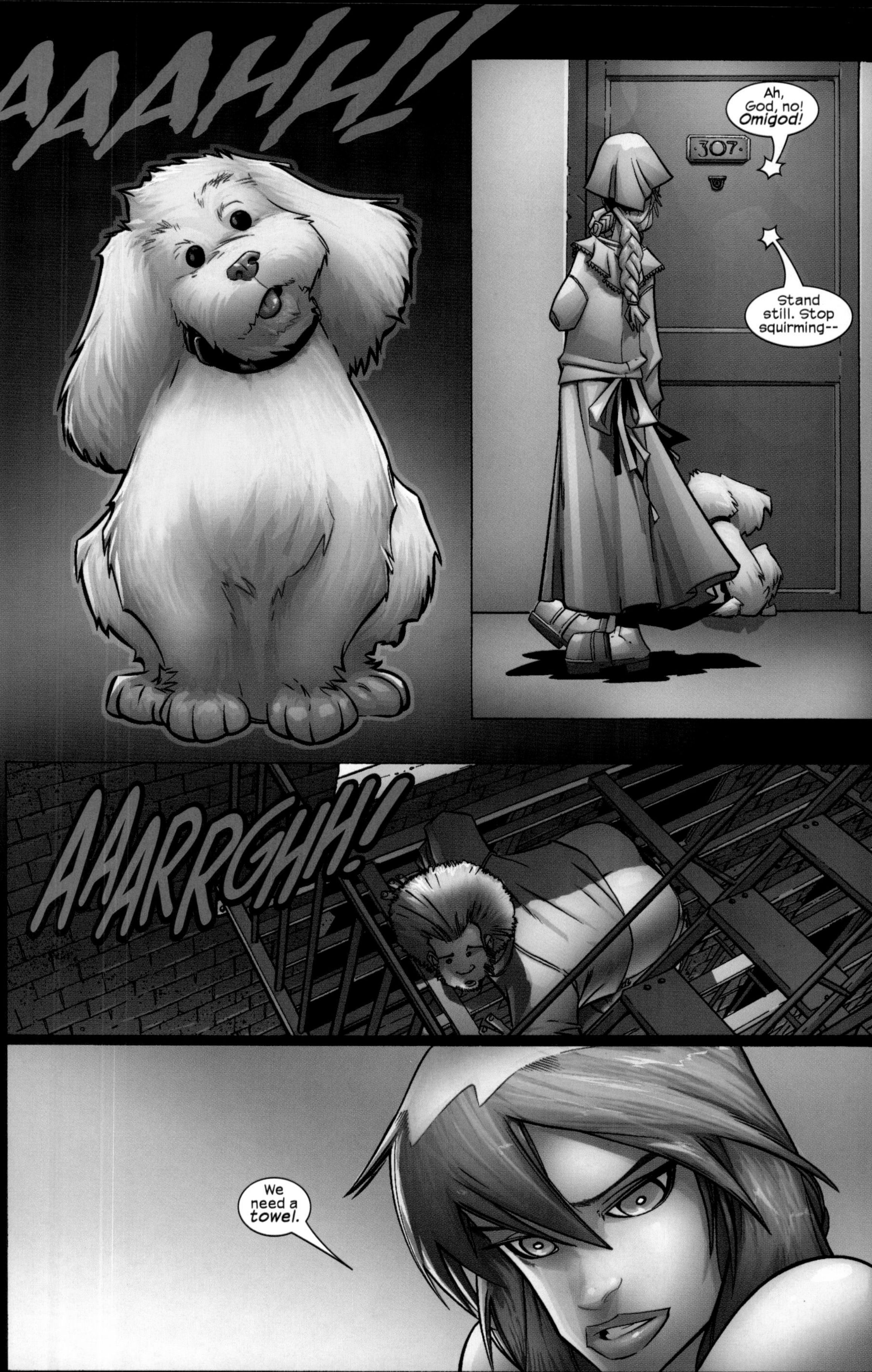
AAAHH!
Ah, God, no! Omigod!
307
Stand still. Stop squirming--
AAARRGHH!
We need a towel.

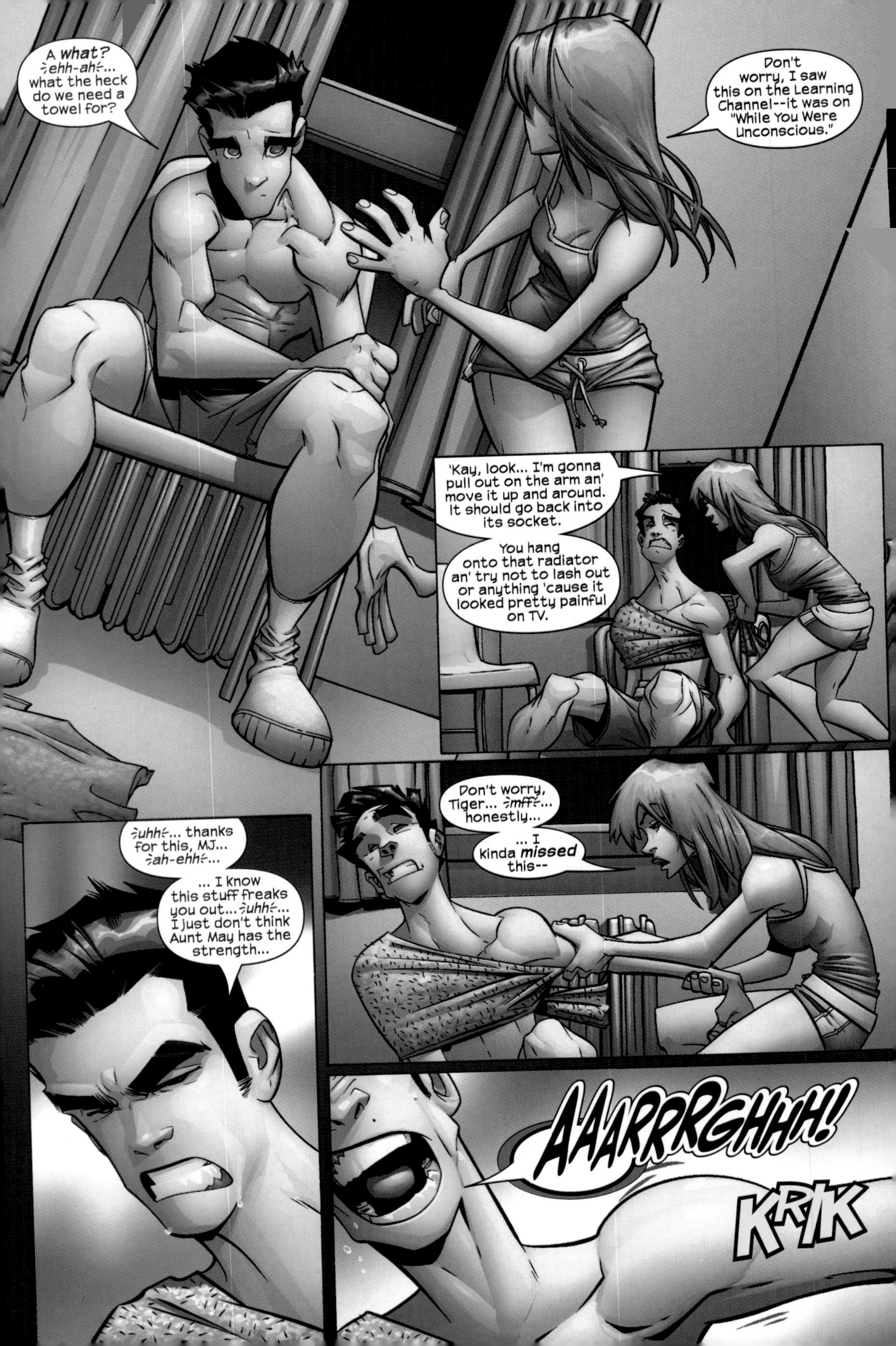
A what? ≈ehh-ah≈... what the heck do we need a towel for?
Don't worry, I saw this on the Learning Channel--it was on "While You Were Unconscious."
'Kay, look... I'm gonna pull out on the arm an' move it up and around. It should go back into its socket.
You hang onto that radiator an' try not to lash out or anything 'cause it looked pretty painful on TV.
Don't worry, Tiger... ≈mff≈... honestly...
... I kinda missed this--
≈uhh≈... thanks for this, MJ... ≈ah-ehh≈...
... I know this stuff freaks you out... ≈uhh≈... I just don't think Aunt May has the strength...
AAARRRGHHH!
KRIK

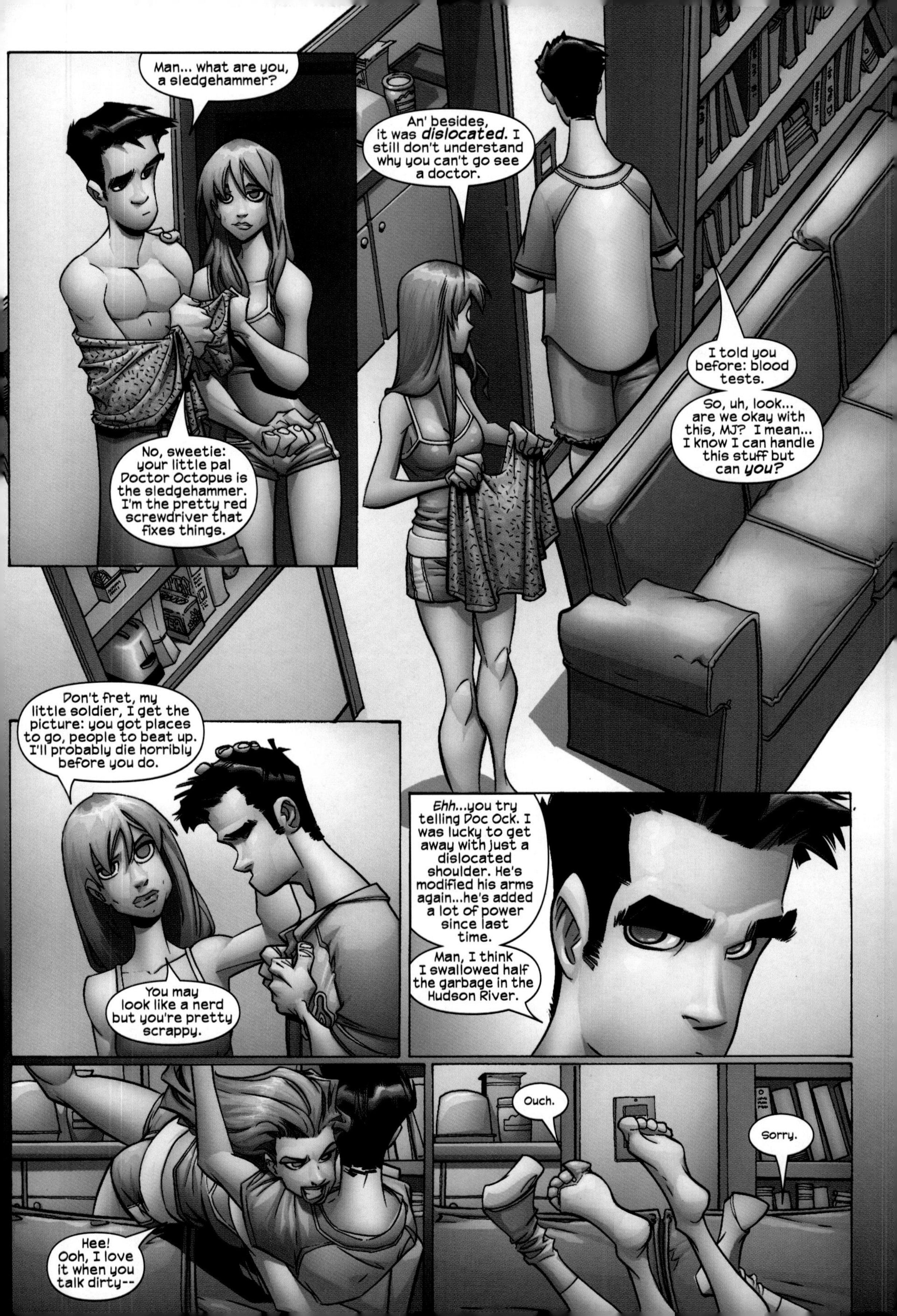
Man... what are you, a sledgehammer?
No, sweetie: your little pal Doctor Octopus is the sledgehammer. I'm the pretty red screwdriver that fixes things.
An' besides, it was *dislocated*. I still don't understand why you can't go see a doctor.
I told you before: blood tests.
So, uh, look... are we okay with this, MJ? I mean... I know I can handle this stuff but can *you?*
Don't fret, my little soldier, I get the picture: you got places to go, people to beat up. I'll probably die horribly before you do.
You may look like a nerd but you're pretty scrappy.
Ehh...you try telling Doc Ock. I was lucky to get away with just a dislocated shoulder. He's modified his arms again...he's added a lot of power since last time.
Man, I think I swallowed half the garbage in the Hudson River.
Hee! Ooh, I love it when you talk dirty--
Ouch.
Sorry.

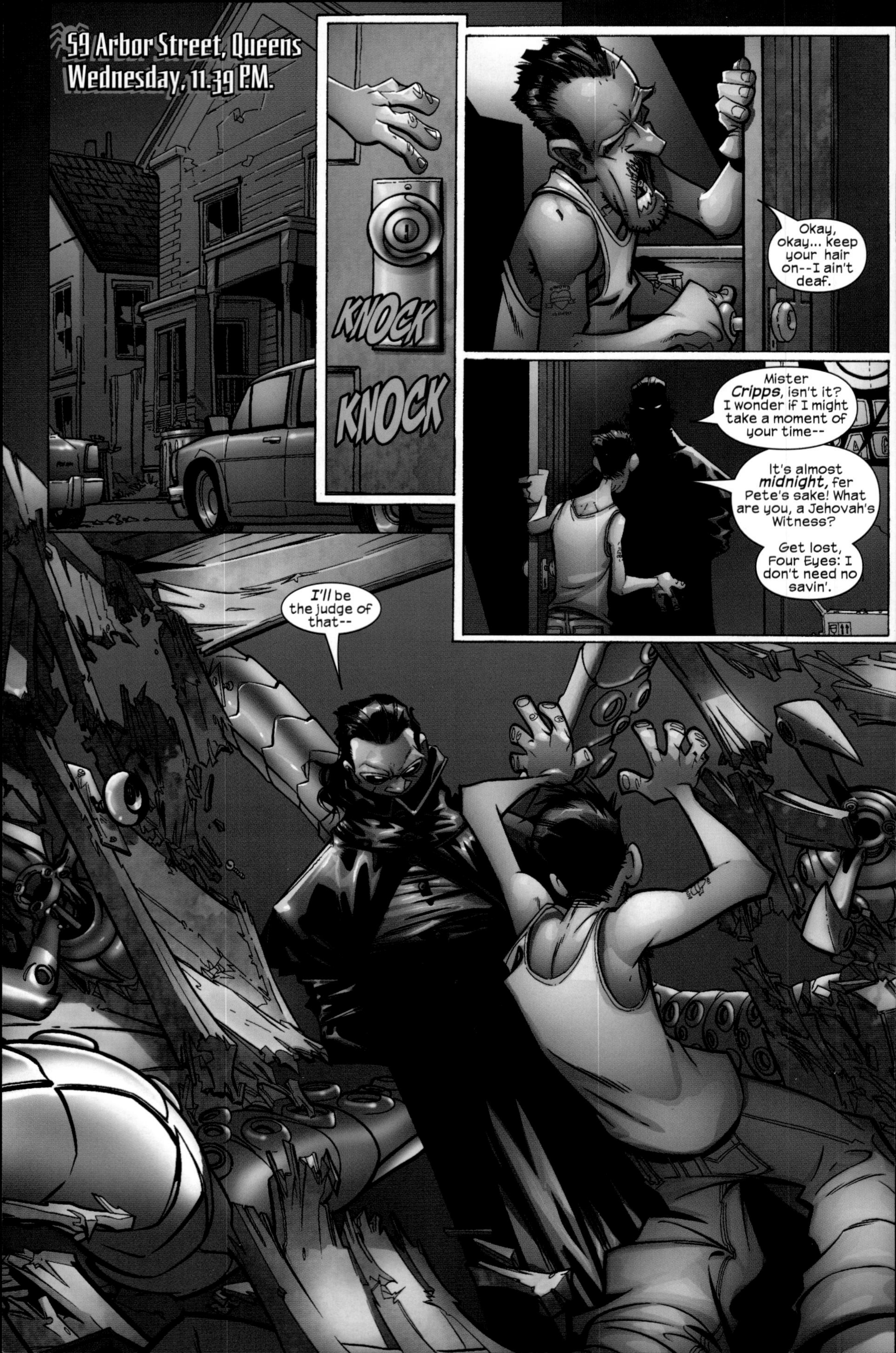
59 Arbor Street, Queens
Wednesday, 11.39 P.M.
KNOCK
KNOCK
Okay, okay... keep your hair on--I ain't deaf.
Mister Cripps, isn't it? I wonder if I might take a moment of your time--
It's almost midnight, fer Pete's sake! What are you, a Jehovah's Witness?
Get lost, Four Eyes: I don't need no savin'.
I'll be the judge of that--

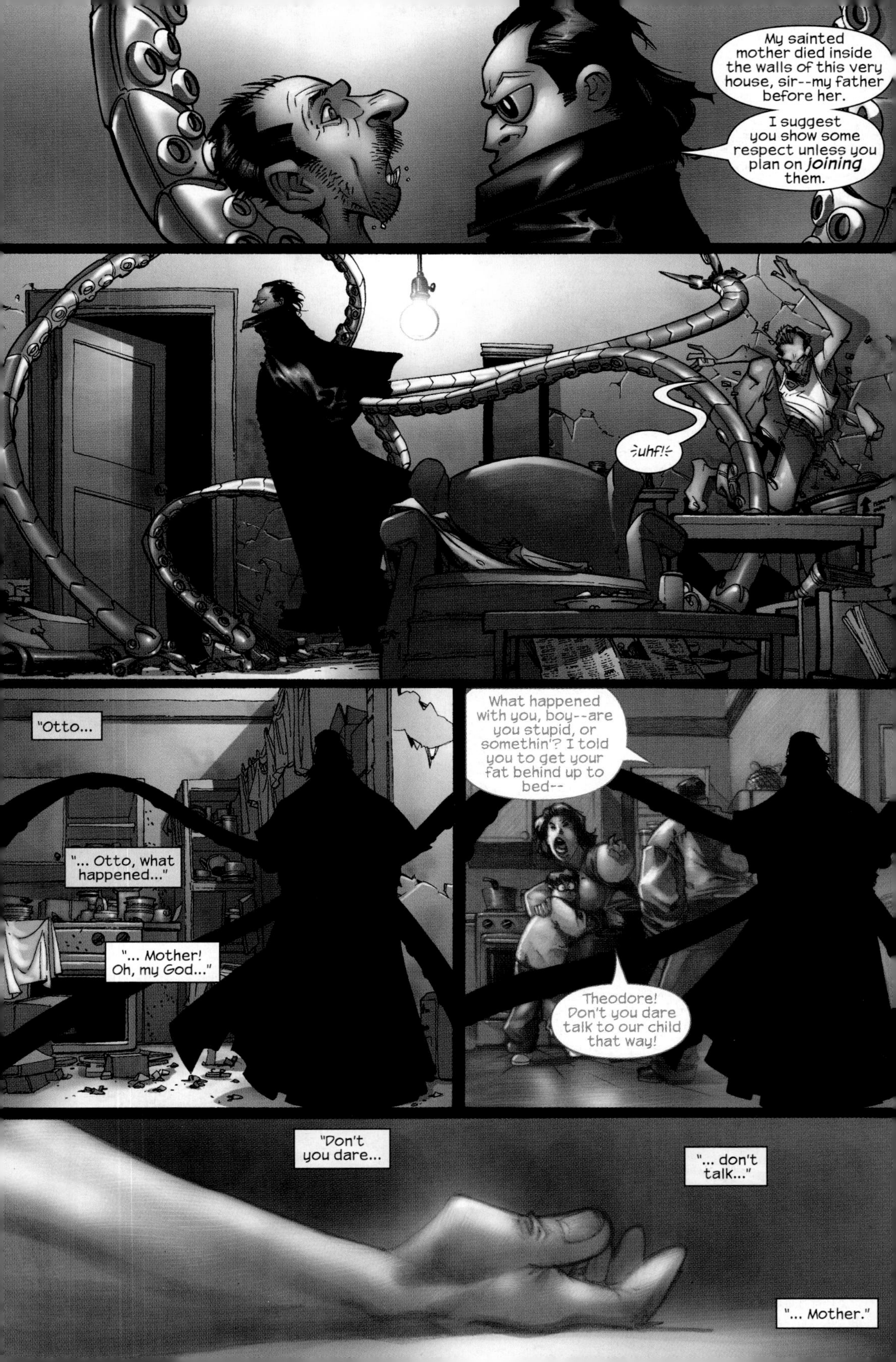
My sainted mother died inside the walls of this very house, sir--my father before her.
I suggest you show some respect unless you plan on *joining* them.
uhf!
"Otto...
"... Otto, what happened..."
"... Mother! Oh, my God..."
What happened with you, boy--are you stupid, or somethin'? I told you to get your fat behind up to bed--
Theodore! Don't you dare talk to our child that way!
"Don't you dare...
"... don't talk..."
"... Mother."

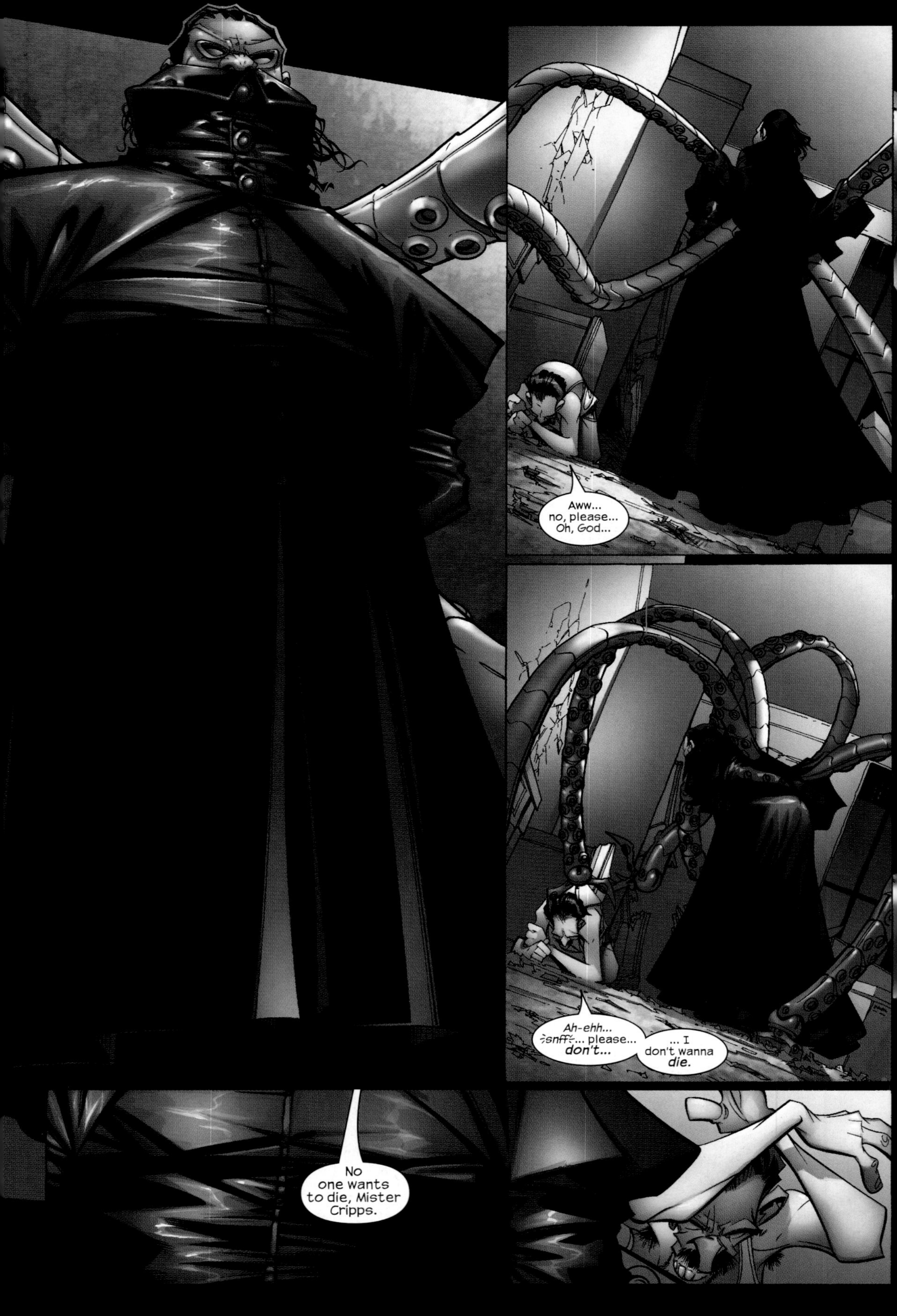
Aww... no, please... Oh, God...
Ah-ehh... ~snff~... please... *don't...*
... I don't wanna *die.*
No one wants to die, Mister Cripps.

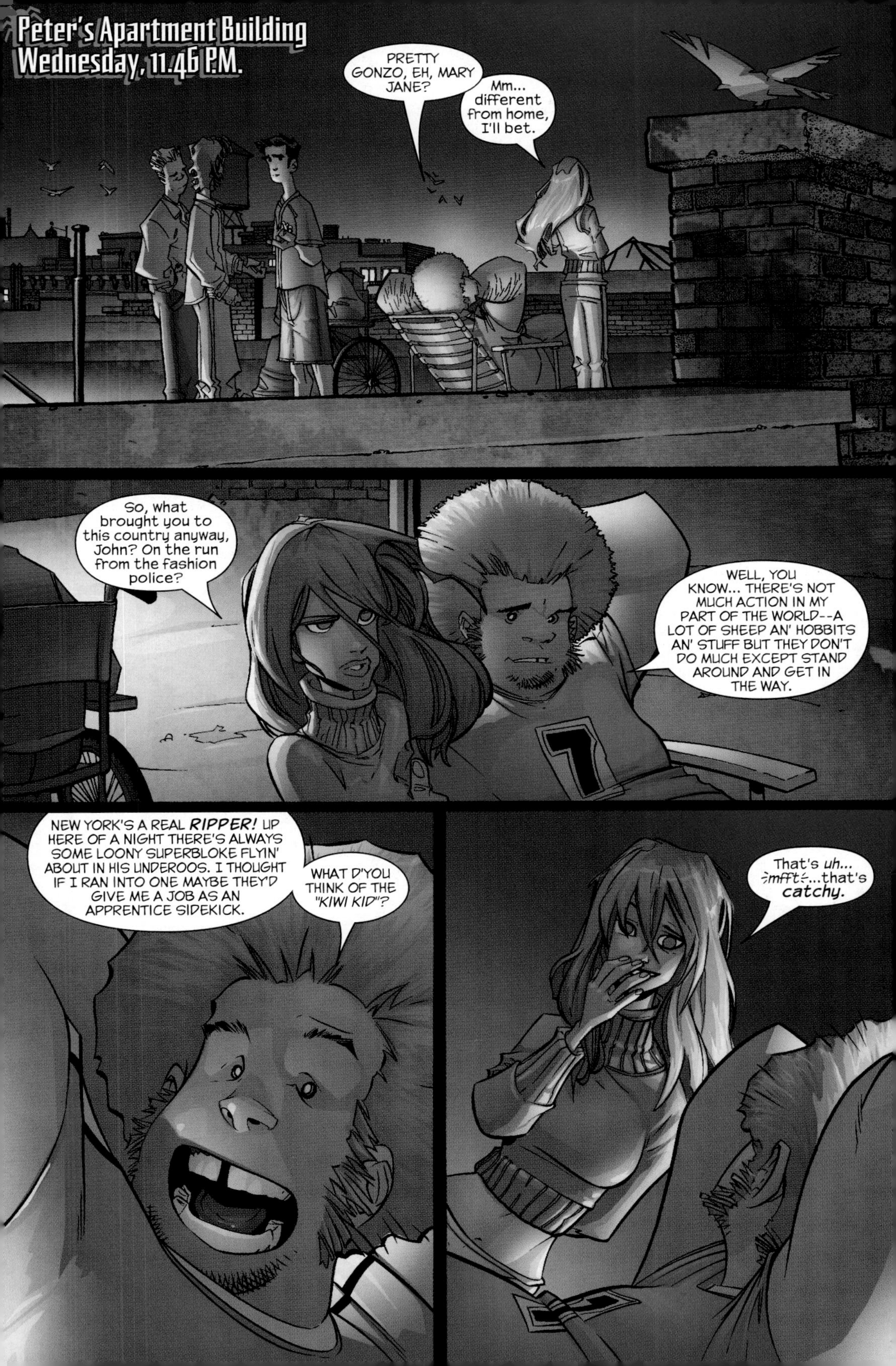
Peter's Apartment Building
Wednesday, 11.46 P.M.
PRETTY GONZO, EH, MARY JANE?
Mm... different from home, I'll bet.
So, what brought you to this country anyway, John? On the run from the fashion police?
WELL, YOU KNOW... THERE'S NOT MUCH ACTION IN MY PART OF THE WORLD--A LOT OF SHEEP AN' HOBBITS AN' STUFF BUT THEY DON'T DO MUCH EXCEPT STAND AROUND AND GET IN THE WAY.
NEW YORK'S A REAL RIPPER! UP HERE OF A NIGHT THERE'S ALWAYS SOME LOONY SUPERBLOKE FLYIN' ABOUT IN HIS UNDEROOS. I THOUGHT IF I RAN INTO ONE MAYBE THEY'D GIVE ME A JOB AS AN APPRENTICE SIDEKICK.
WHAT D'YOU THINK OF THE "KIWI KID"?
That's uh... mfft...that's catchy.

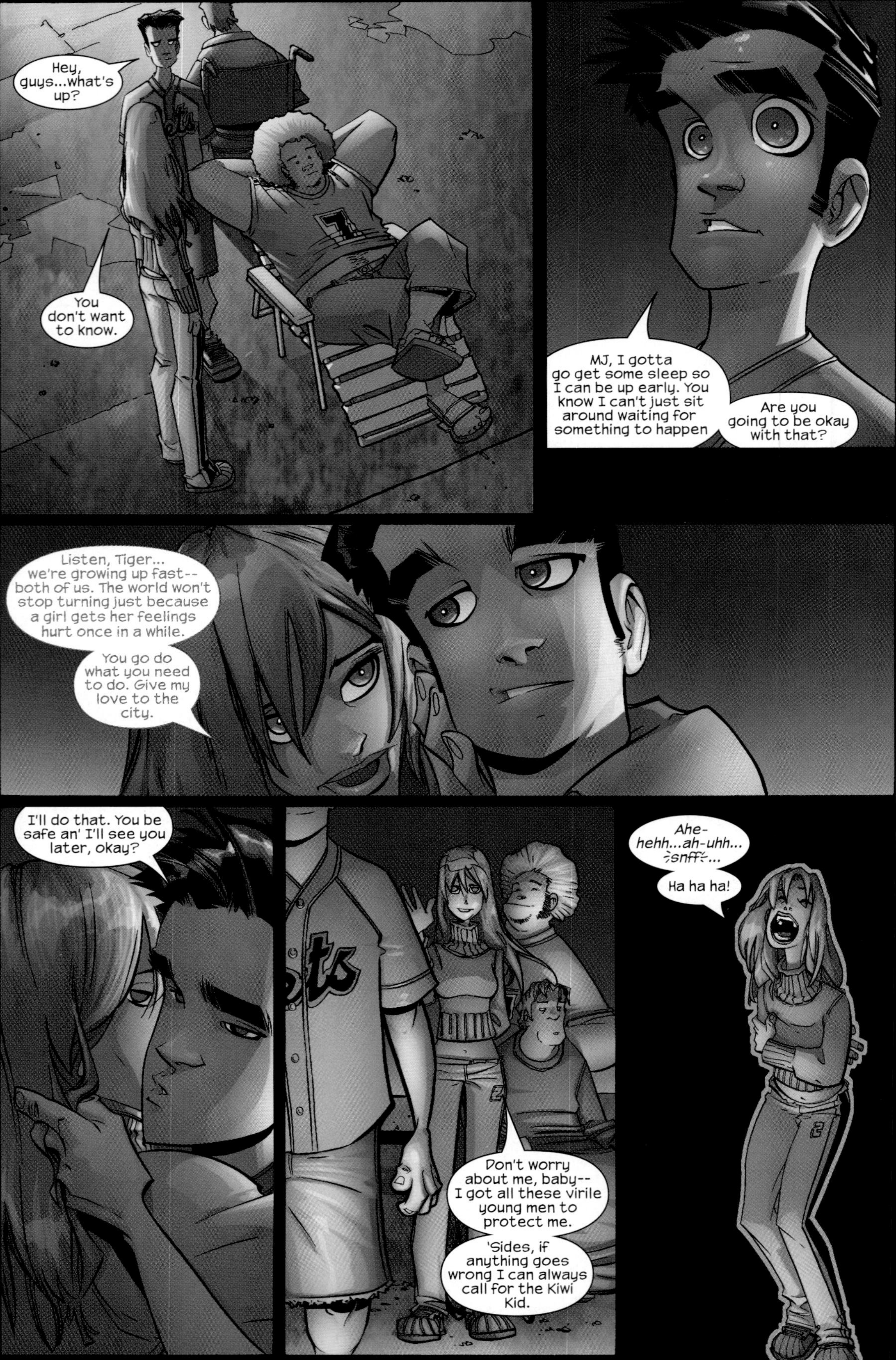
Hey, guys...what's up?
You don't want to know.
MJ, I gotta go get some sleep so I can be up early. You know I can't just sit around waiting for something to happen
Are you going to be okay with that?
Listen, Tiger... we're growing up fast-- both of us. The world won't stop turning just because a girl gets her feelings hurt once in a while.
You go do what you need to do. Give my love to the city.
I'll do that. You be safe an' I'll see you later, okay?
Don't worry about me, baby-- I got all these virile young men to protect me.
'Sides, if anything goes wrong I can always call for the Kiwi Kid.
Ahe-hehh...ah-uhh... snff...
Ha ha ha!

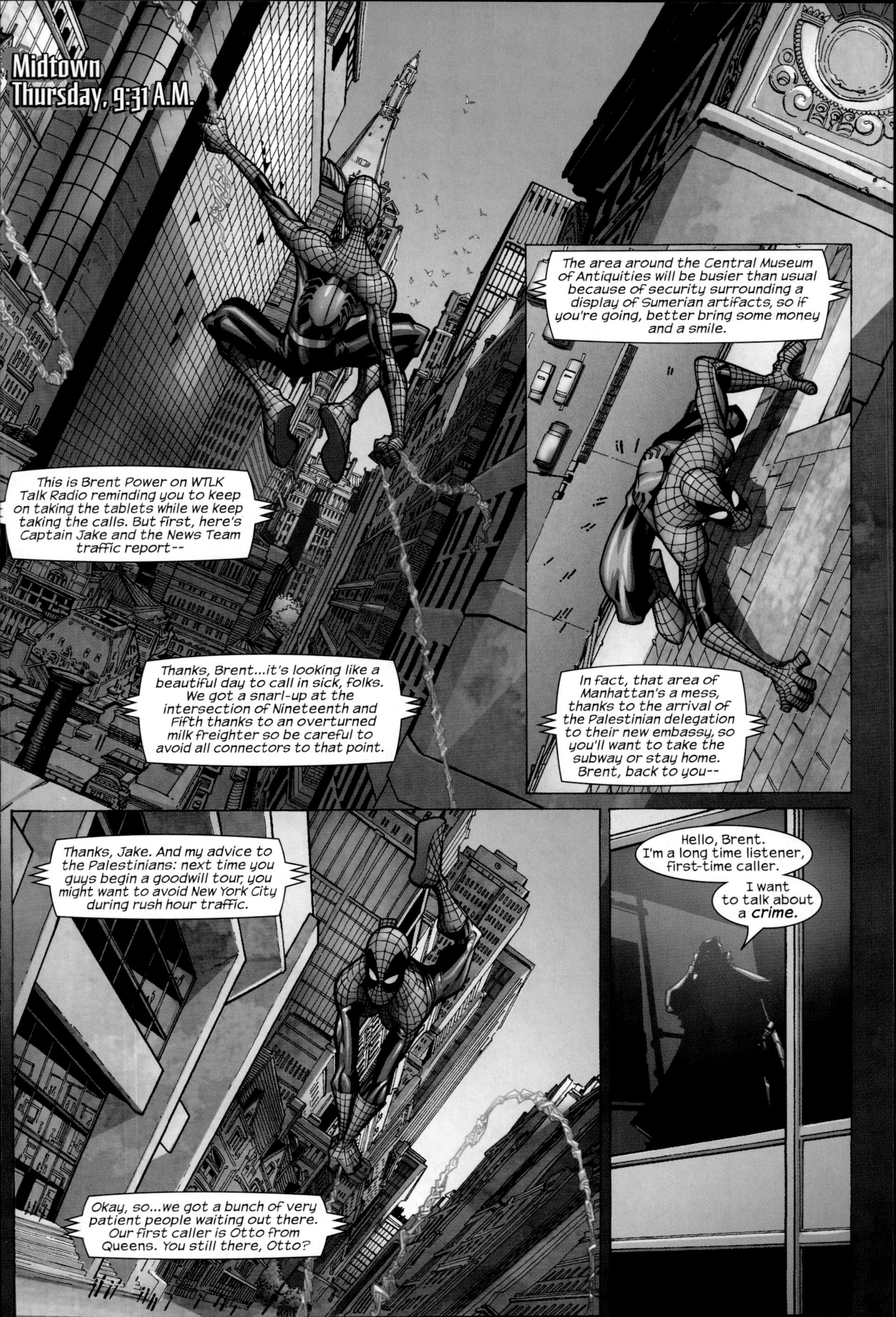

Midtown
Thursday, 9:31 A.M.
This is Brent Power on WTLK Talk Radio reminding you to keep on taking the tablets while we keep taking the calls. But first, here's Captain Jake and the News Team traffic report--
Thanks, Brent...it's looking like a beautiful day to call in sick, folks. We got a snarl-up at the intersection of Nineteenth and Fifth thanks to an overturned milk freighter so be careful to avoid all connectors to that point.
The area around the Central Museum of Antiquities will be busier than usual because of security surrounding a display of Sumerian artifacts, so if you're going, better bring some money and a smile.
In fact, that area of Manhattan's a mess, thanks to the arrival of the Palestinian delegation to their new embassy, so you'll want to take the subway or stay home. Brent, back to you--
Thanks, Jake. And my advice to the Palestinians: next time you guys begin a goodwill tour, you might want to avoid New York City during rush hour traffic.
Okay, so...we got a bunch of very patient people waiting out there. Our first caller is Otto from Queens. You still there, Otto?
Hello, Brent. I'm a long time listener, first-time caller.
I want to talk about a *crime.*

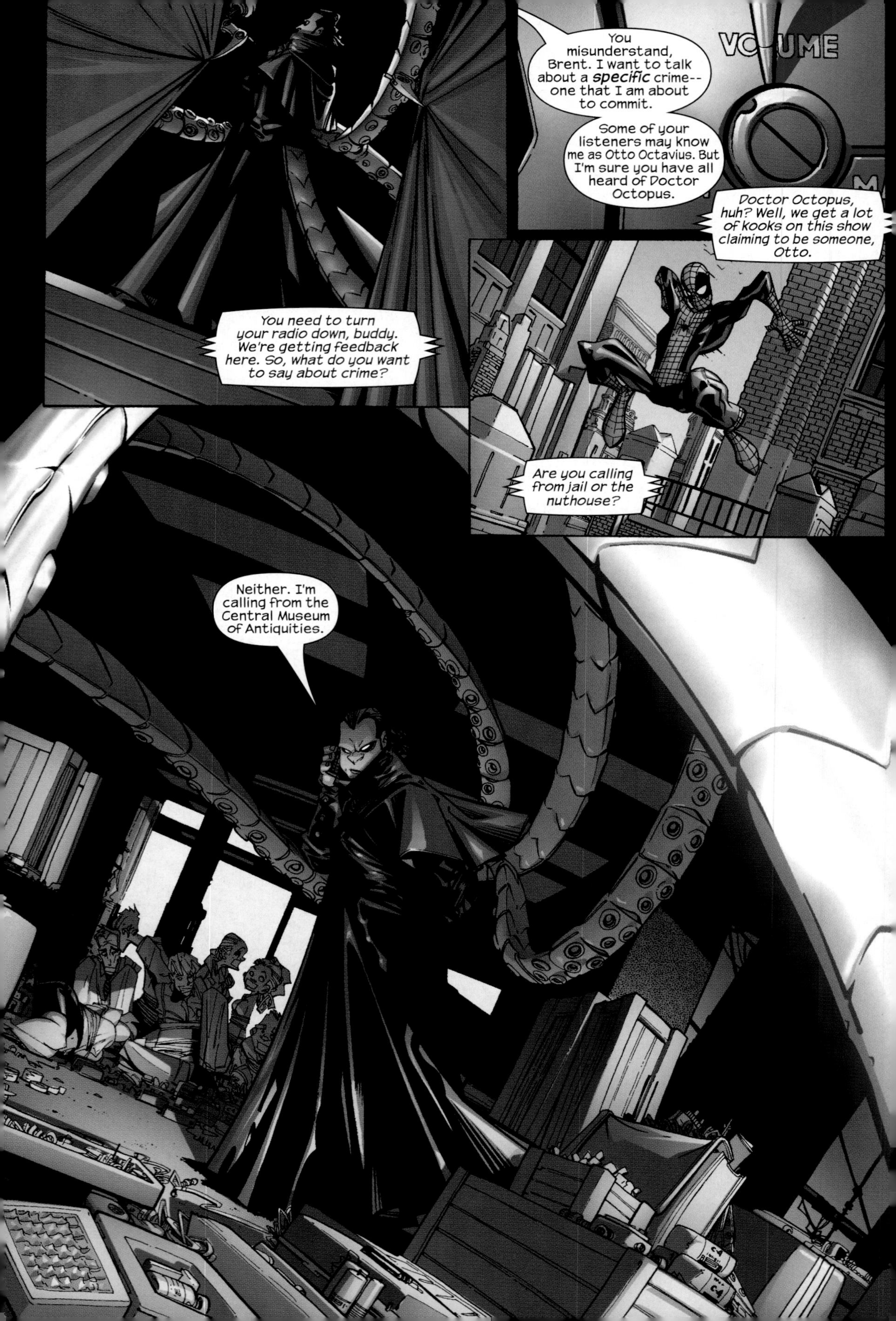
VOLUME
You need to turn your radio down, buddy. We're getting feedback here. So, what do you want to say about crime?
You misunderstand, Brent. I want to talk about a *specific* crime-- one that I am about to commit.
Some of your listeners may know me as Otto Octavius. But I'm sure you have all heard of Doctor Octopus.
Doctor Octopus, huh? Well, we get a lot of kooks on this show claiming to be someone, Otto.
Are you calling from jail or the nuthouse?
Neither. I'm calling from the Central Museum of Antiquities.
C4

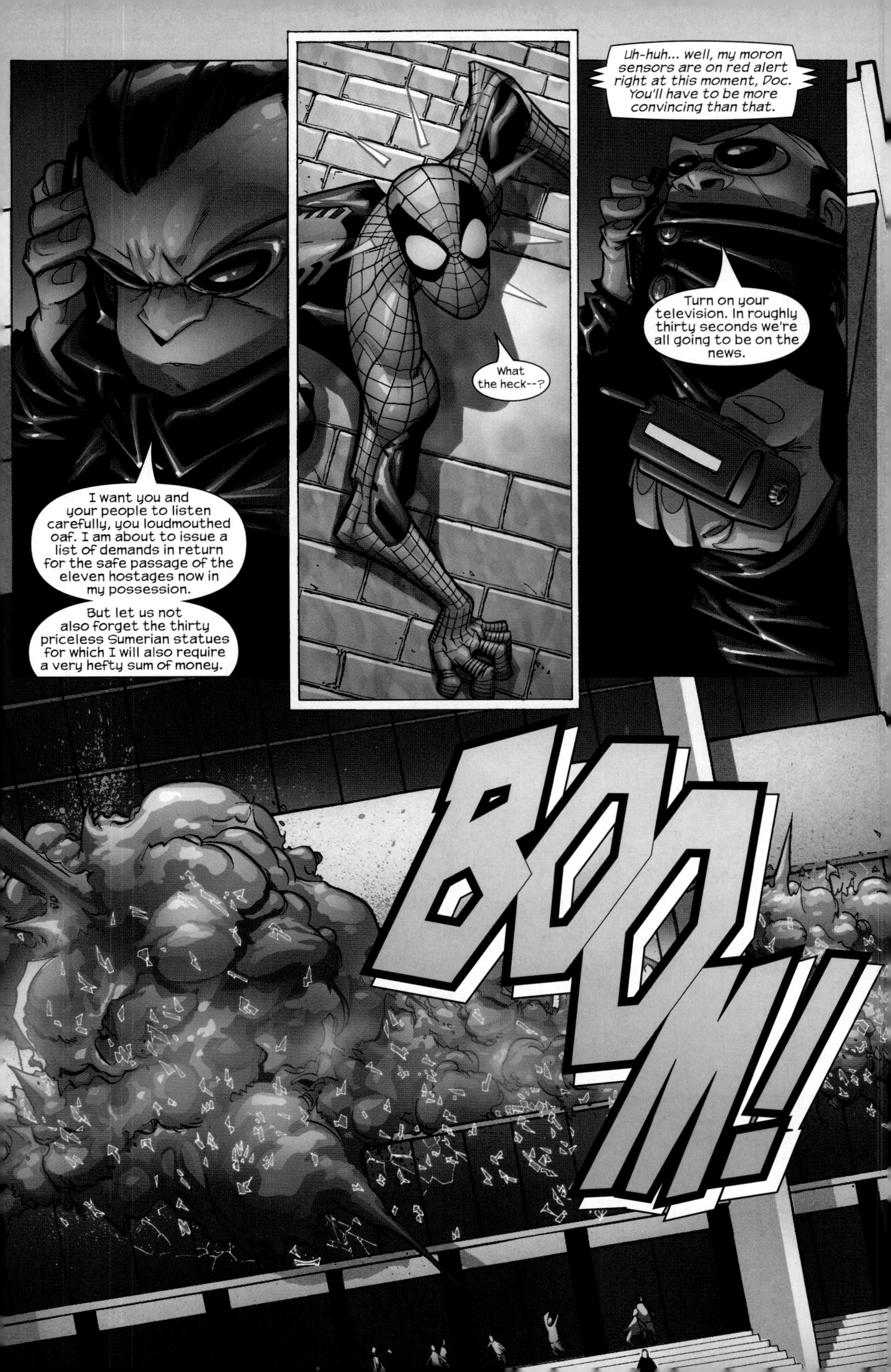
I want you and your people to listen carefully, you loudmouthed oaf. I am about to issue a list of demands in return for the safe passage of the eleven hostages now in my possession.
But let us not also forget the thirty priceless Sumerian statues for which I will also require a very hefty sum of money.
What the heck--?
Uh-huh... well, my moron sensors are on red alert right at this moment, Doc. You'll have to be more convincing than that.
Turn on your television. In roughly thirty seconds we're all going to be on the news.
BOOM!!

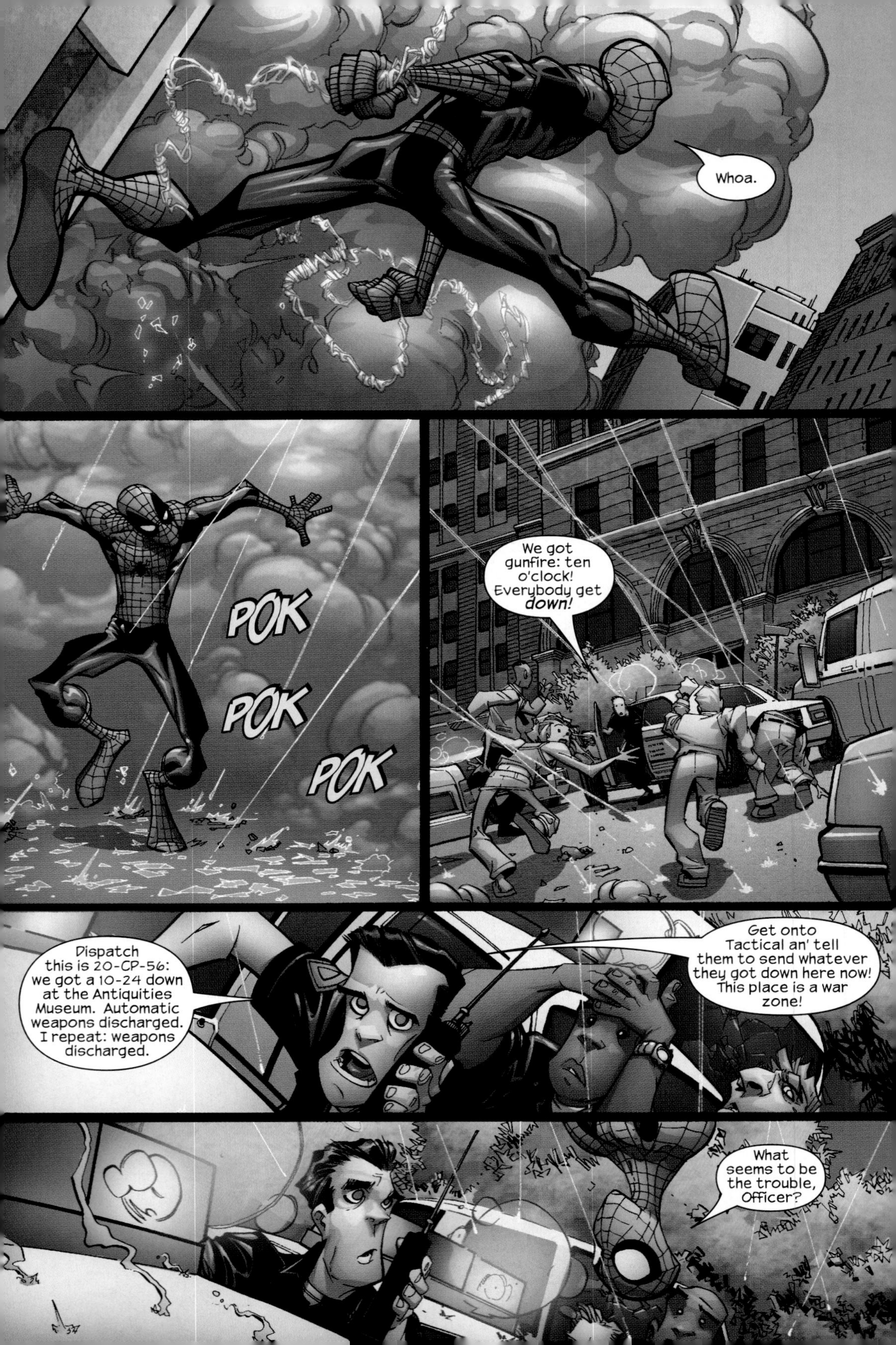
Whoa.
POK
POK
POK
We got gunfire: ten o'clock! Everybody get *down!*
Dispatch this is 20-CP-56: we got a 10-24 down at the Antiquities Museum. Automatic weapons discharged. I repeat: weapons discharged.
Get onto Tactical an' tell them to send whatever they got down here now! This place is a war zone!
What seems to be the trouble, Officer?

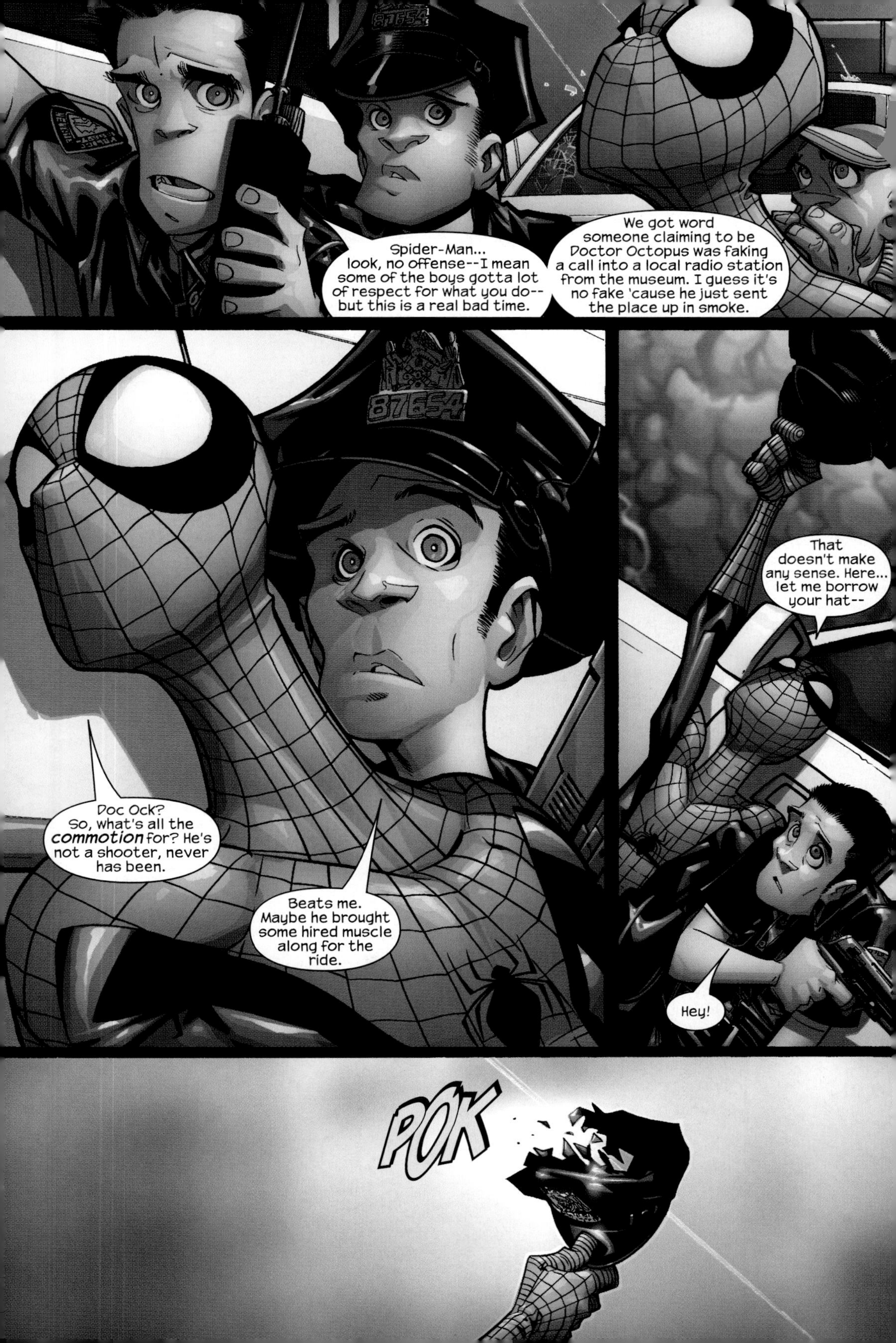
Spider-Man...
look, no offense--I mean some of the boys gotta lot of respect for what you do--but this is a real bad time.
We got word someone claiming to be Doctor Octopus was faking a call into a local radio station from the museum. I guess it's no fake 'cause he just sent the place up in smoke.
Doc Ock? So, what's all the *commotion* for? He's not a shooter, never has been.
Beats me. Maybe he brought some hired muscle along for the ride.
That doesn't make any sense. Here... let me borrow your hat--
Hey!
POK

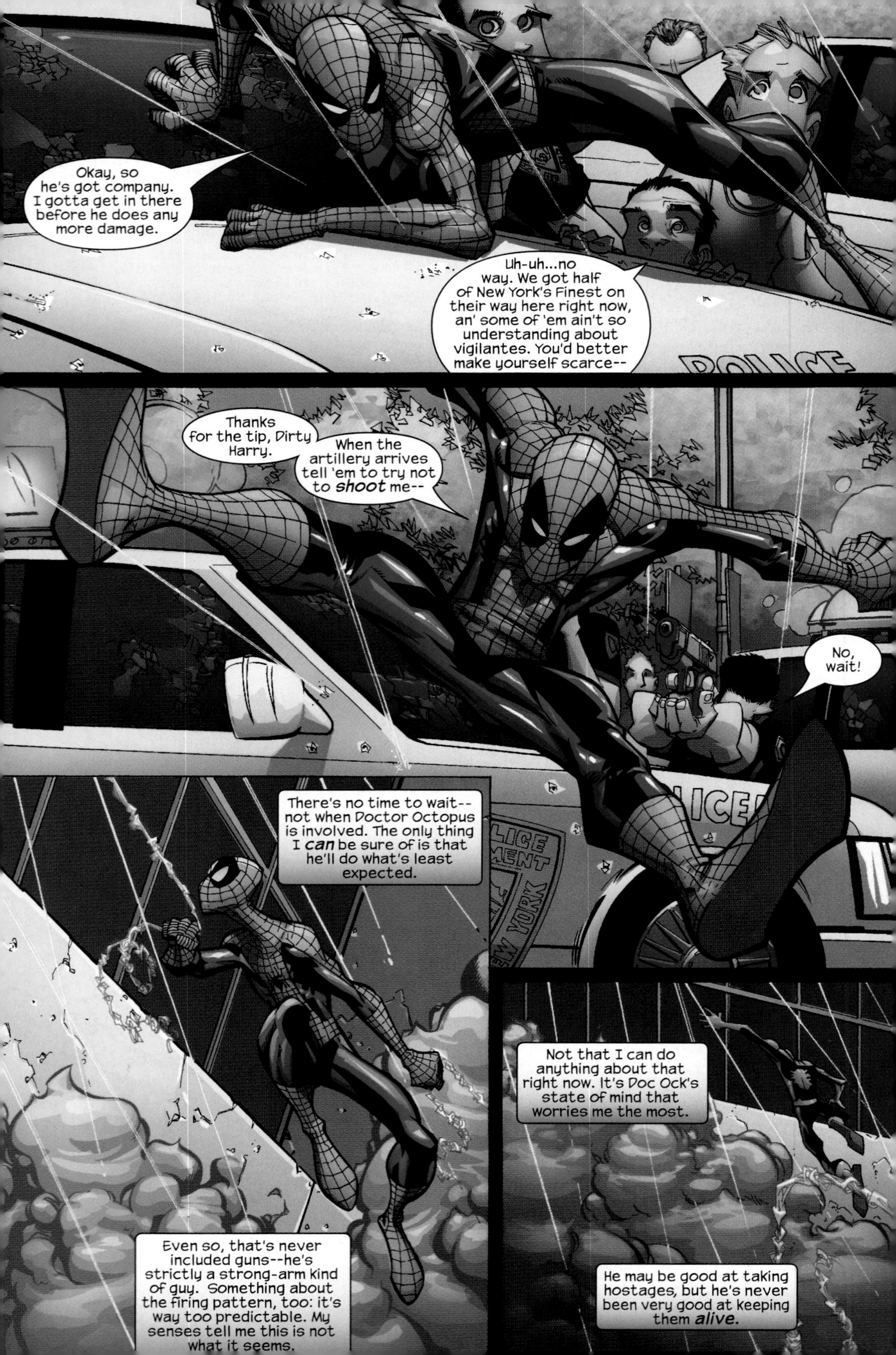
Okay, so he's got company. I gotta get in there before he does any more damage.
Uh-uh...no way. We got half of New York's Finest on their way here right now, an' some of 'em ain't so understanding about vigilantes. You'd better make yourself scarce--
POLICE
Thanks for the tip, Dirty Harry.
When the artillery arrives tell 'em to try not to *shoot* me--
No, wait!
There's no time to wait--not when Doctor Octopus is involved. The only thing I *can* be sure of is that he'll do what's least expected.
Even so, that's never included guns--he's strictly a strong-arm kind of guy. Something about the firing pattern, too: it's way too predictable. My senses tell me this is not what it seems.
Not that I can do anything about that right now. It's Doc Ock's state of mind that worries me the most.
He may be good at taking hostages, but he's never been very good at keeping them *alive*.

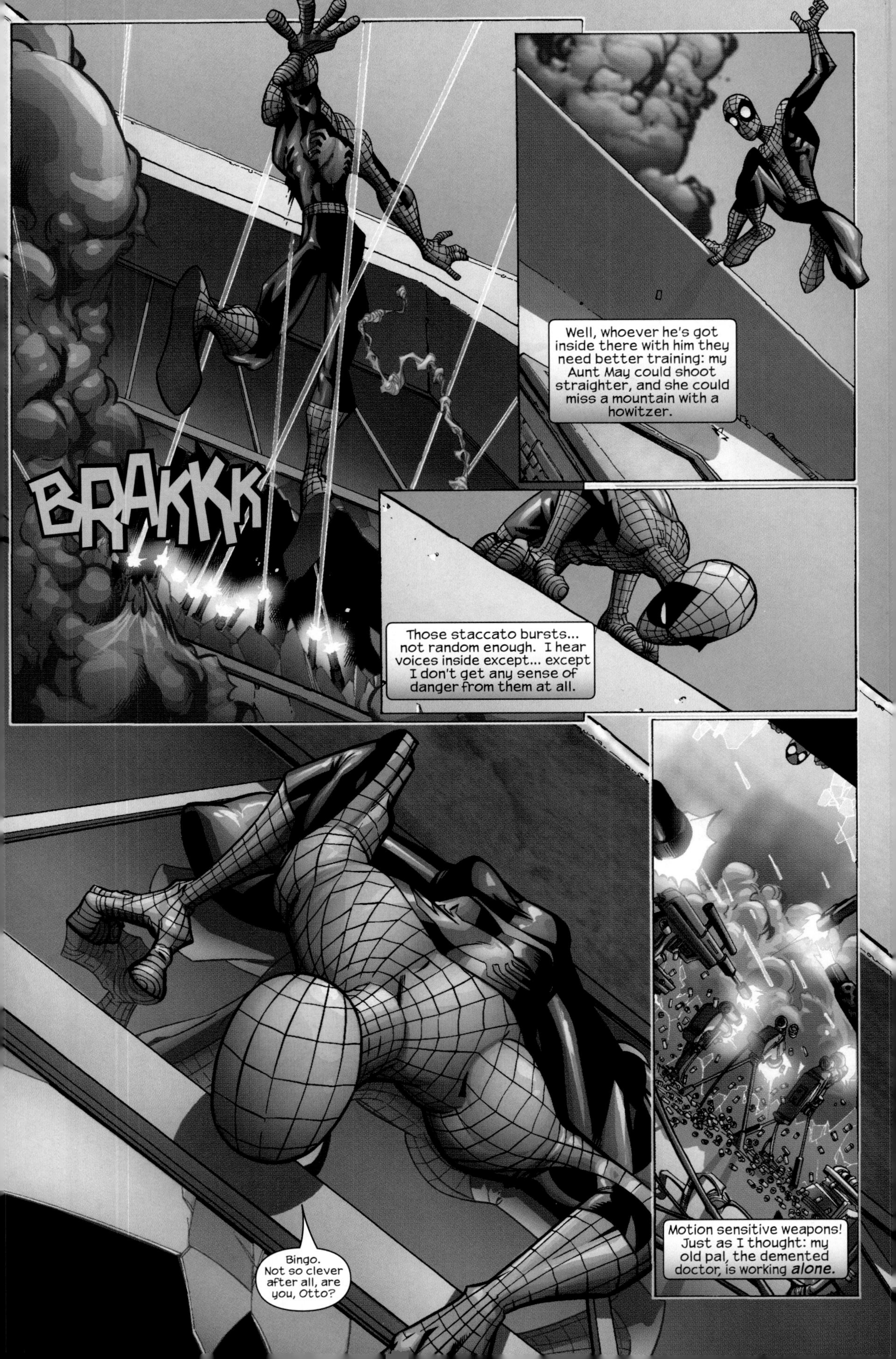
BRAKKK
Well, whoever he's got inside there with him they need better training: my Aunt May could shoot straighter, and she could miss a mountain with a howitzer.
Those staccato bursts... not random enough. I hear voices inside except... except I don't get any sense of danger from them at all.
Bingo. Not so clever after all, are you, Otto?
Motion sensitive weapons! Just as I thought: my old pal, the demented doctor, is working *alone.*

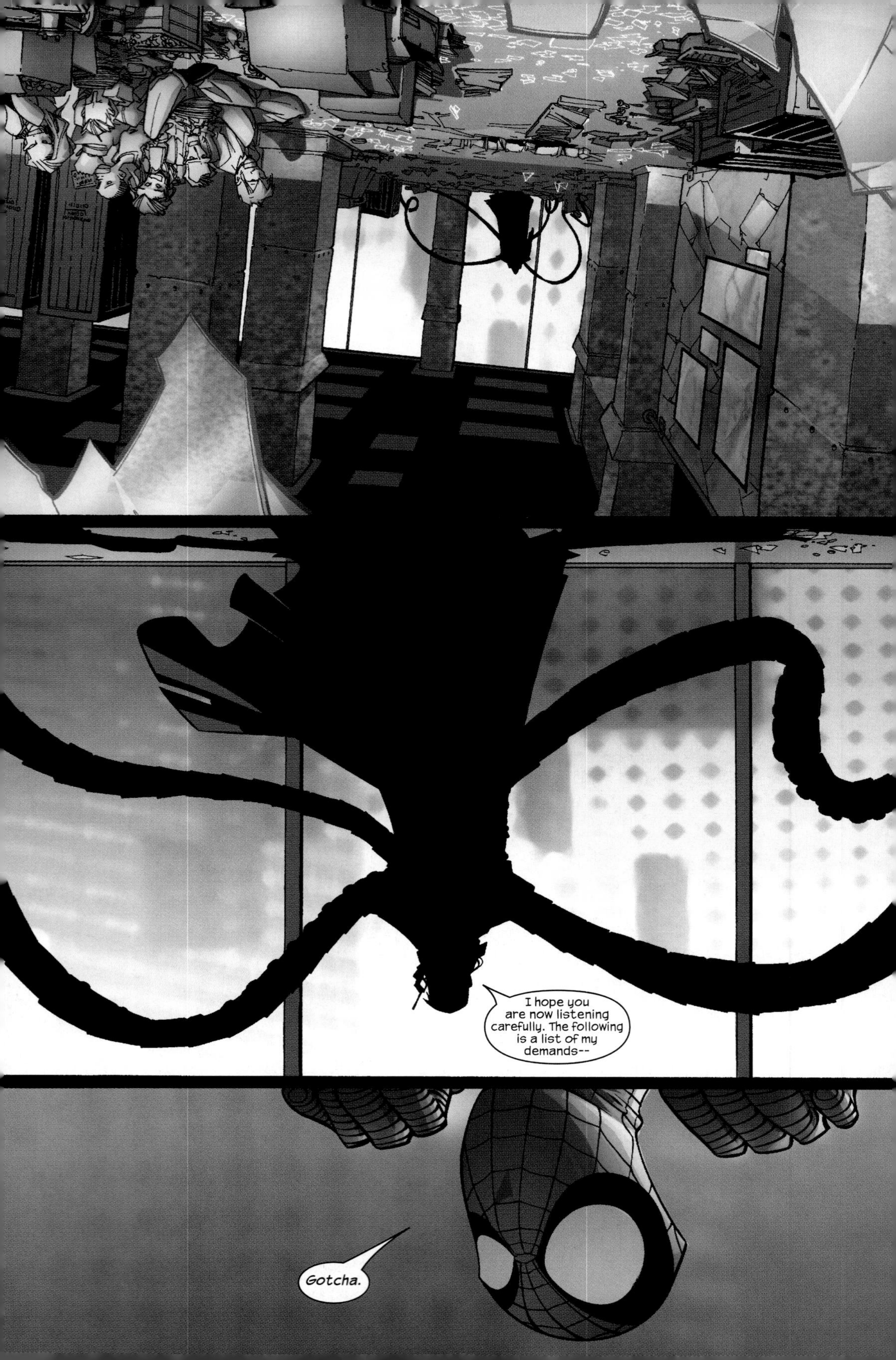
I hope you are now listening carefully. The following is a list of my demands--
Gotcha.

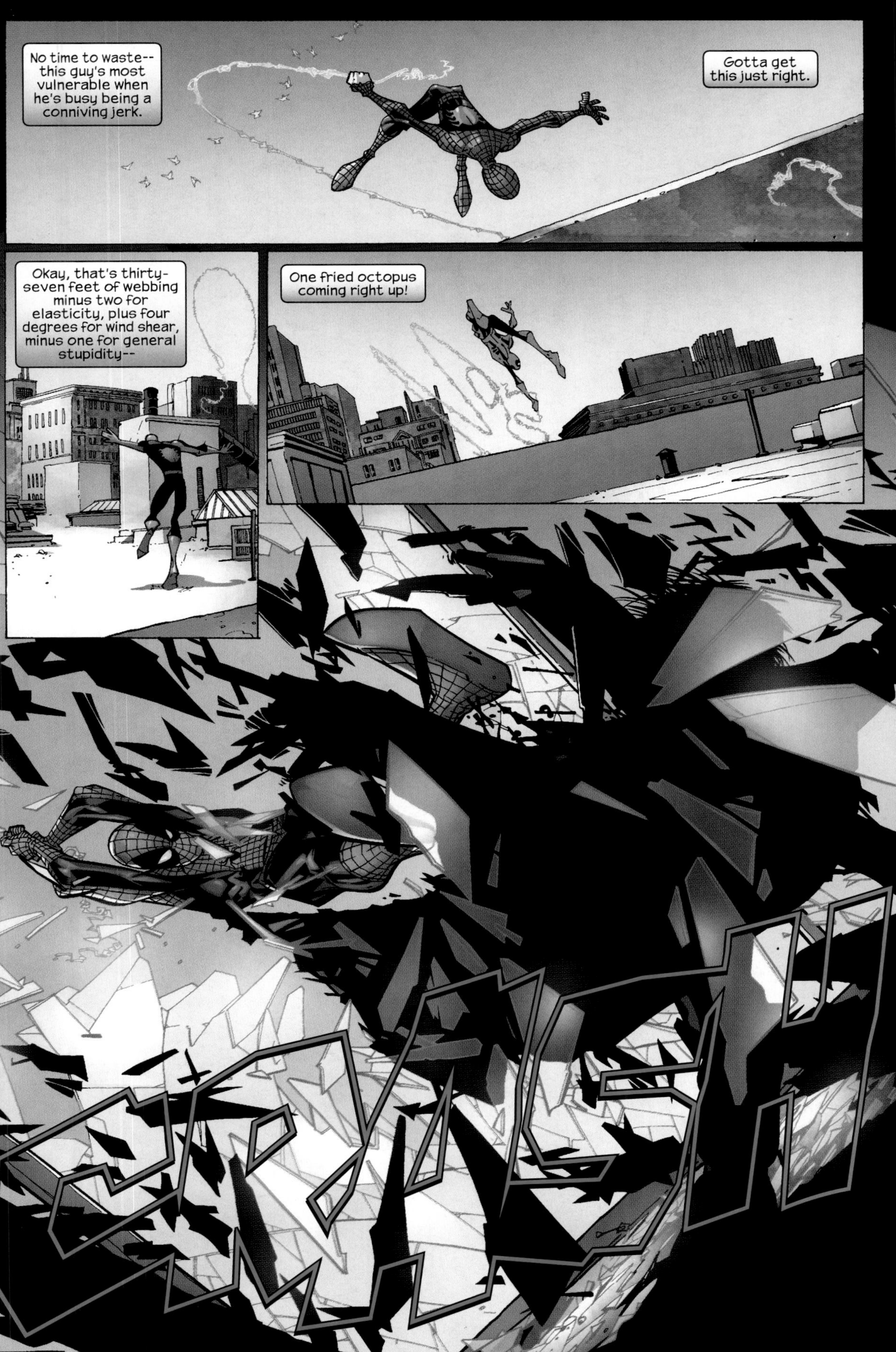
No time to waste-- this guy's most vulnerable when he's busy being a conniving jerk.
Gotta get this just right.
Okay, that's thirty-seven feet of webbing minus two for elasticity, plus four degrees for wind shear, minus one for general stupidity--
One fried octopus coming right up!

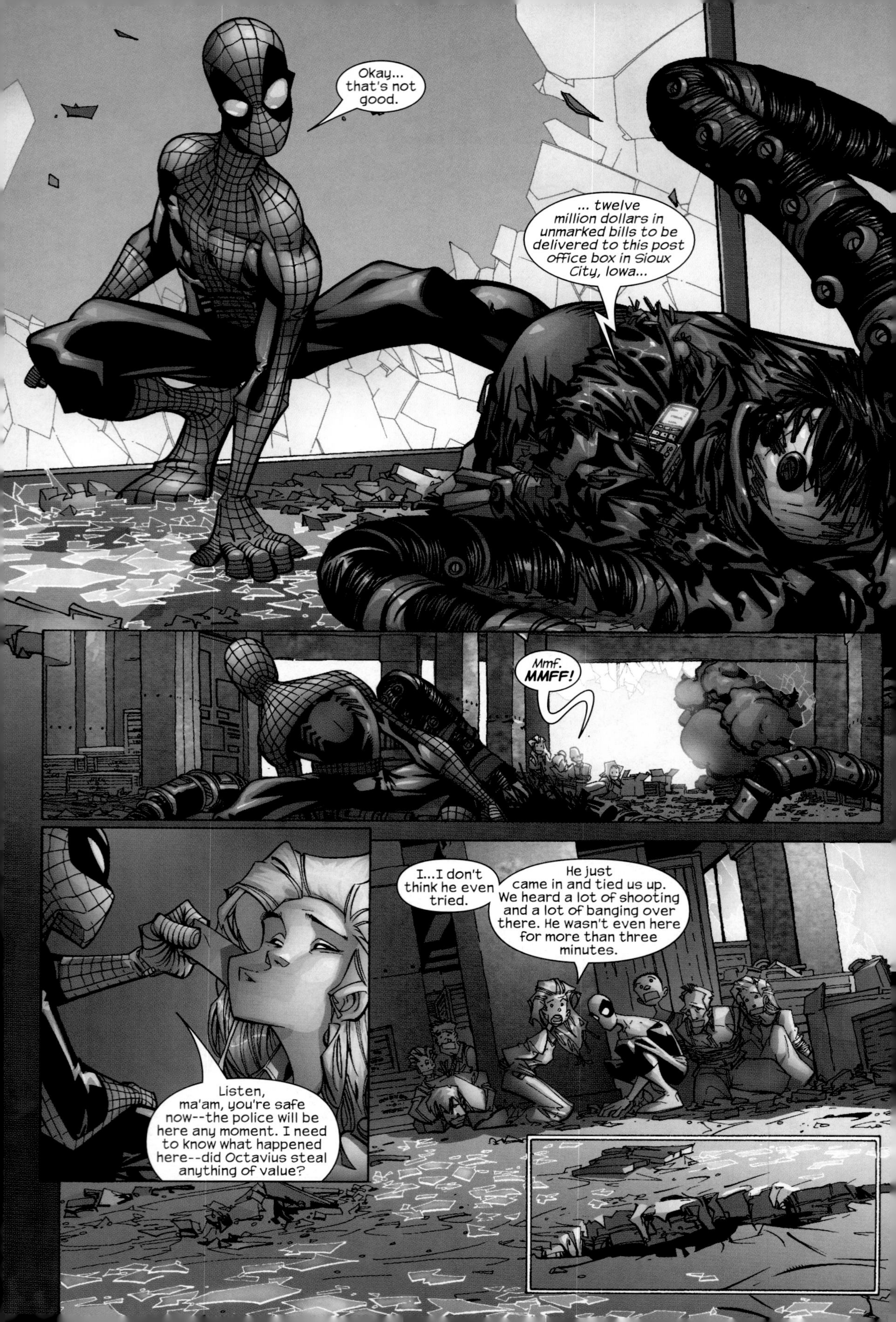
Okay... that's not good.
... twelve million dollars in unmarked bills to be delivered to this post office box in Sioux City, Iowa...
Mmf. MMFF!
Listen, ma'am, you're safe now--the police will be here any moment. I need to know what happened here--did Octavius steal anything of value?
I...I don't think he even tried.
He just came in and tied us up. We heard a lot of shooting and a lot of banging over there. He wasn't even here for more than three minutes.

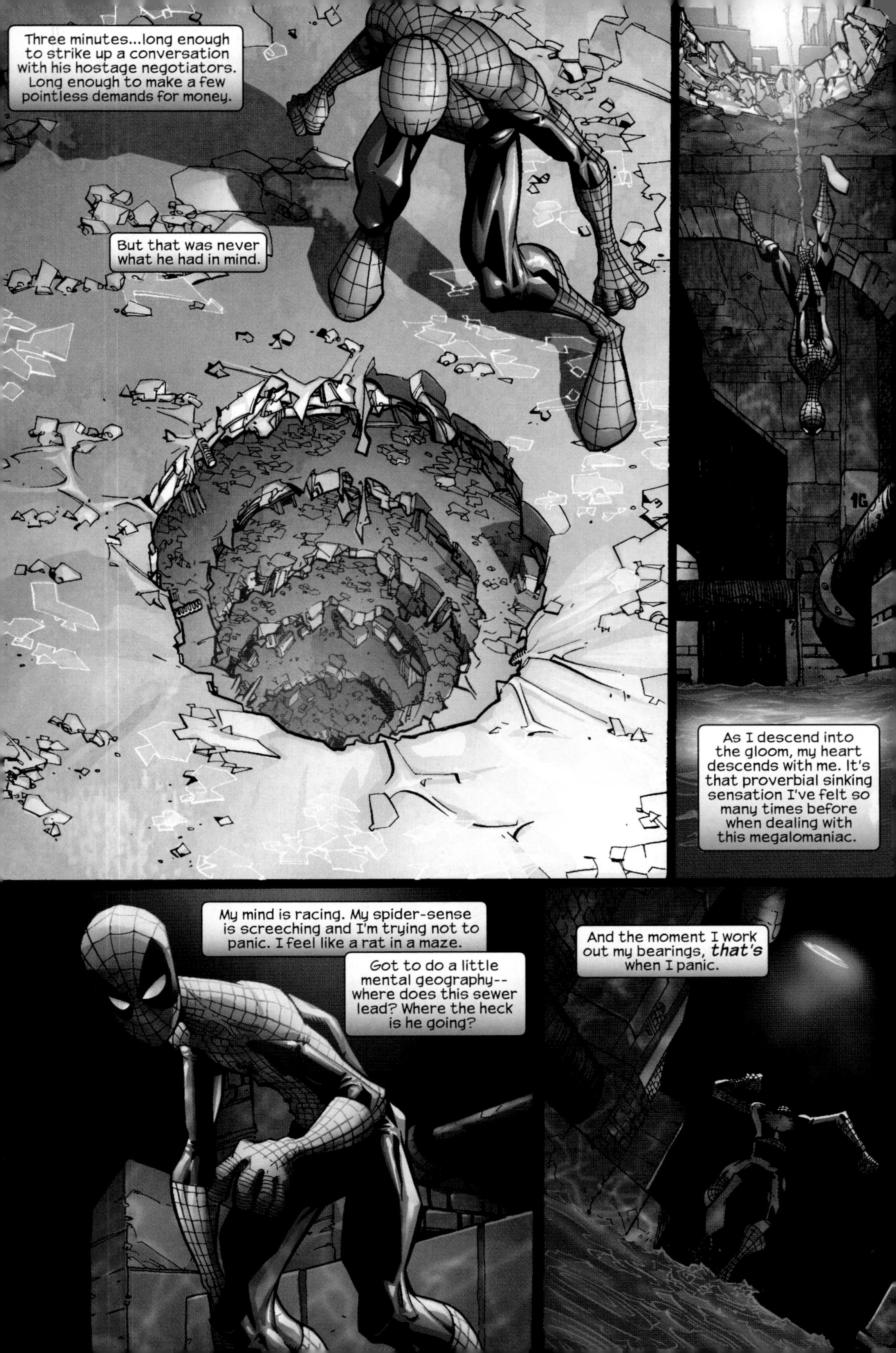
Three minutes...long enough to strike up a conversation with his hostage negotiators. Long enough to make a few pointless demands for money.
But that was never what he had in mind.
As I descend into the gloom, my heart descends with me. It's that proverbial sinking sensation I've felt so many times before when dealing with this megalomaniac.
My mind is racing. My spider-sense is screeching and I'm trying not to panic. I feel like a rat in a maze.
Got to do a little mental geography--where does this sewer lead? Where the heck is he going?
And the moment I work out my bearings, *that's* when I panic.

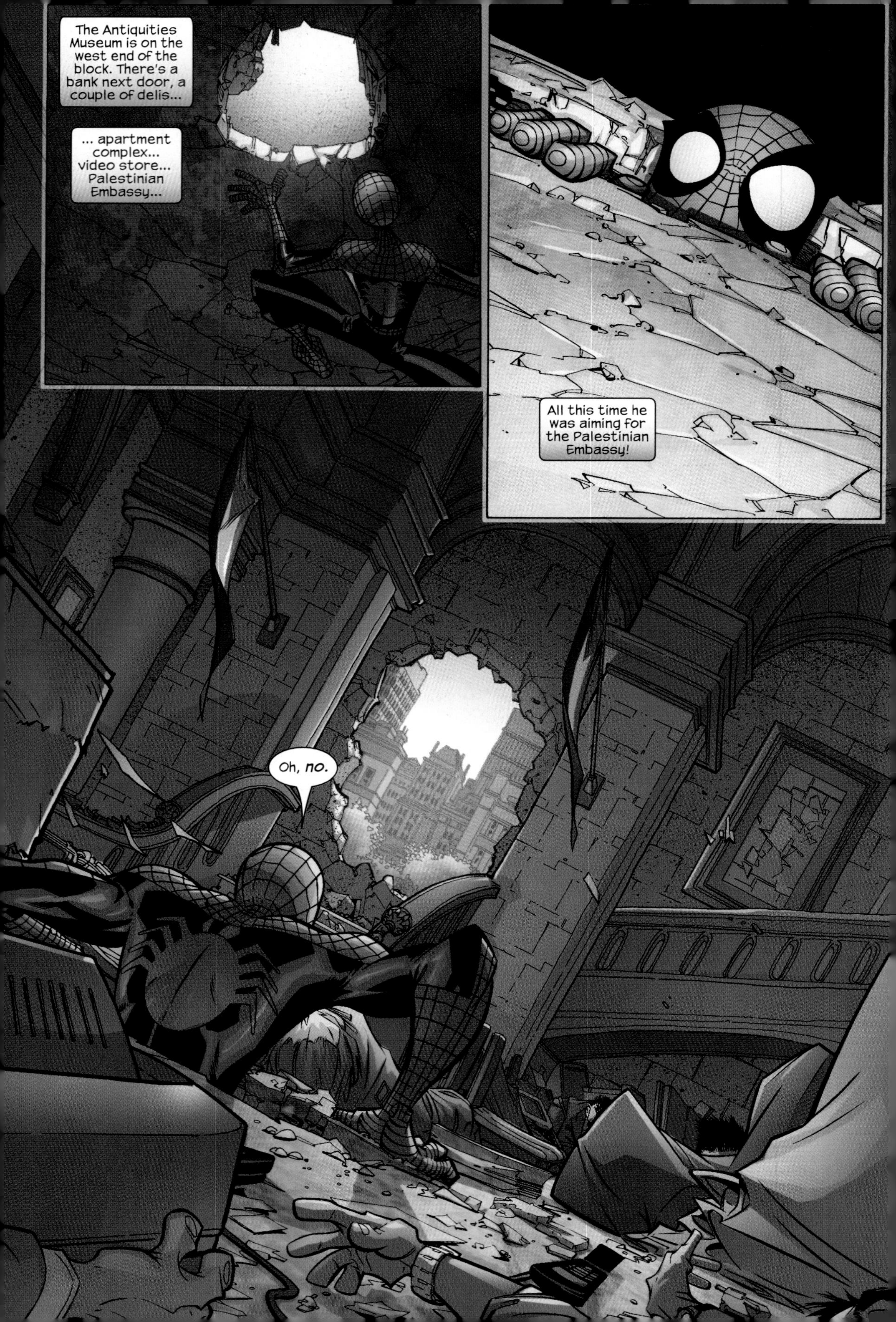
The Antiquities Museum is on the west end of the block. There's a bank next door, a couple of delis...
... apartment complex... video store... Palestinian Embassy...
All this time he was aiming for the Palestinian Embassy!
Oh, *no*.

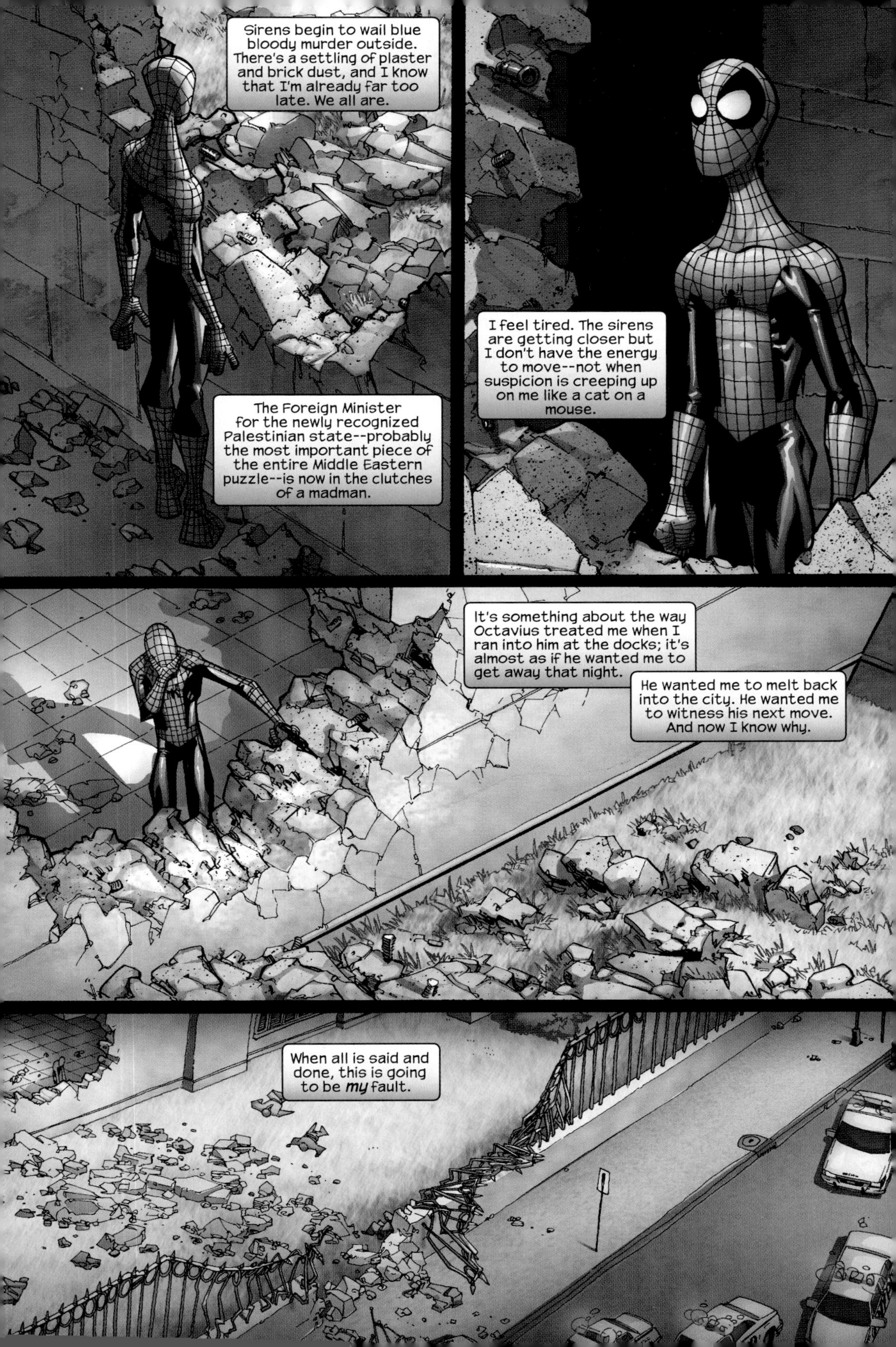
Sirens begin to wail blue bloody murder outside. There's a settling of plaster and brick dust, and I know that I'm already far too late. We all are.
The Foreign Minister for the newly recognized Palestinian state--probably the most important piece of the entire Middle Eastern puzzle--is now in the clutches of a madman.
I feel tired. The sirens are getting closer but I don't have the energy to move--not when suspicion is creeping up on me like a cat on a mouse.
It's something about the way Octavius treated me when I ran into him at the docks; it's almost as if he wanted me to get away that night.
He wanted me to melt back into the city. He wanted me to witness his next move. And now I know why.
When all is said and done, this is going to be *my* fault.

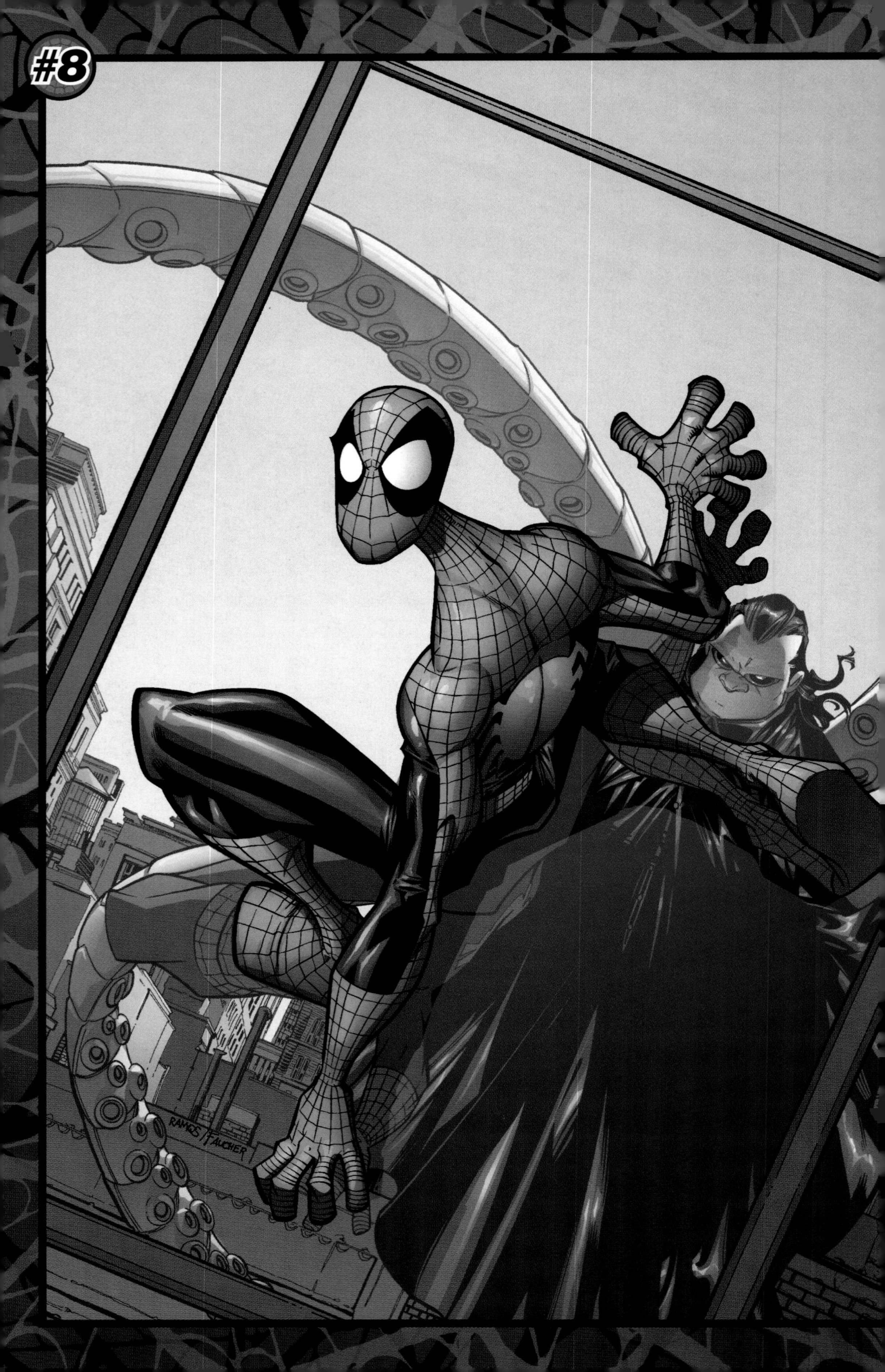
#8
RAMOS / FAUCHER

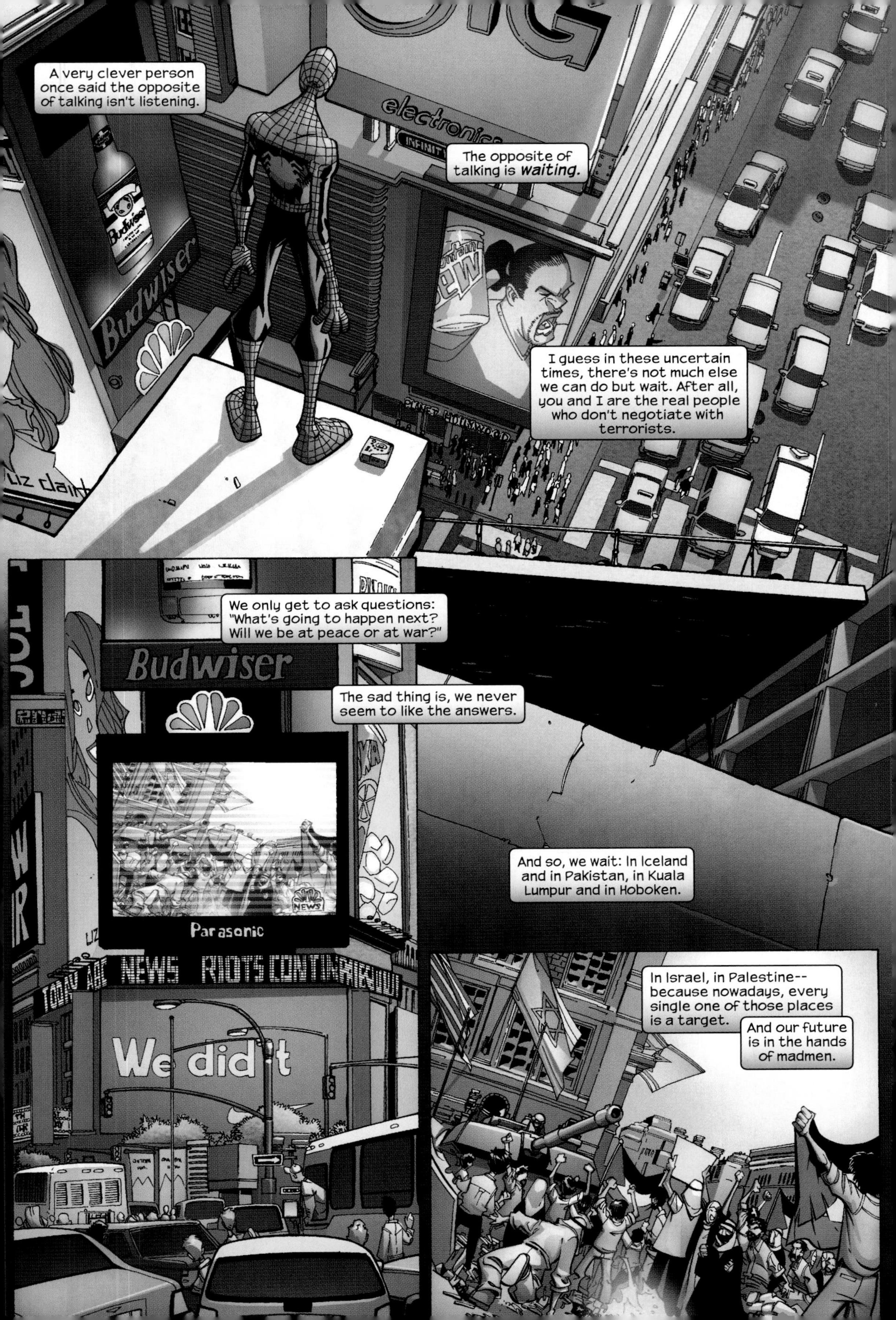
A very clever person once said the opposite of talking isn't listening.
The opposite of talking is *waiting.*
I guess in these uncertain times, there's not much else we can do but wait. After all, you and I are the real people who don't negotiate with terrorists.
We only get to ask questions: "What's going to happen next? Will we be at peace or at war?"
Budwiser
The sad thing is, we never seem to like the answers.
Parasonic
TODAY ABC NEWS RIOTS CONTIN
We did it
And so, we wait: In Iceland and in Pakistan, in Kuala Lumpur and in Hoboken.
In Israel, in Palestine-- because nowadays, every single one of those places is a target.
And our future is in the hands of madmen.

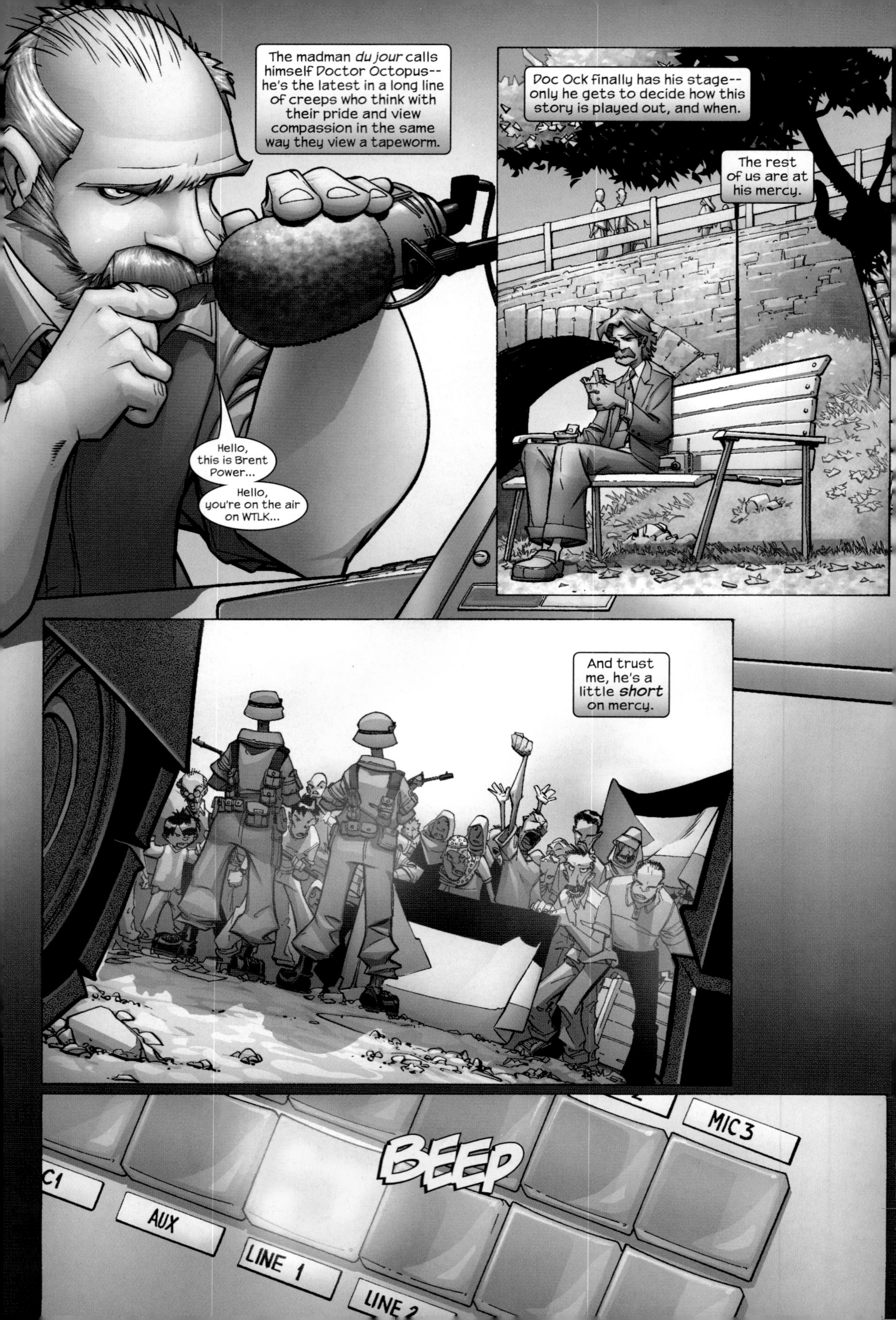
The madman *du jour* calls himself Doctor Octopus--he's the latest in a long line of creeps who think with their pride and view compassion in the same way they view a tapeworm.
Hello, this is Brent Power...
Hello, you're on the air on WTLK...
Doc Ock finally has his stage--only he gets to decide how this story is played out, and when.
The rest of us are at his mercy.
And trust me, he's a little *short* on mercy.
BEEP
MIC3
C1
AUX
LINE 1
LINE 2

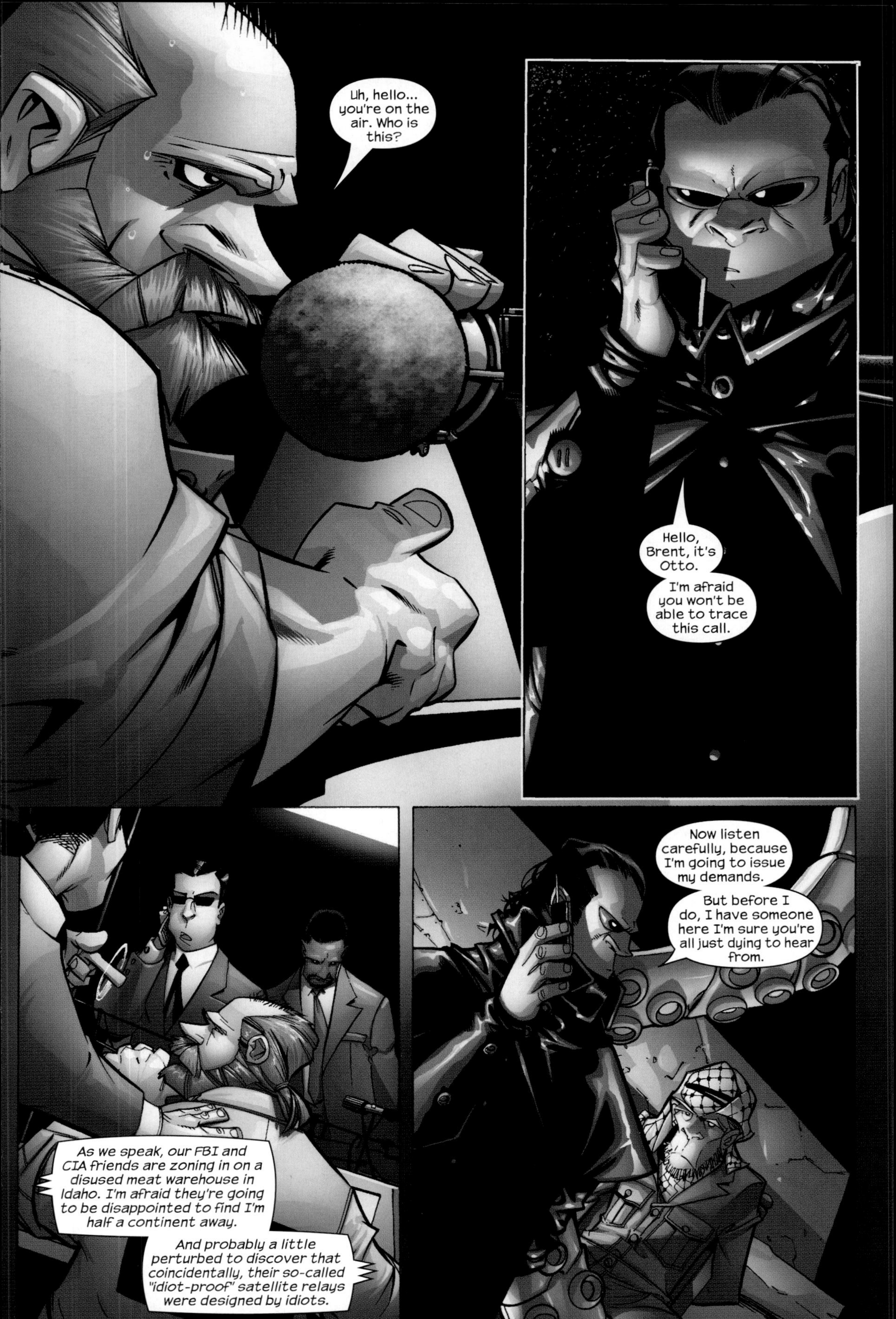
Uh, hello... you're on the air. Who is this?
Hello, Brent, it's Otto.
I'm afraid you won't be able to trace this call.
As we speak, our FBI and CIA friends are zoning in on a disused meat warehouse in Idaho. I'm afraid they're going to be disappointed to find I'm half a continent away.
And probably a little perturbed to discover that coincidentally, their so-called "idiot-proof" satellite relays were designed by idiots.
Now listen carefully, because I'm going to issue my demands.
But before I do, I have someone here I'm sure you're all just dying to hear from.

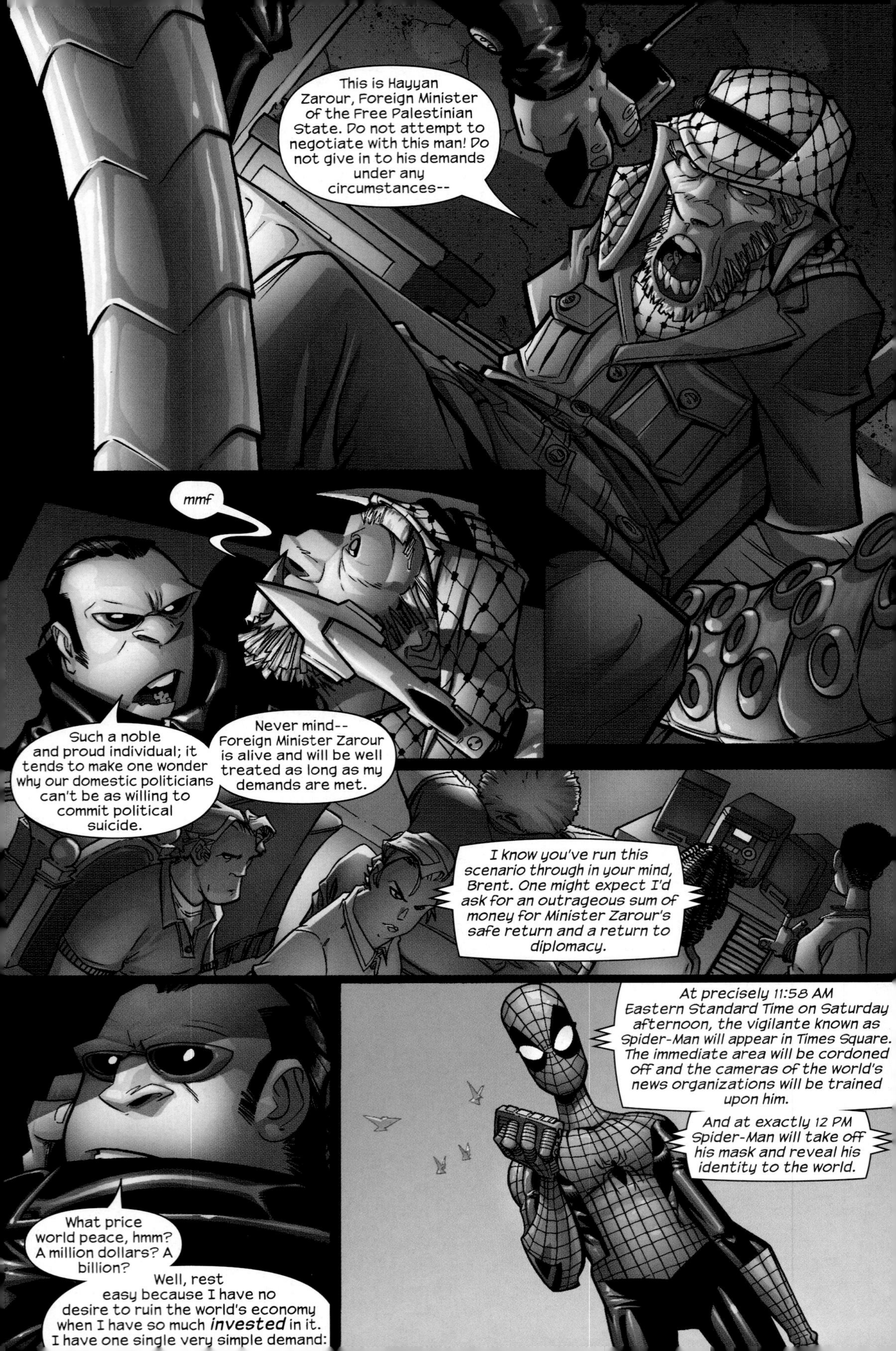

This is Hayyan Zarour, Foreign Minister of the Free Palestinian State. Do not attempt to negotiate with this man! Do not give in to his demands under any circumstances--
mmf
Such a noble and proud individual; it tends to make one wonder why our domestic politicians can't be as willing to commit political suicide.
Never mind-- Foreign Minister Zarour is alive and will be well treated as long as my demands are met.
I know you've run this scenario through in your mind, Brent. One might expect I'd ask for an outrageous sum of money for Minister Zarour's safe return and a return to diplomacy.
What price world peace, hmm? A million dollars? A billion?
Well, rest easy because I have no desire to ruin the world's economy when I have so much *invested* in it. I have one single very simple demand:
At precisely 11:58 AM Eastern Standard Time on Saturday afternoon, the vigilante known as Spider-Man will appear in Times Square. The immediate area will be cordoned off and the cameras of the world's news organizations will be trained upon him.
And at exactly 12 PM Spider-Man will take off his mask and reveal his identity to the world.

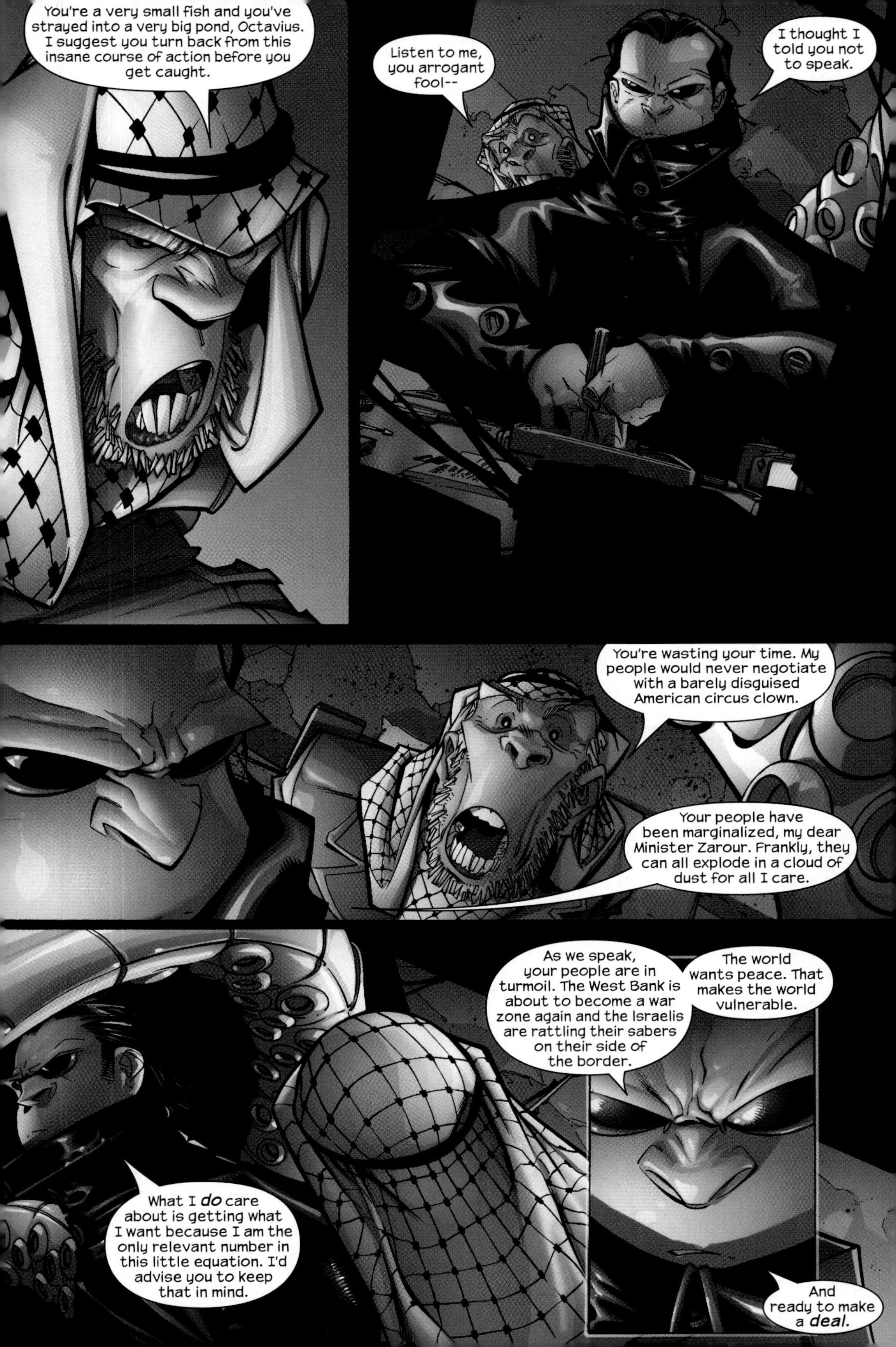
You're a very small fish and you've strayed into a very big pond, Octavius. I suggest you turn back from this insane course of action before you get caught.
Listen to me, you arrogant fool--
I thought I told you not to speak.
You're wasting your time. My people would never negotiate with a barely disguised American circus clown.
Your people have been marginalized, my dear Minister Zarour. Frankly, they can all explode in a cloud of dust for all I care.
What I *do* care about is getting what I want because I am the only relevant number in this little equation. I'd advise you to keep that in mind.
As we speak, your people are in turmoil. The West Bank is about to become a war zone again and the Israelis are rattling their sabers on their side of the border.
The world wants peace. That makes the world vulnerable.
And ready to make a ***deal.***

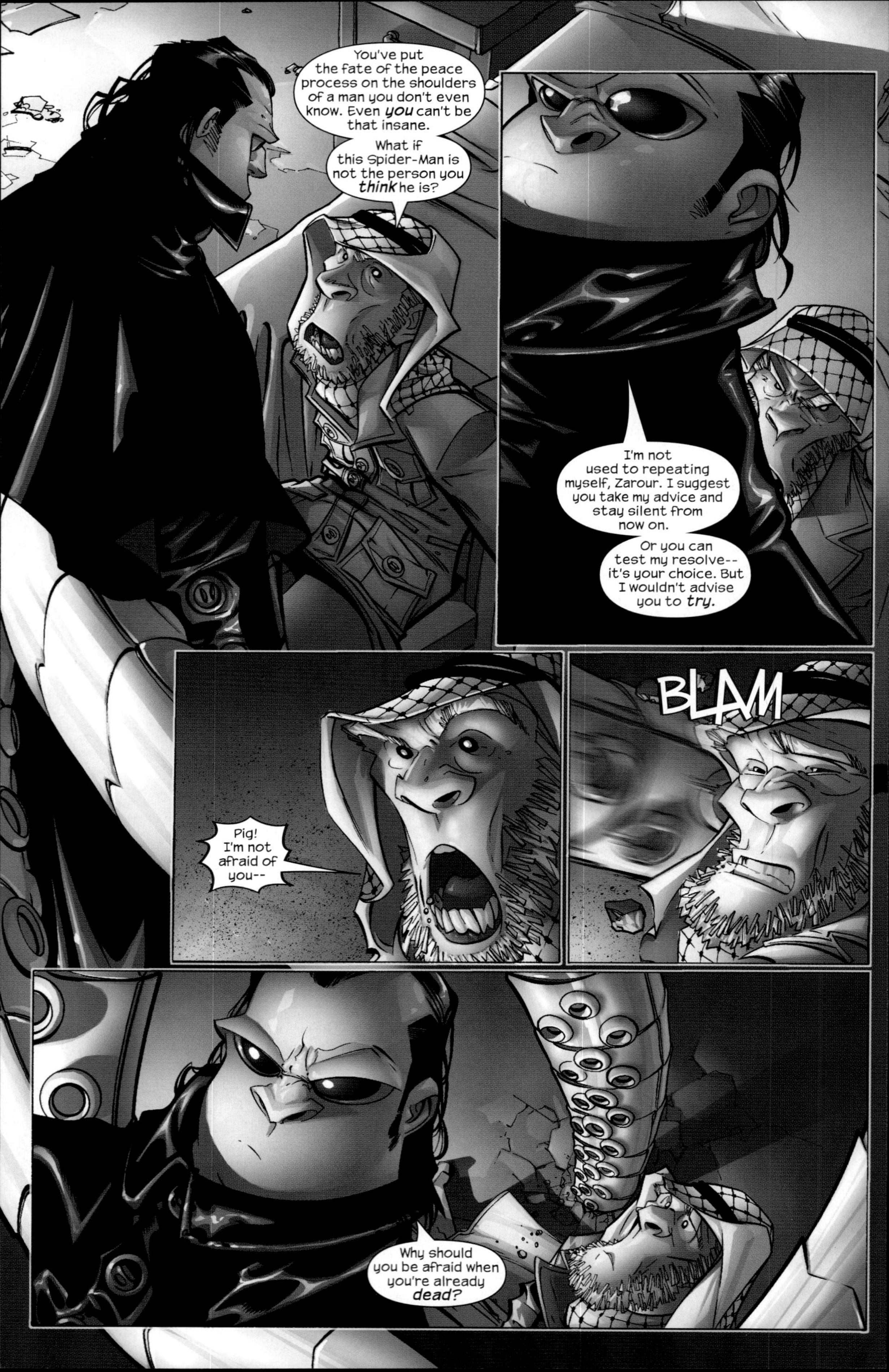
You've put the fate of the peace process on the shoulders of a man you don't even know. Even *you* can't be that insane.
What if this Spider-Man is not the person you *think* he is?
I'm not used to repeating myself, Zarour. I suggest you take my advice and stay silent from now on.
Or you can test my resolve-- it's your choice. But I wouldn't advise you to *try.*
Pig! I'm not afraid of you--
BLAM
Why should you be afraid when you're already *dead?*

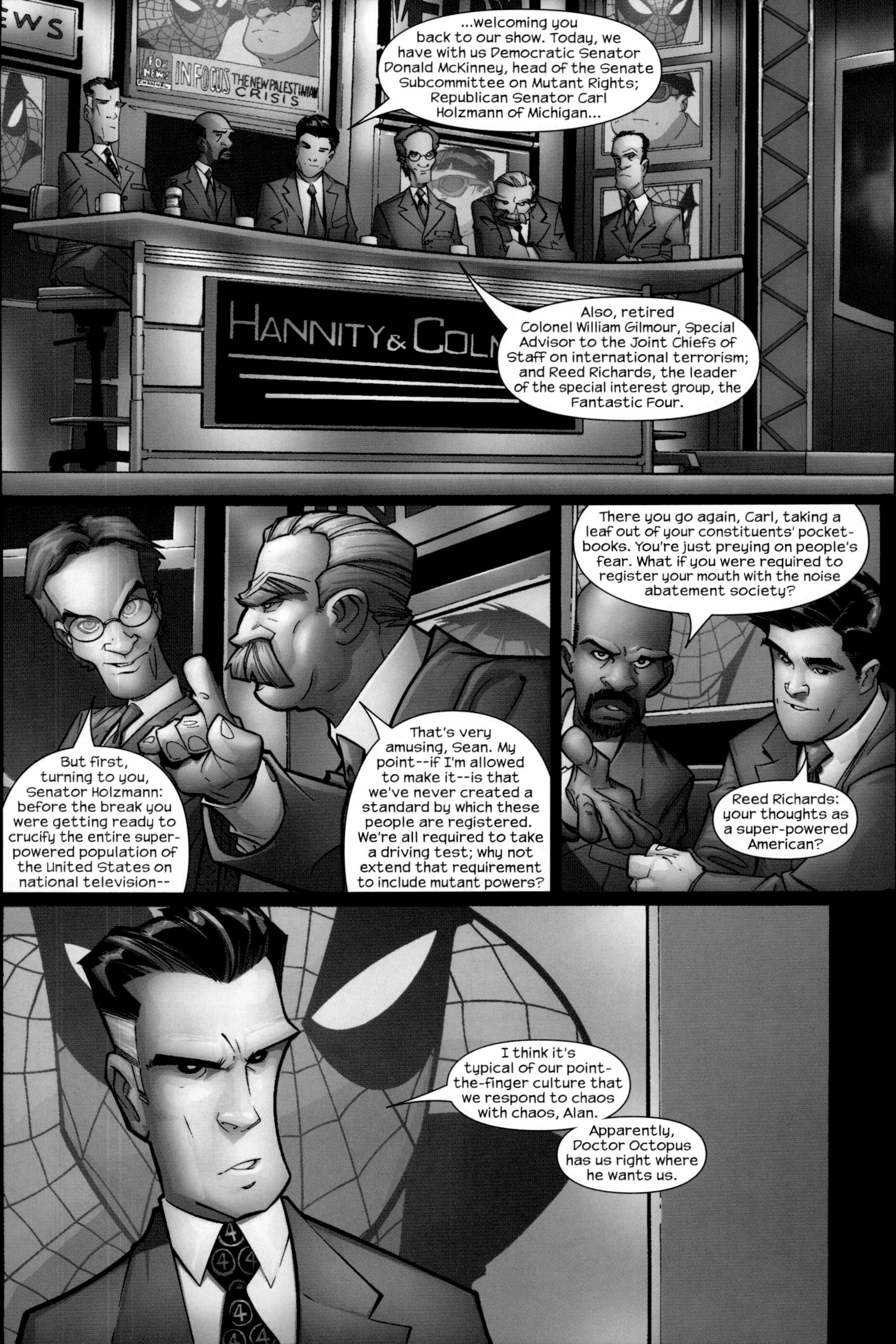
...welcoming you back to our show. Today, we have with us Democratic Senator Donald McKinney, head of the Senate Subcommittee on Mutant Rights; Republican Senator Carl Holzmann of Michigan...
Also, retired Colonel William Gilmour, Special Advisor to the Joint Chiefs of Staff on international terrorism; and Reed Richards, the leader of the special interest group, the Fantastic Four.
But first, turning to you, Senator Holzmann: before the break you were getting ready to crucify the entire super-powered population of the United States on national television--
That's very amusing, Sean. My point--if I'm allowed to make it--is that we've never created a standard by which these people are registered. We're all required to take a driving test; why not extend that requirement to include mutant powers?
There you go again, Carl, taking a leaf out of your constituents' pocket-books. You're just preying on people's fear. What if you were required to register your mouth with the noise abatement society?
Reed Richards: your thoughts as a super-powered American?
I think it's typical of our point-the-finger culture that we respond to chaos with chaos, Alan.
Apparently, Doctor Octopus has us right where he wants us.

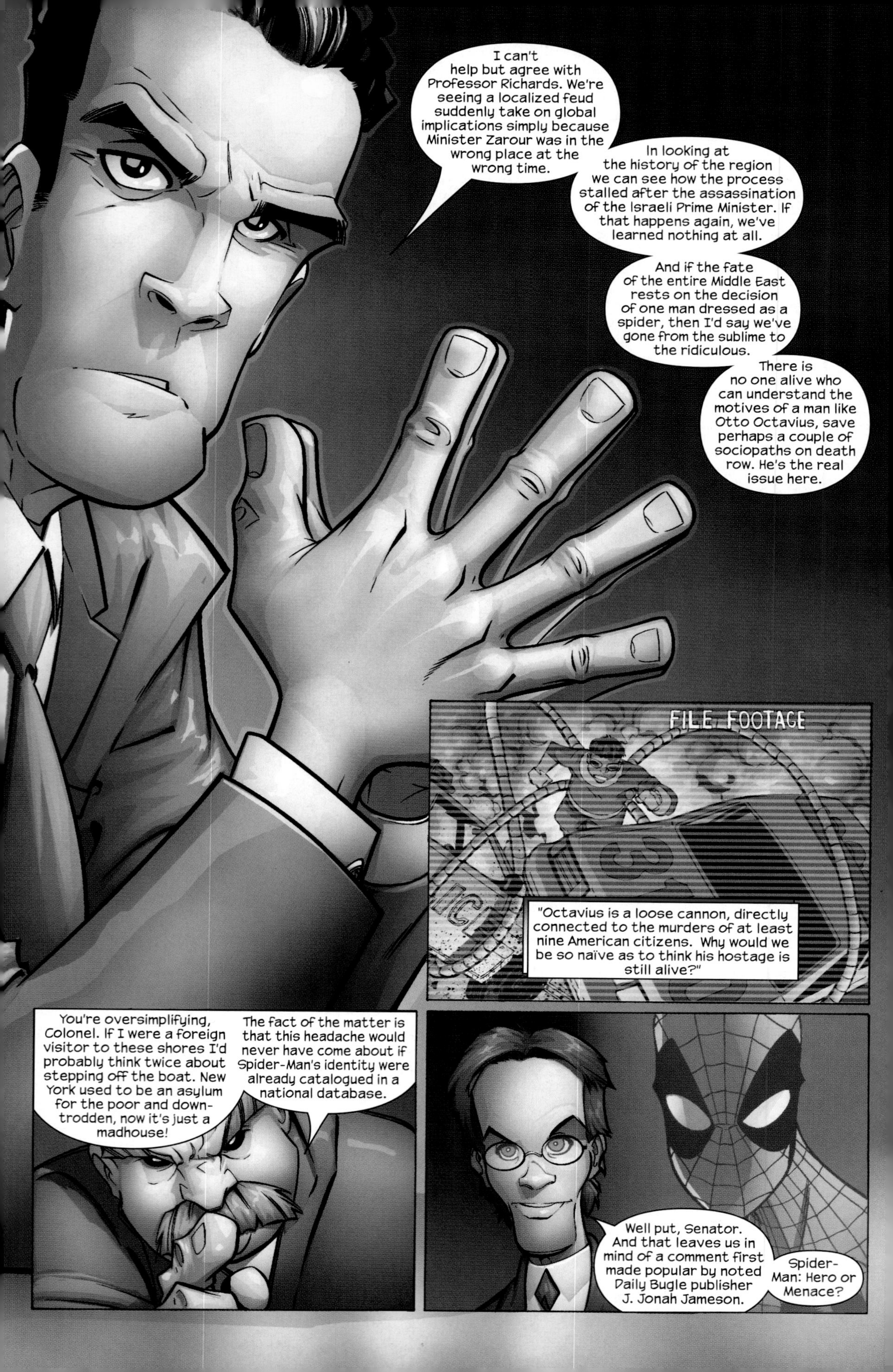
I can't help but agree with Professor Richards. We're seeing a localized feud suddenly take on global implications simply because Minister Zarour was in the wrong place at the wrong time.
In looking at the history of the region we can see how the process stalled after the assassination of the Israeli Prime Minister. If that happens again, we've learned nothing at all.
And if the fate of the entire Middle East rests on the decision of one man dressed as a spider, then I'd say we've gone from the sublime to the ridiculous.
There is no one alive who can understand the motives of a man like Otto Octavius, save perhaps a couple of sociopaths on death row. He's the real issue here.
FILE FOOTAGE
"Octavius is a loose cannon, directly connected to the murders of at least nine American citizens. Why would we be so naïve as to think his hostage is still alive?"
You're oversimplifying, Colonel. If I were a foreign visitor to these shores I'd probably think twice about stepping off the boat. New York used to be an asylum for the poor and down-trodden, now it's just a madhouse!
The fact of the matter is that this headache would never have come about if Spider-Man's identity were already catalogued in a national database.
Well put, Senator. And that leaves us in mind of a comment first made popular by noted Daily Bugle publisher J. Jonah Jameson.
Spider-Man: Hero or Menace?

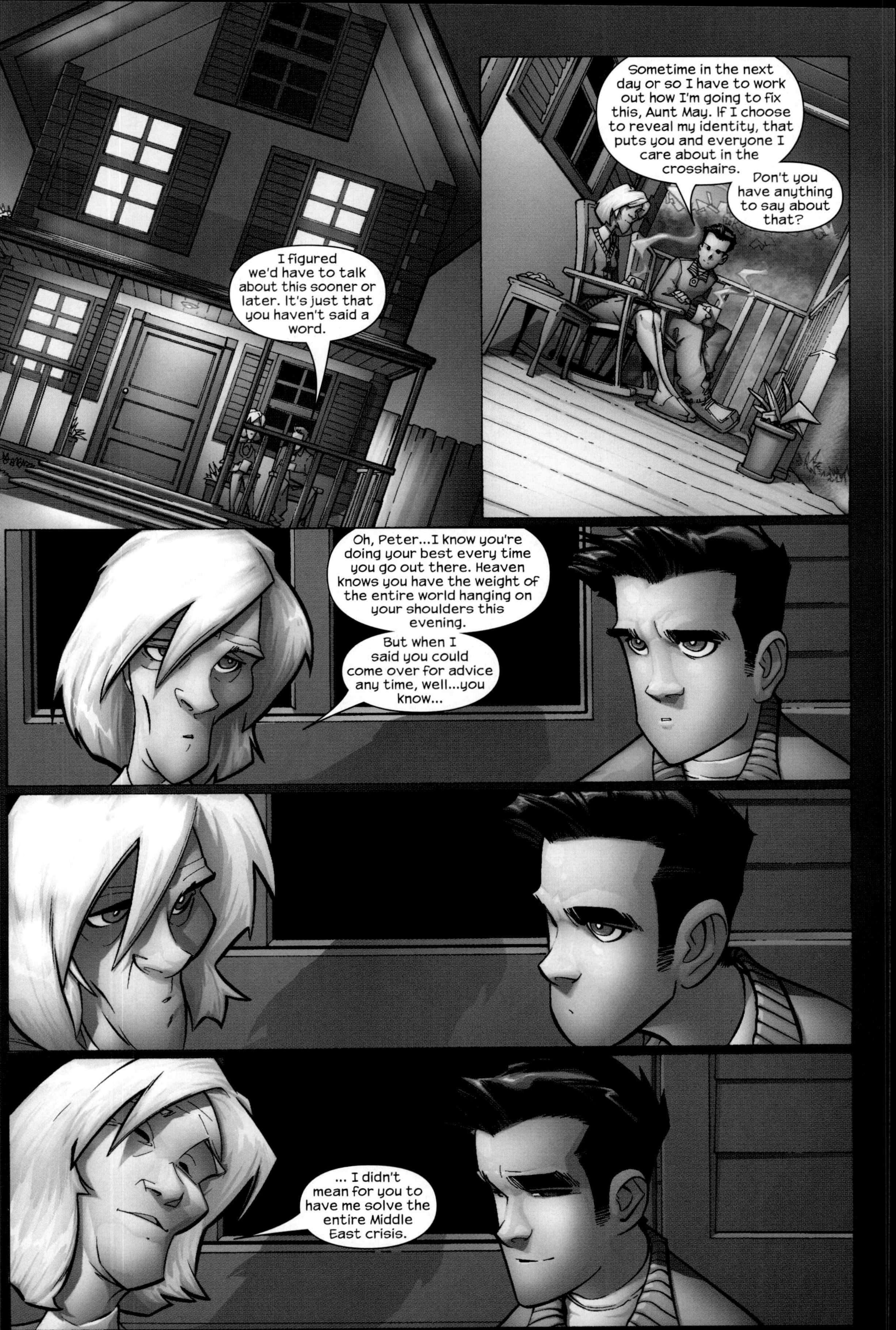
I figured we'd have to talk about this sooner or later. It's just that you haven't said a word.
Sometime in the next day or so I have to work out how I'm going to fix this, Aunt May. If I choose to reveal my identity, that puts you and everyone I care about in the crosshairs.
Don't you have anything to say about that?
Oh, Peter...I know you're doing your best every time you go out there. Heaven knows you have the weight of the entire world hanging on your shoulders this evening.
But when I said you could come over for advice any time, well...you know...
... I didn't mean for you to have me solve the entire Middle East crisis.

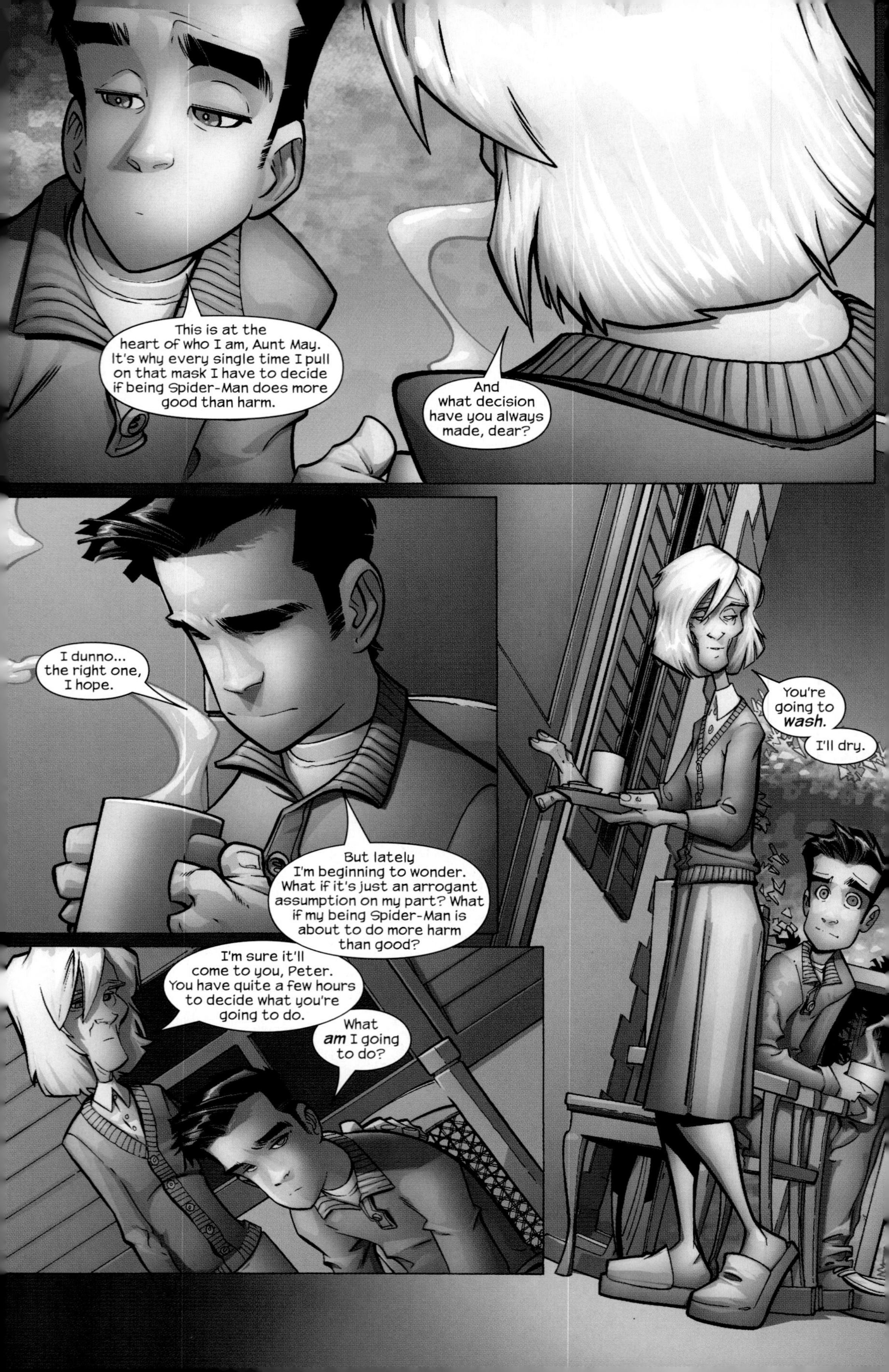

This is at the heart of who I am, Aunt May. It's why every single time I pull on that mask I have to decide if being Spider-Man does more good than harm.
And what decision have you always made, dear?
I dunno... the right one, I hope.
But lately I'm beginning to wonder. What if it's just an arrogant assumption on my part? What if my being Spider-Man is about to do more harm than good?
I'm sure it'll come to you, Peter. You have quite a few hours to decide what you're going to do.
What am I going to do?
You're going to wash.
I'll dry.

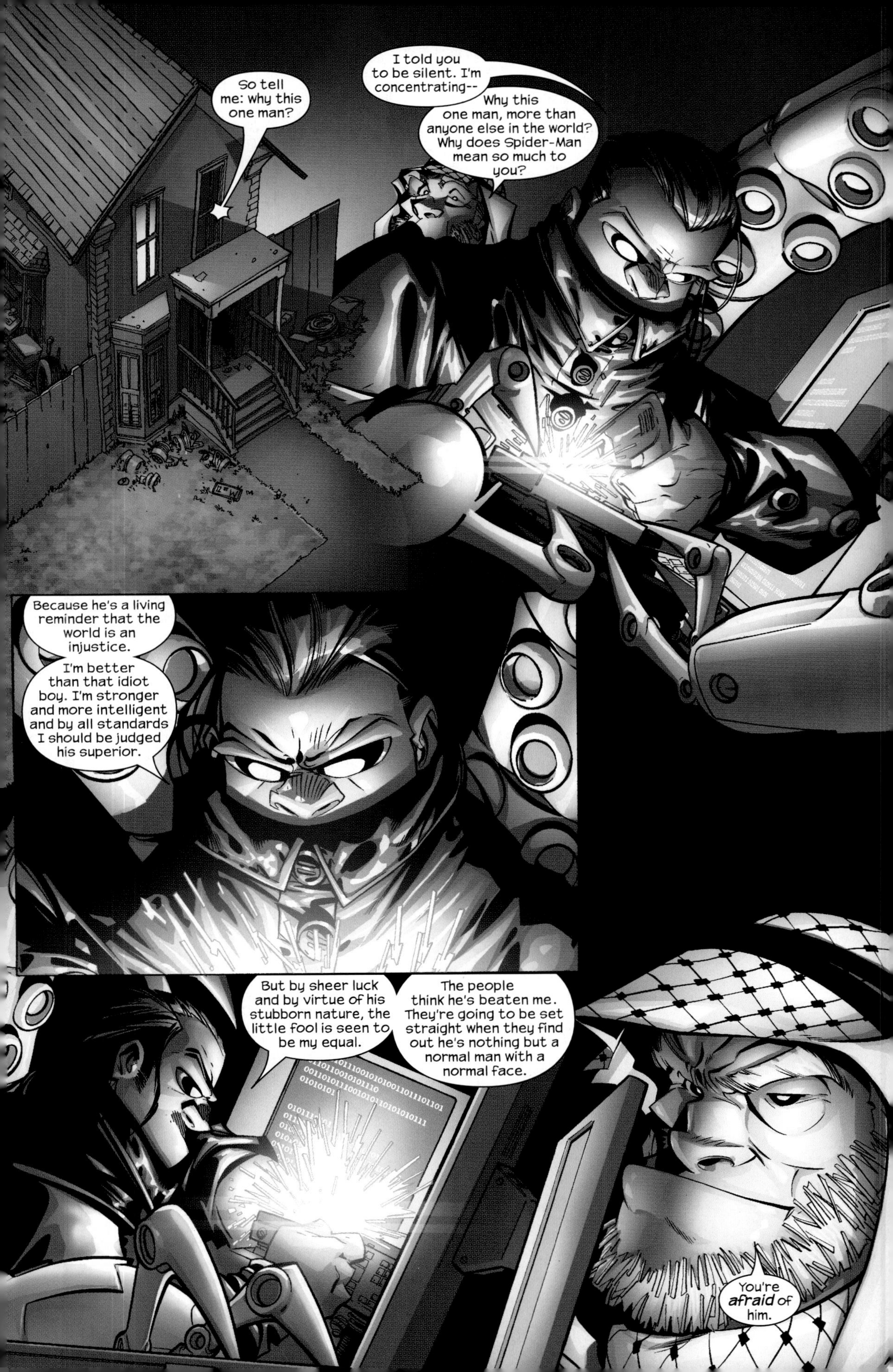

So tell me: why this one man?
I told you to be silent. I'm concentrating--
Why this one man, more than anyone else in the world? Why does Spider-Man mean so much to you?
Because he's a living reminder that the world is an injustice.
I'm better than that idiot boy. I'm stronger and more intelligent and by all standards I should be judged his superior.
But by sheer luck and by virtue of his stubborn nature, the little fool is seen to be my equal.
The people think he's beaten me. They're going to be set straight when they find out he's nothing but a normal man with a normal face.
You're *afraid* of him.

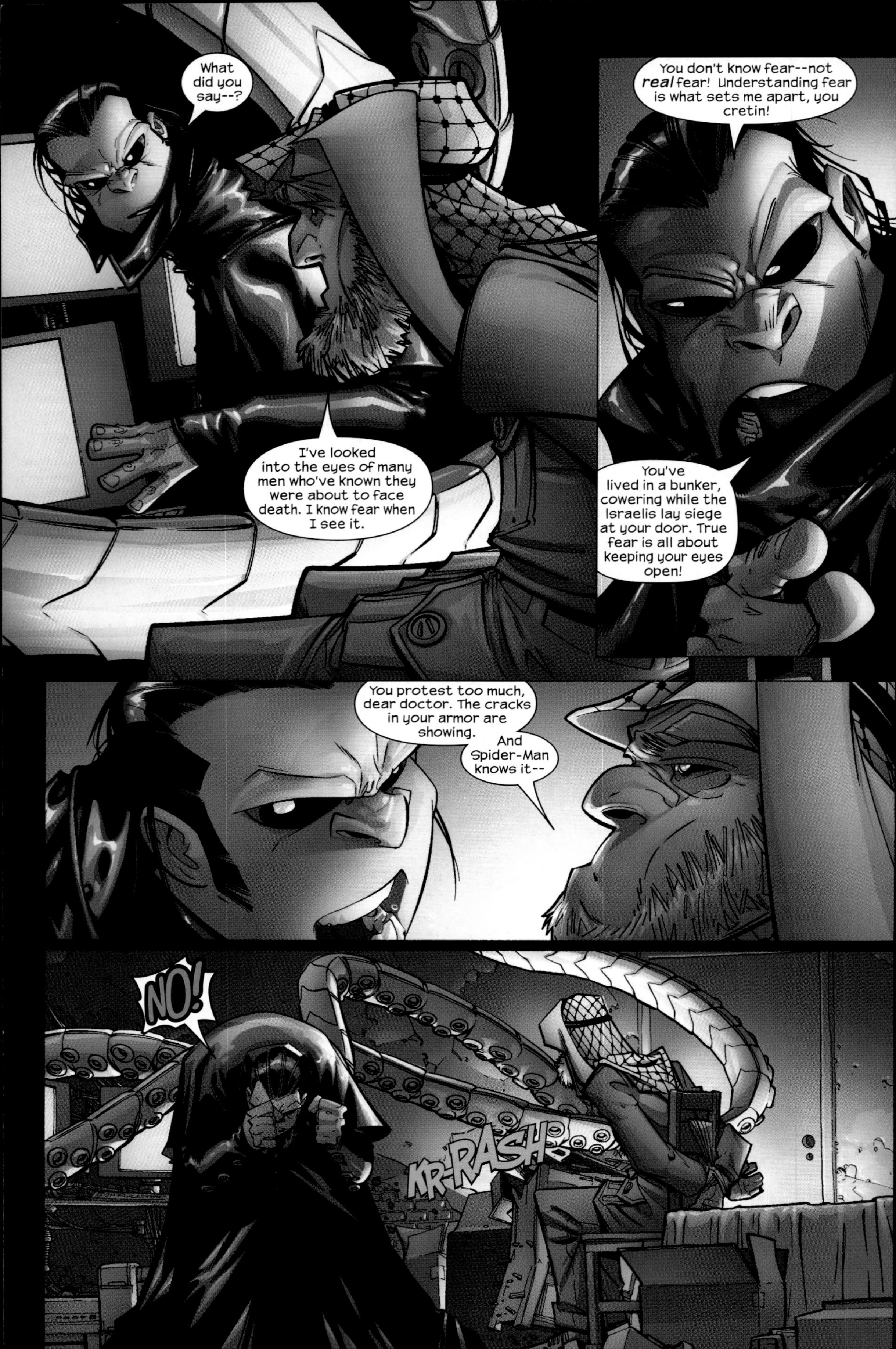
What did you say--?
I've looked into the eyes of many men who've known they were about to face death. I know fear when I see it.
You don't know fear--not *real* fear! Understanding fear is what sets me apart, you cretin!
You've lived in a bunker, cowering while the Israelis lay siege at your door. True fear is all about keeping your eyes open!
You protest too much, dear doctor. The cracks in your armor are showing.
And Spider-Man knows it--
NO!
KR-RASH

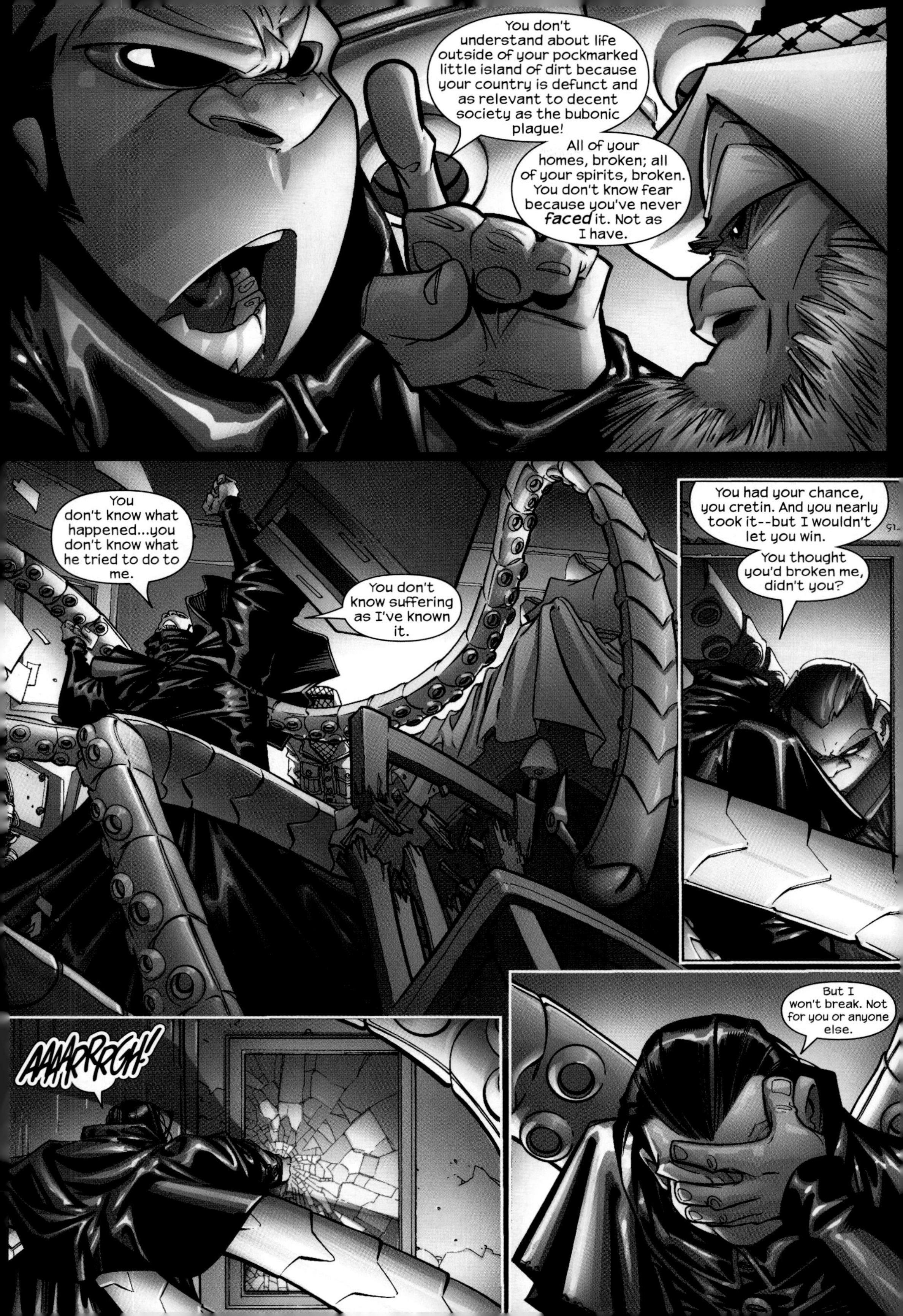

You don't understand about life outside of your pockmarked little island of dirt because your country is defunct and as relevant to decent society as the bubonic plague!
All of your homes, broken; all of your spirits, broken. You don't know fear because you've never *faced* it. Not as I have.
You don't know what happened...you don't know what he tried to do to me.
You don't know suffering as I've known it.
You had your chance, you cretin. And you nearly took it--but I wouldn't let you win.
You thought you'd broken me, didn't you?
AAAARRRGH!
But I won't break. Not for you or anyone else.

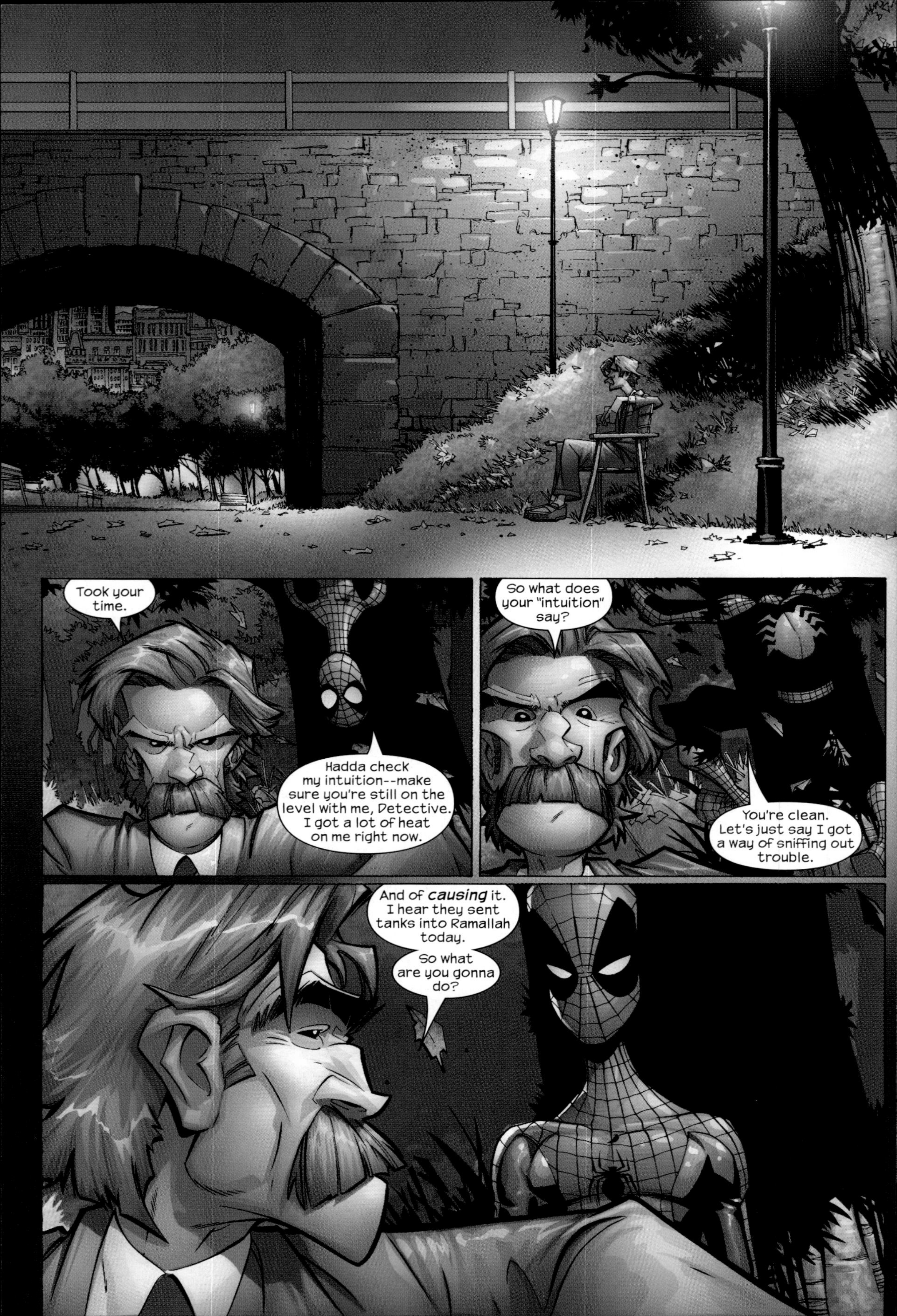
Took your time.
Hadda check my intuition--make sure you're still on the level with me, Detective. I got a lot of heat on me right now.
So what does your "intuition" say?
You're clean. Let's just say I got a way of sniffing out trouble.
And of *causing* it. I hear they sent tanks into Ramallah today.
So what are you gonna do?

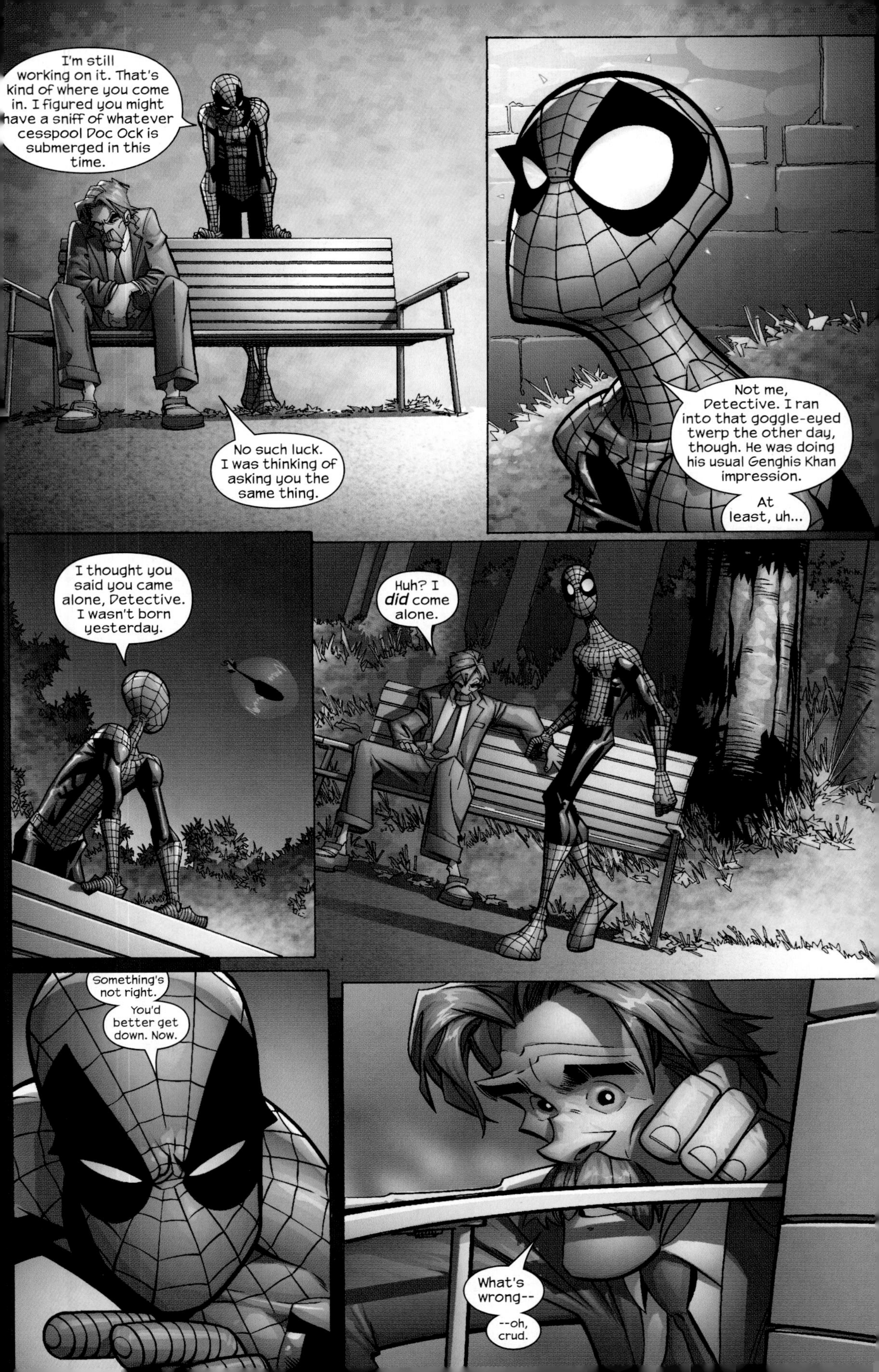
I'm still working on it. That's kind of where you come in. I figured you might have a sniff of whatever cesspool Doc Ock is submerged in this time.
No such luck. I was thinking of asking you the same thing.
Not me, Detective. I ran into that goggle-eyed twerp the other day, though. He was doing his usual Genghis Khan impression.
At least, uh...
I thought you said you came alone, Detective. I wasn't born yesterday.
Huh? I *did* come alone.
Something's not right.
You'd better get down. Now.
What's wrong--
--oh, crud.

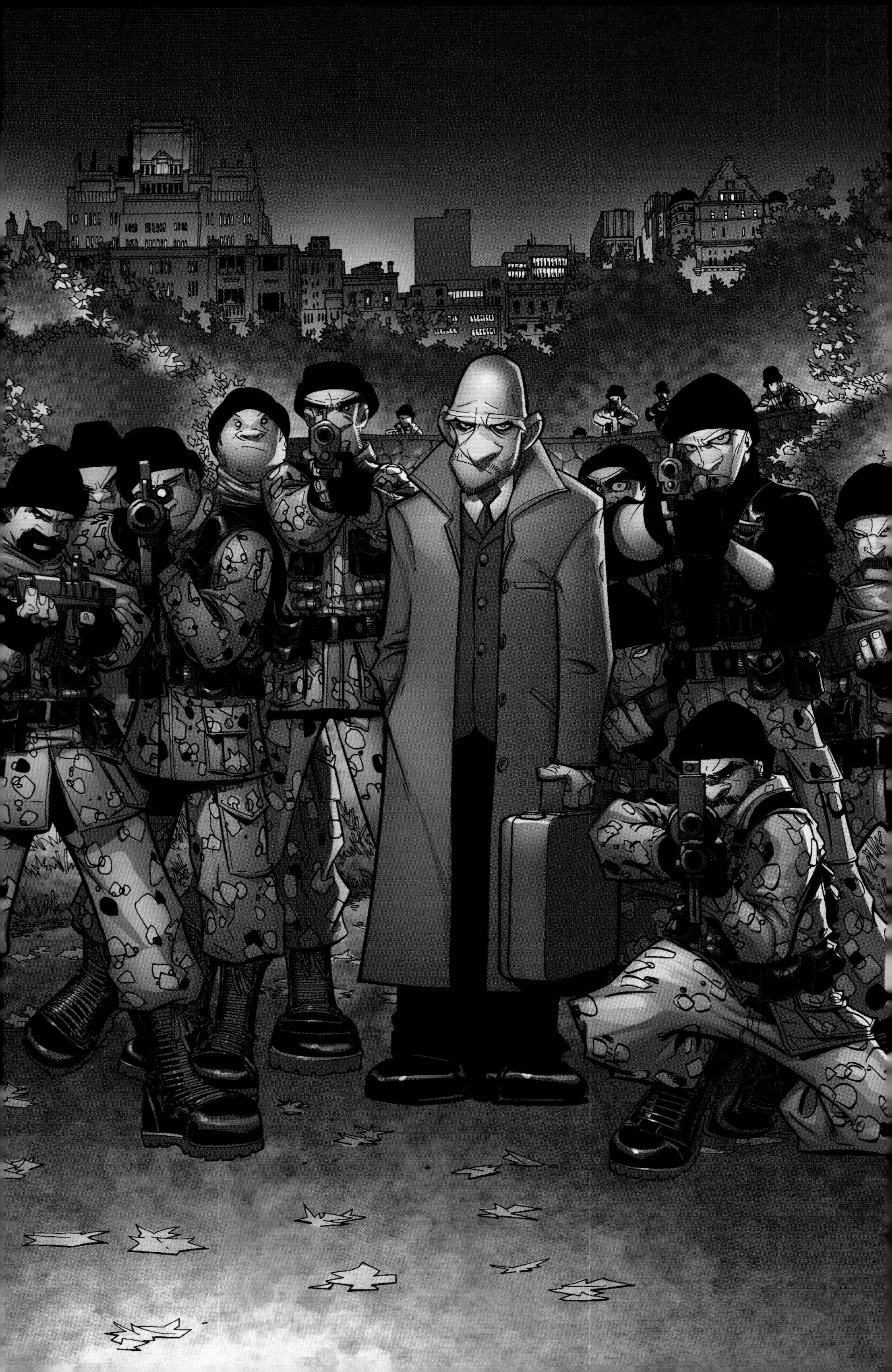

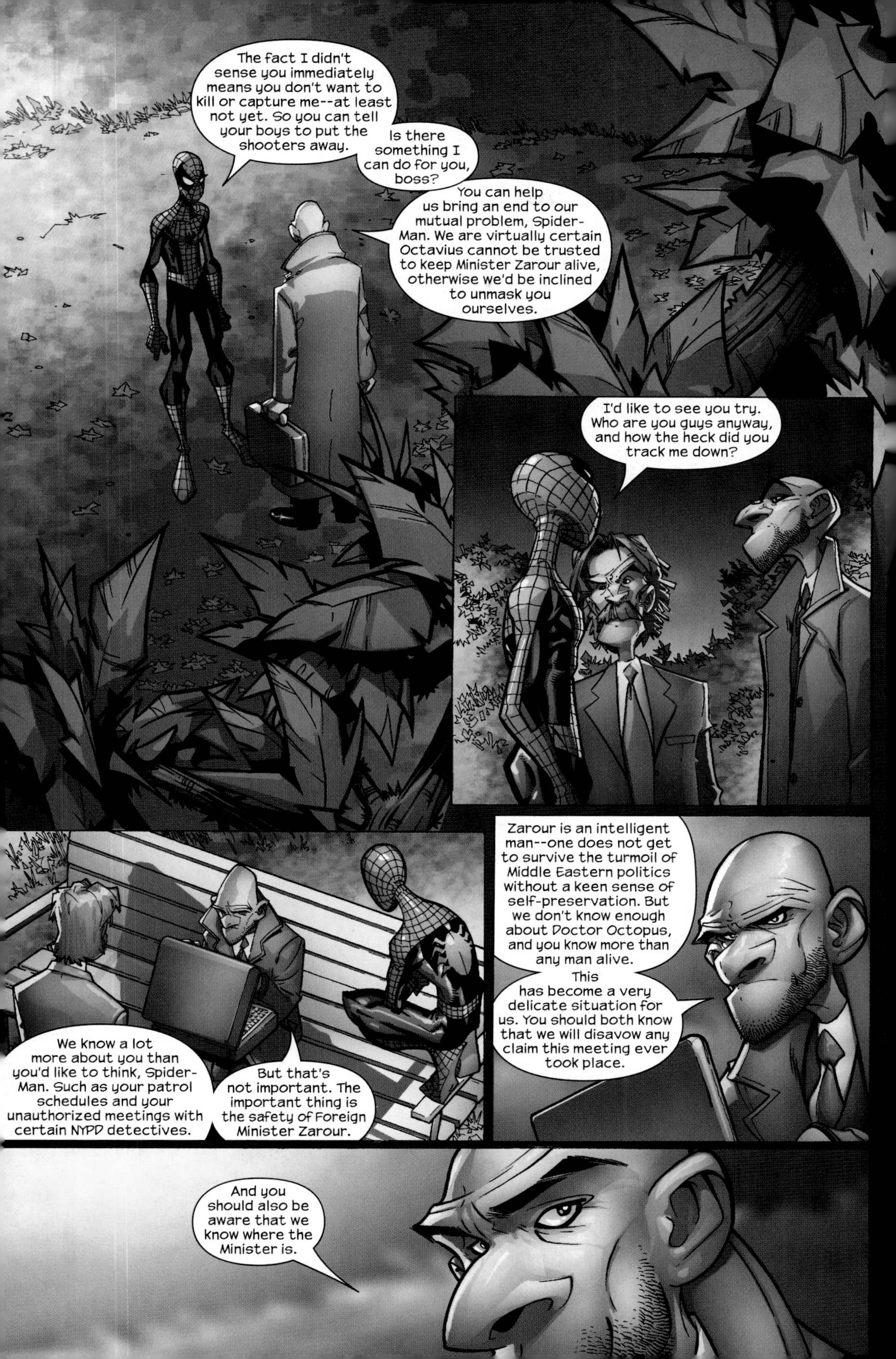
The fact I didn't sense you immediately means you don't want to kill or capture me--at least not yet. So you can tell your boys to put the shooters away.
Is there something I can do for you, boss?
You can help us bring an end to our mutual problem, Spider-Man. We are virtually certain Octavius cannot be trusted to keep Minister Zarour alive, otherwise we'd be inclined to unmask you ourselves.
I'd like to see you try. Who are you guys anyway, and how the heck did you track me down?
We know a lot more about you than you'd like to think, Spider-Man. Such as your patrol schedules and your unauthorized meetings with certain NYPD detectives.
But that's not important. The important thing is the safety of Foreign Minister Zarour.
Zarour is an intelligent man--one does not get to survive the turmoil of Middle Eastern politics without a keen sense of self-preservation. But we don't know enough about Doctor Octopus, and you know more than any man alive.
This has become a very delicate situation for us. You should both know that we will disavow any claim this meeting ever took place.
And you should also be aware that we know where the Minister is.

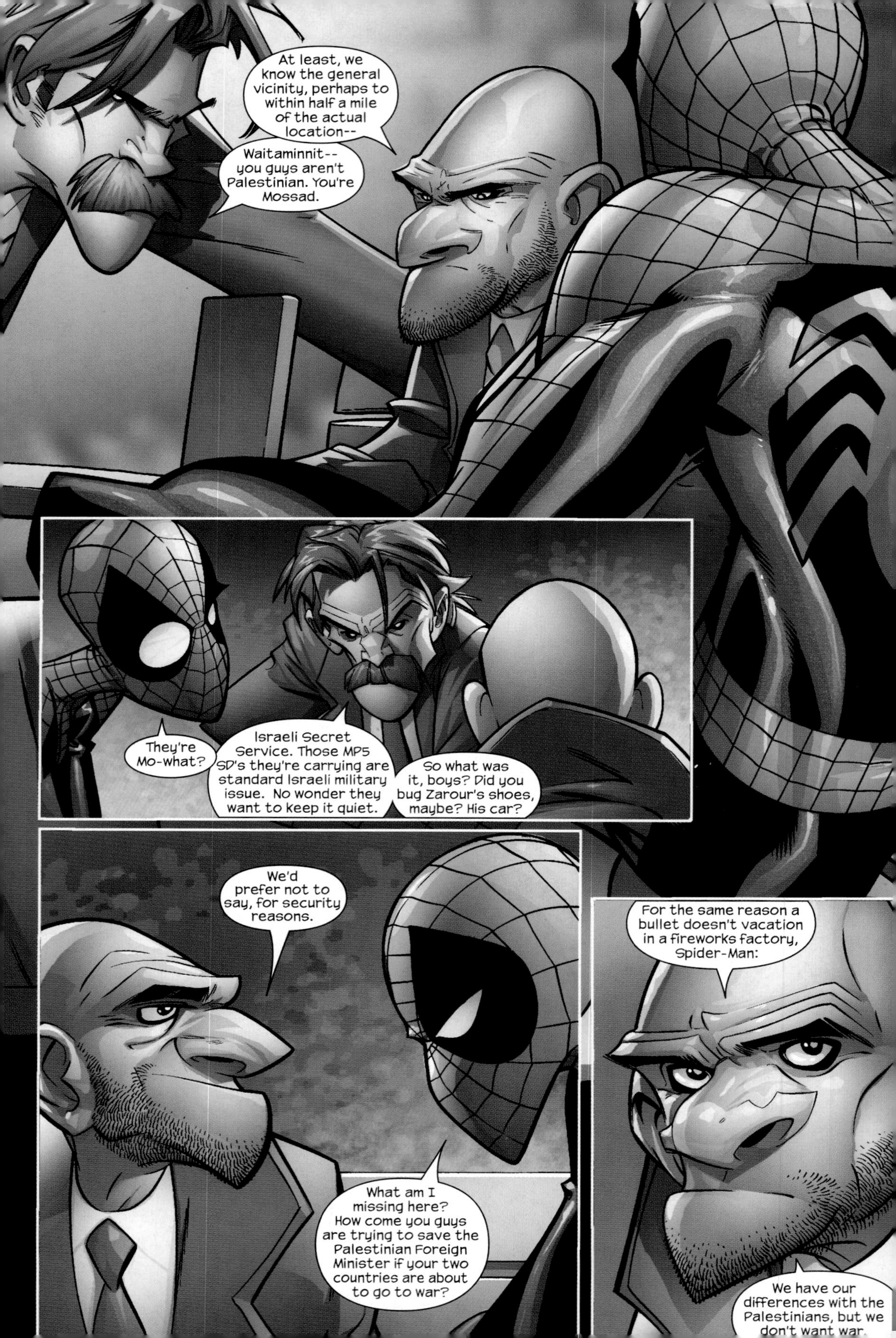
At least, we know the general vicinity, perhaps to within half a mile of the actual location--
Waitaminnit-- you guys aren't Palestinian. You're Mossad.
They're Mo-what?
Israeli Secret Service. Those MP5 SD's they're carrying are standard Israeli military issue. No wonder they want to keep it quiet.
So what was it, boys? Did you bug Zarour's shoes, maybe? His car?
We'd prefer not to say, for security reasons.
What am I missing here? How come you guys are trying to save the Palestinian Foreign Minister if your two countries are about to go to war?
For the same reason a bullet doesn't vacation in a fireworks factory, Spider-Man:
We have our differences with the Palestinians, but we don't want war.

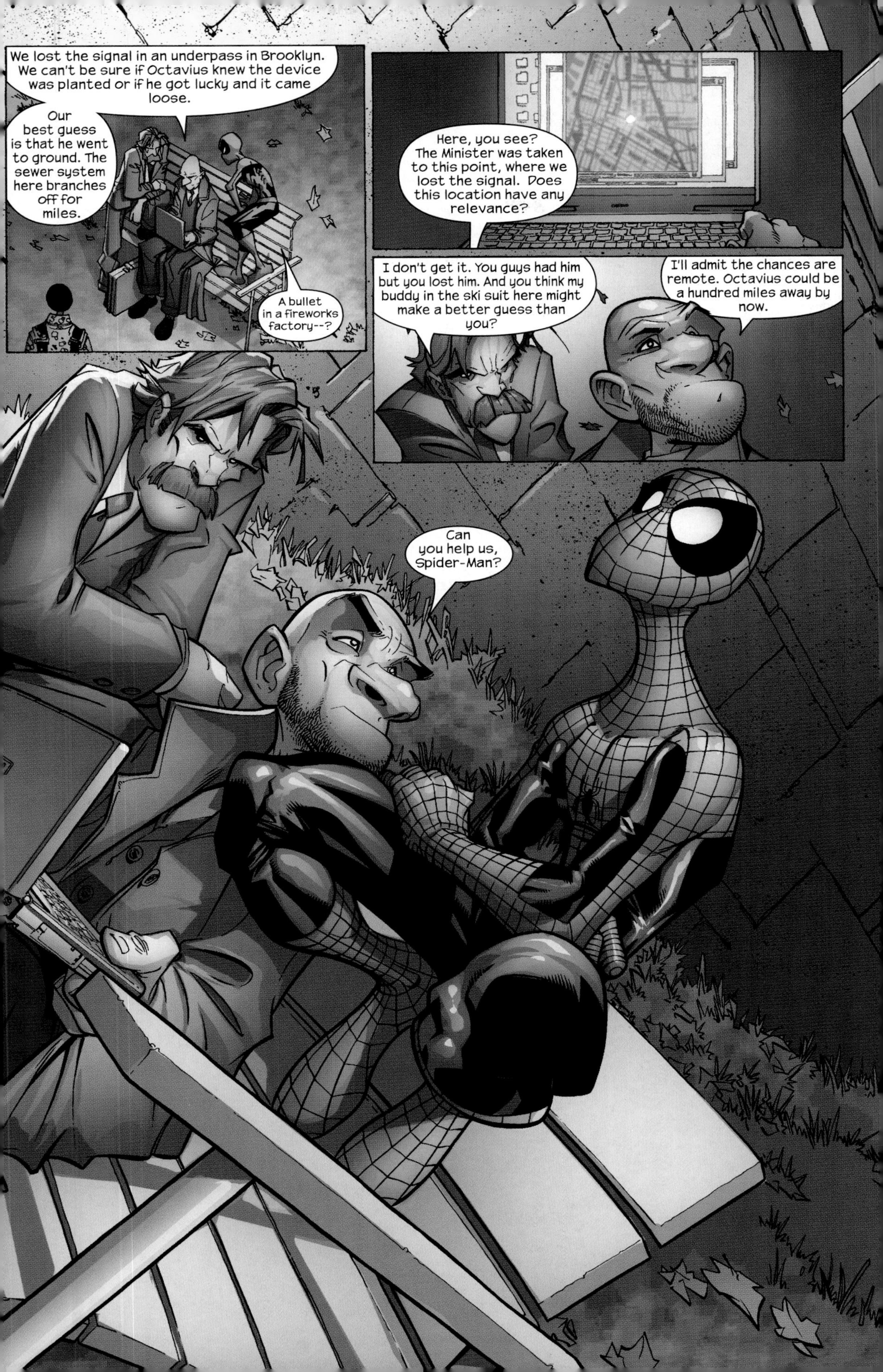
We lost the signal in an underpass in Brooklyn. We can't be sure if Octavius knew the device was planted or if he got lucky and it came loose.
Our best guess is that he went to ground. The sewer system here branches off for miles.
A bullet in a fireworks factory--?
Here, you see? The Minister was taken to this point, where we lost the signal. Does this location have any relevance?
I don't get it. You guys had him but you lost him. And you think my buddy in the ski suit here might make a better guess than you?
I'll admit the chances are remote. Octavius could be a hundred miles away by now.
Can you help us, Spider-Man?

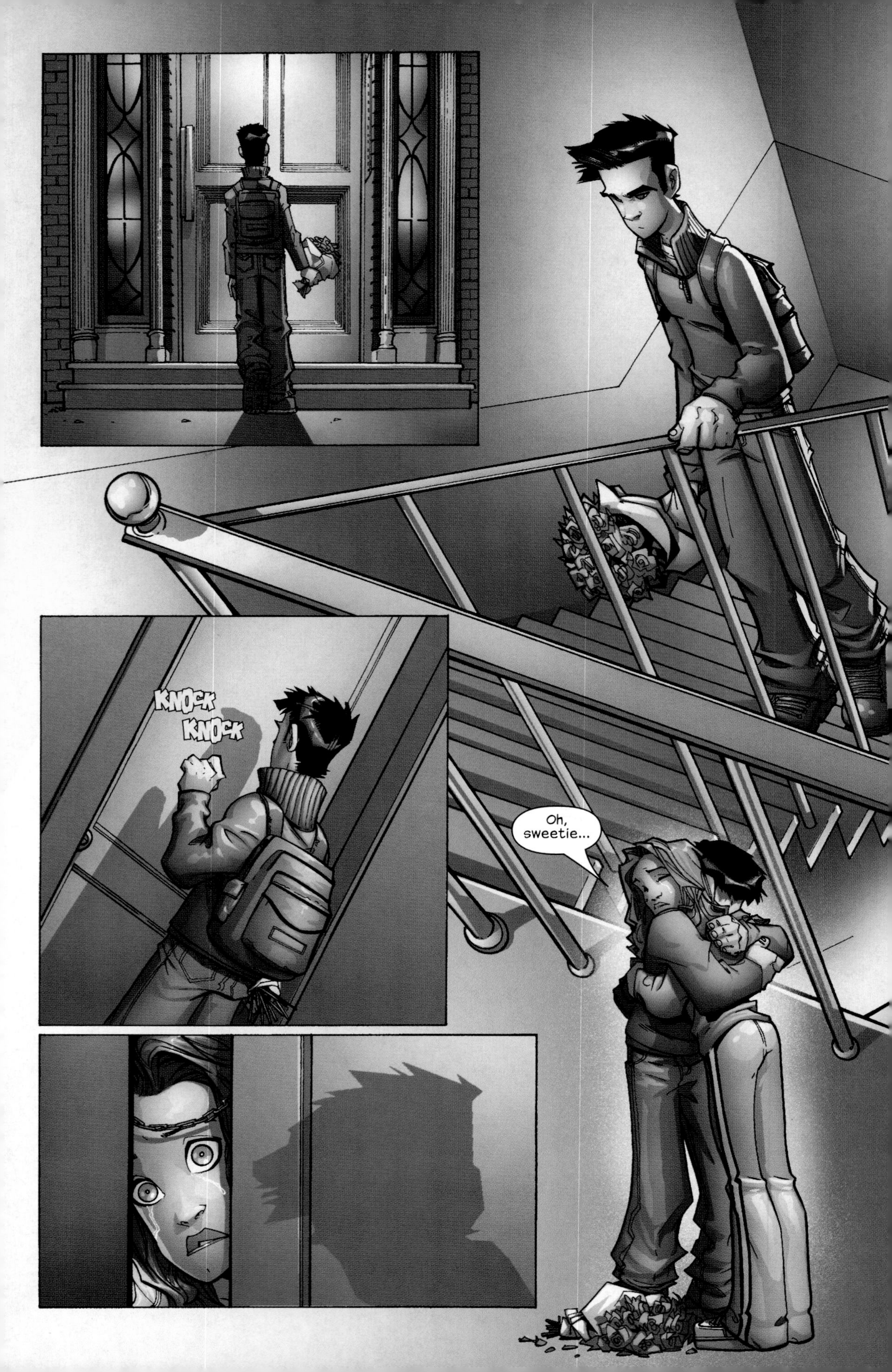
KNOCK
KNOCK
Oh, sweetie...

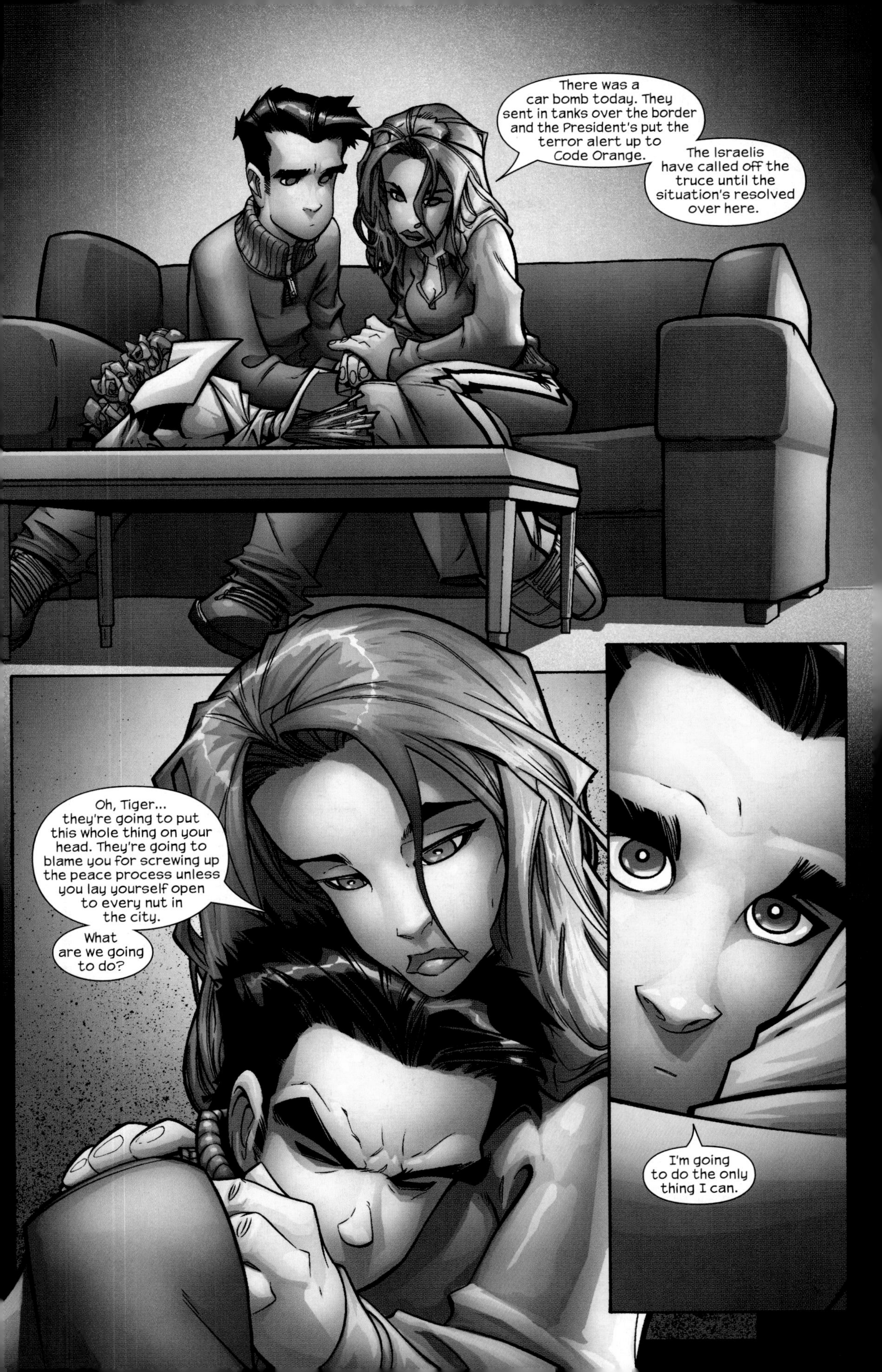
There was a car bomb today. They sent in tanks over the border and the President's put the terror alert up to Code Orange.
The Israelis have called off the truce until the situation's resolved over here.
Oh, Tiger... they're going to put this whole thing on your head. They're going to blame you for screwing up the peace process unless you lay yourself open to every nut in the city.
What are we going to do?
I'm going to do the only thing I can.

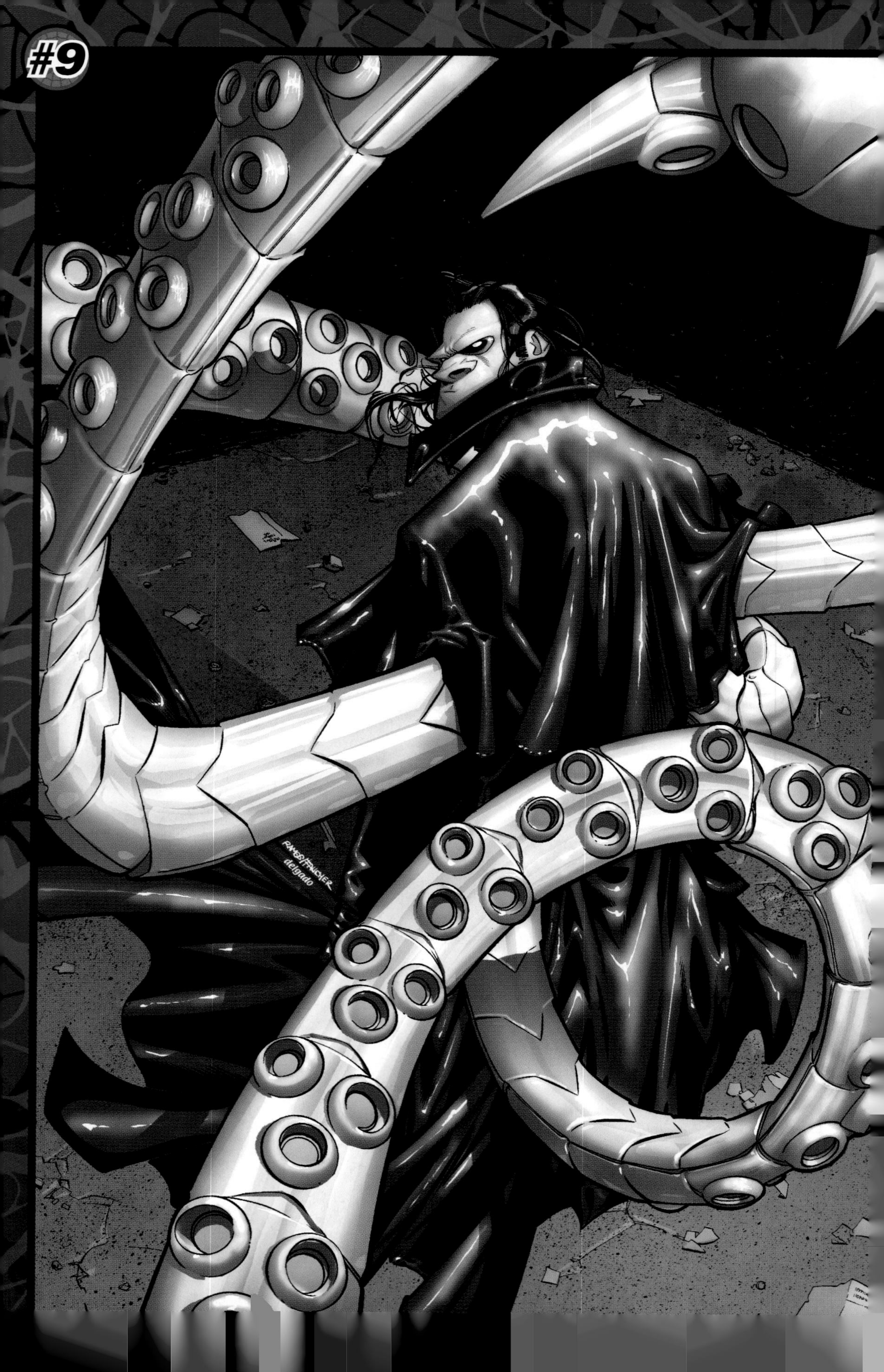
#9
RAMOS/FAUCHER
delgado

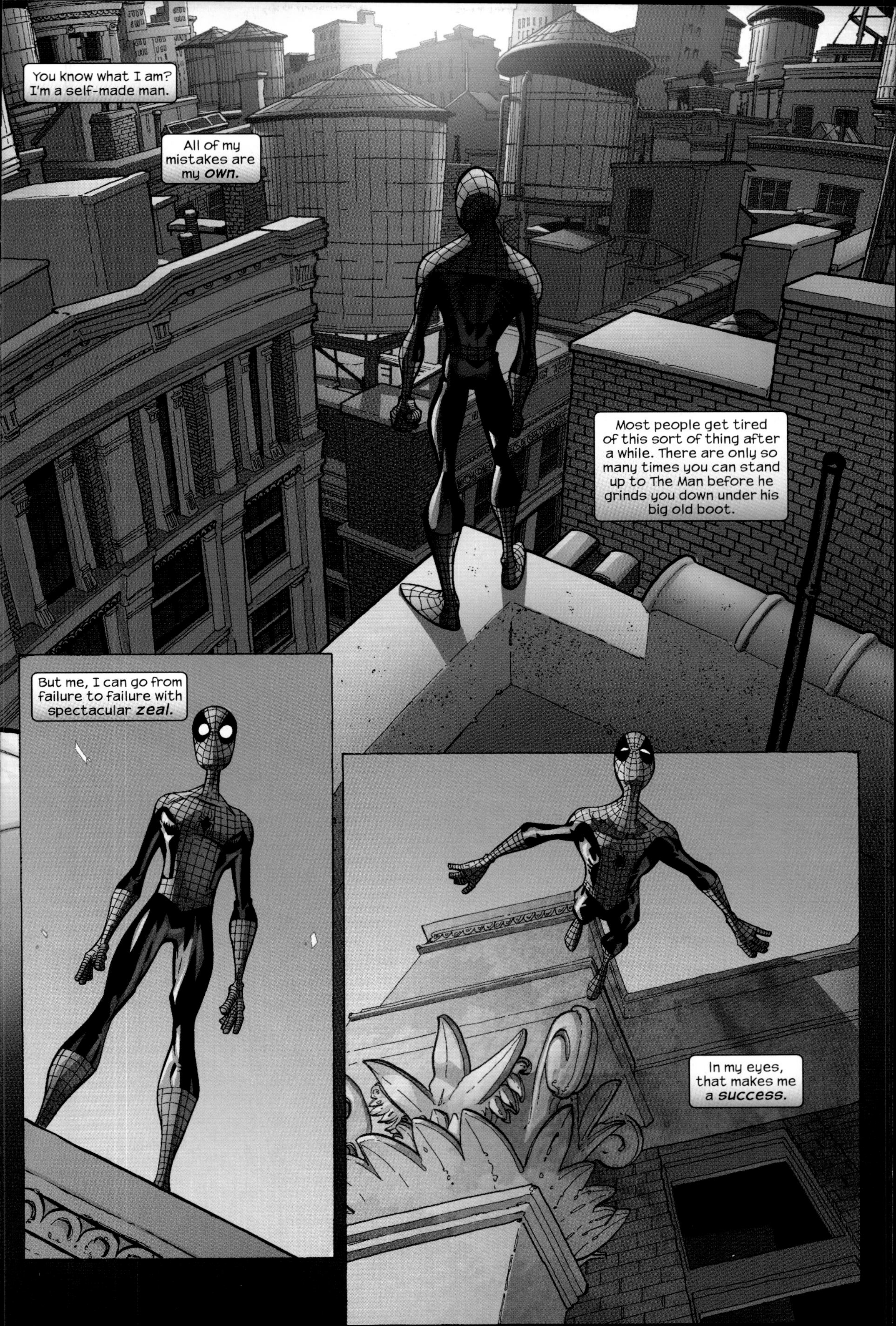
You know what I am? I'm a self-made man.
All of my mistakes are my *own.*
Most people get tired of this sort of thing after a while. There are only so many times you can stand up to The Man before he grinds you down under his big old boot.
But me, I can go from failure to failure with spectacular *zeal.*
In my eyes, that makes me a *success.*

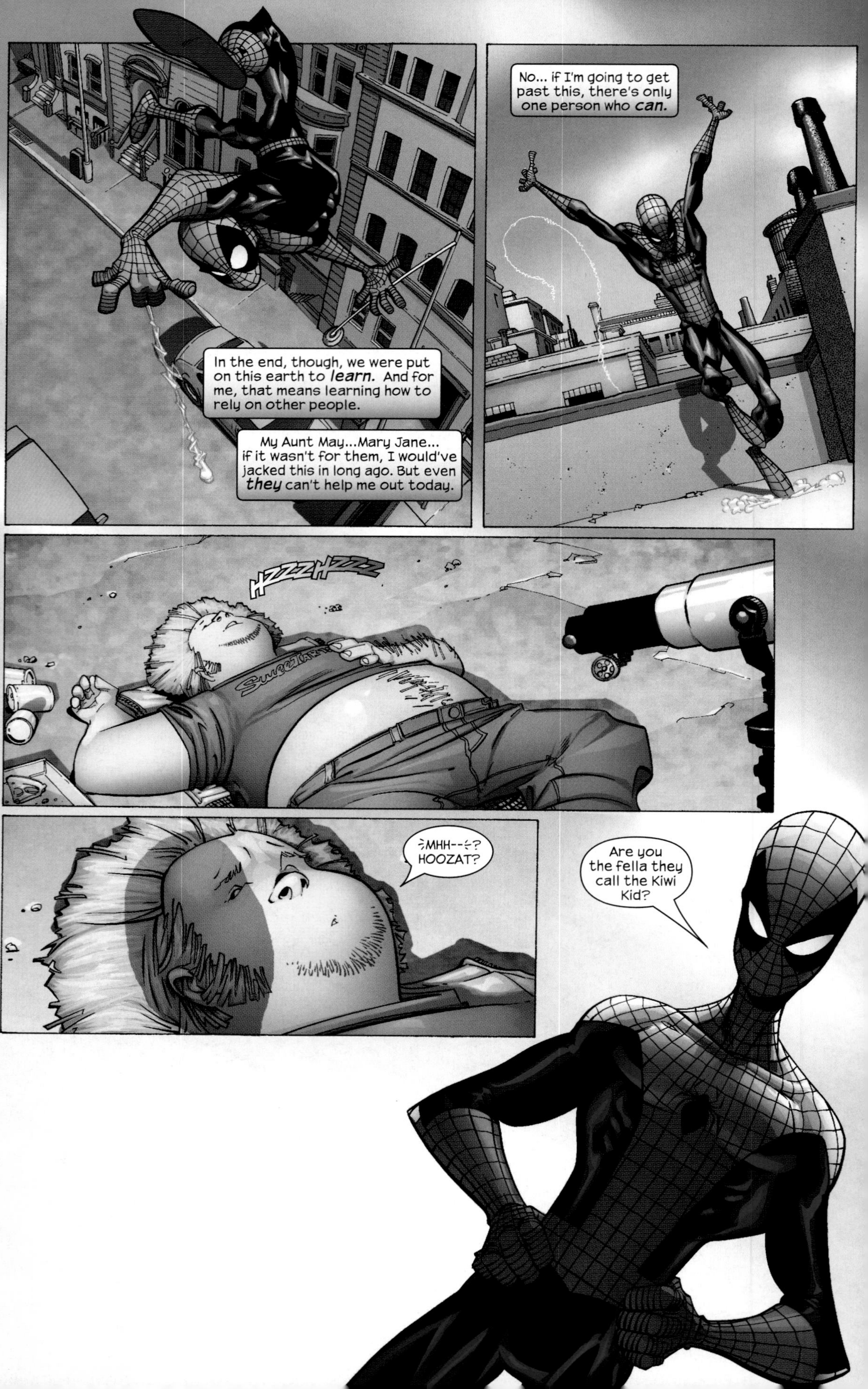

In the end, though, we were put on this earth to *learn.* And for me, that means learning how to rely on other people.
My Aunt May...Mary Jane... if it wasn't for them, I would've jacked this in long ago. But even *they* can't help me out today.
No... if I'm going to get past this, there's only one person who *can.*
HZZZHZZZ
MHH--? HOOZAT?
Are you the fella they call the Kiwi Kid?

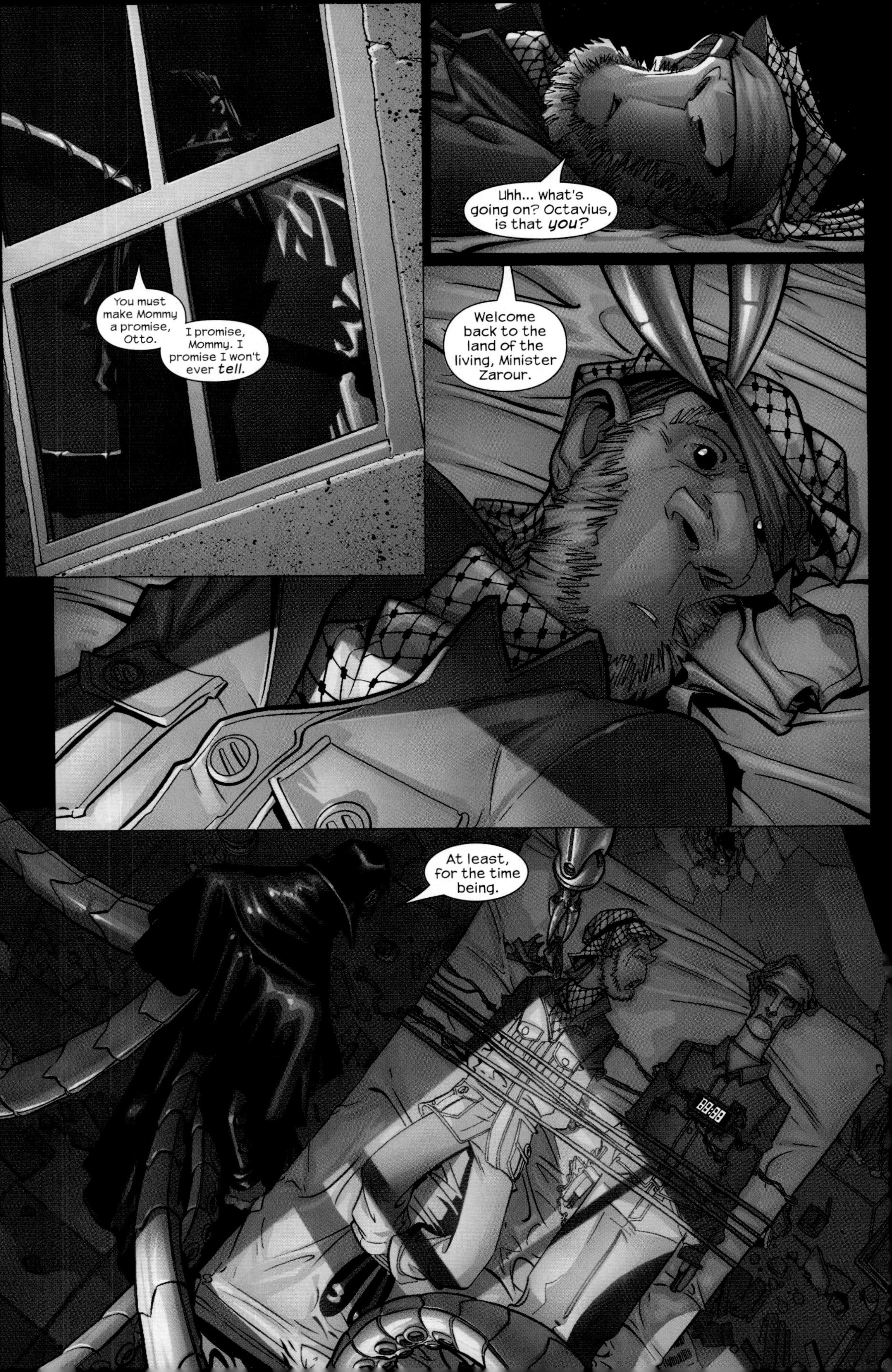
You must make Mommy a promise, Otto.
I promise, Mommy. I promise I won't ever *tell.*
Uhh... what's going on? Octavius, is that *you?*
Welcome back to the land of the living, Minister Zarour.
At least, for the time being.

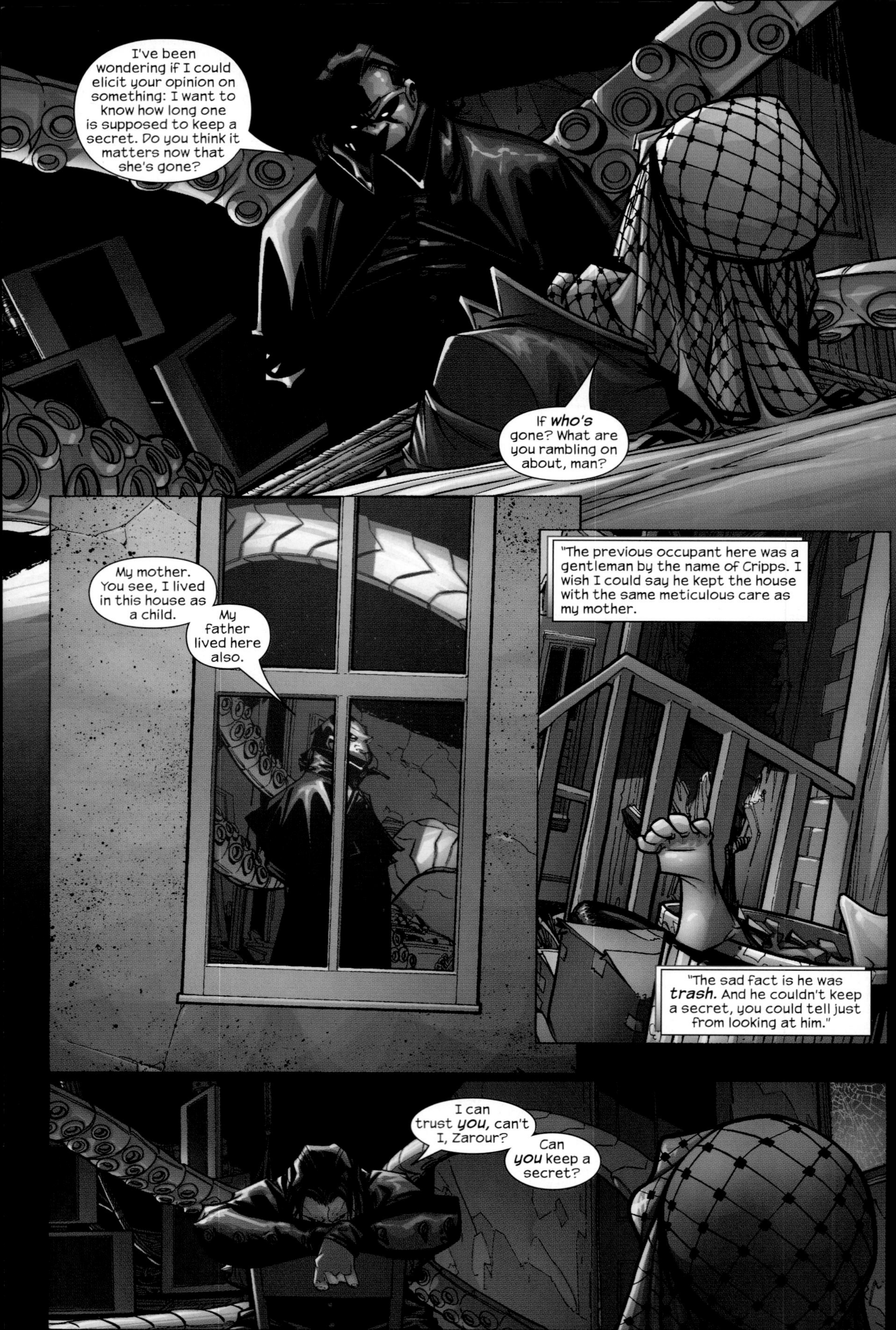
I've been wondering if I could elicit your opinion on something: I want to know how long one is supposed to keep a secret. Do you think it matters now that she's gone?
If *who's* gone? What are you rambling on about, man?
My mother. You see, I lived in this house as a child.
My father lived here also.
"The previous occupant here was a gentleman by the name of Cripps. I wish I could say he kept the house with the same meticulous care as my mother.
"The sad fact is he was *trash.* And he couldn't keep a secret, you could tell just from looking at him."
I can trust *you,* can't I, Zarour?
Can *you* keep a secret?

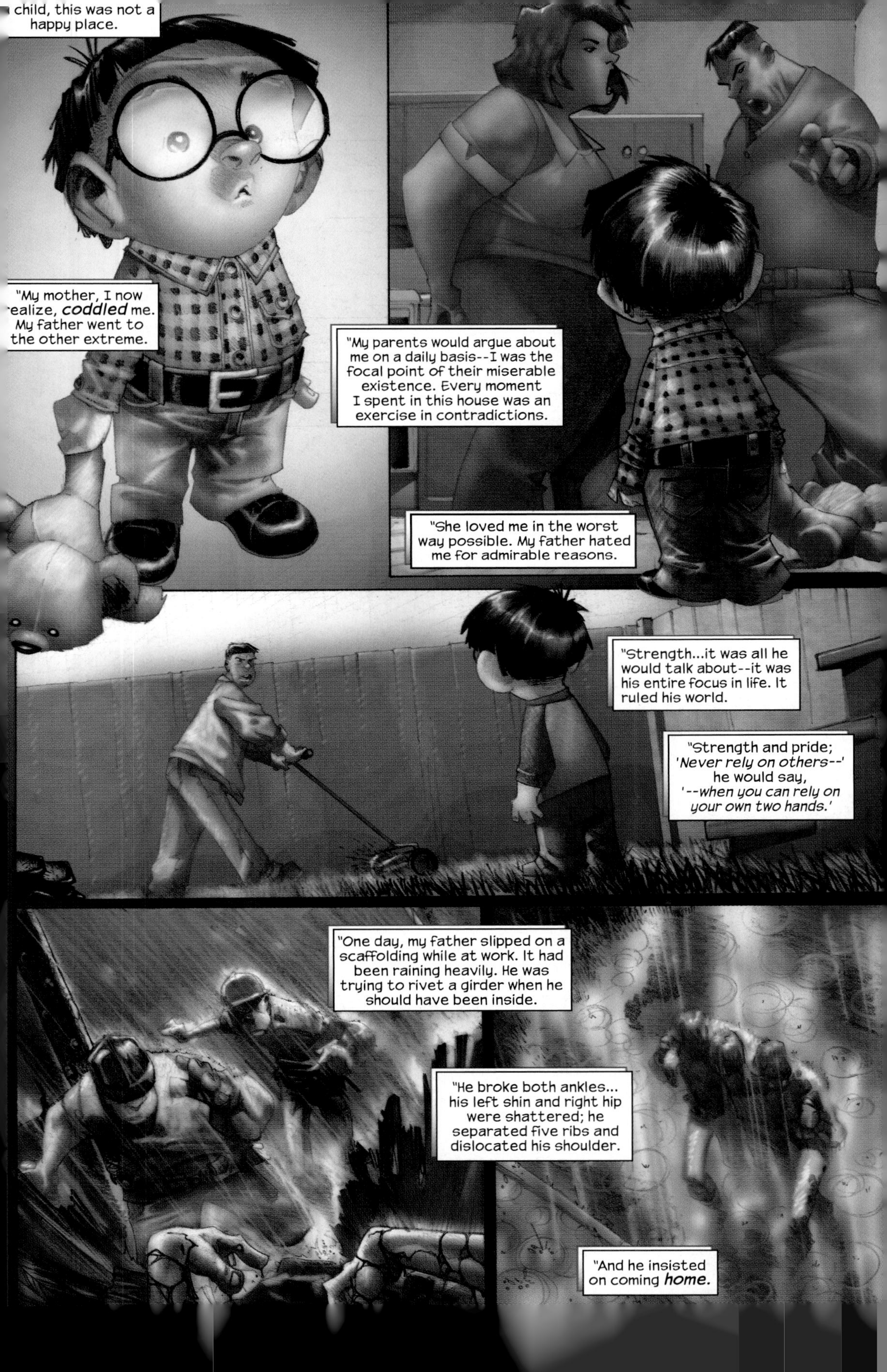
child, this was not a happy place.
"My mother, I now realize, *coddled* me. My father went to the other extreme.
"My parents would argue about me on a daily basis--I was the focal point of their miserable existence. Every moment I spent in this house was an exercise in contradictions.
"She loved me in the worst way possible. My father hated me for admirable reasons.
"Strength...it was all he would talk about--it was his entire focus in life. It ruled his world.
"Strength and pride; *'Never rely on others--'* he would say, *'--when you can rely on your own two hands.'*
"One day, my father slipped on a scaffolding while at work. It had been raining heavily. He was trying to rivet a girder when he should have been inside.
"He broke both ankles... his left shin and right hip were shattered; he separated five ribs and dislocated his shoulder.
"And he insisted on coming ***home.***

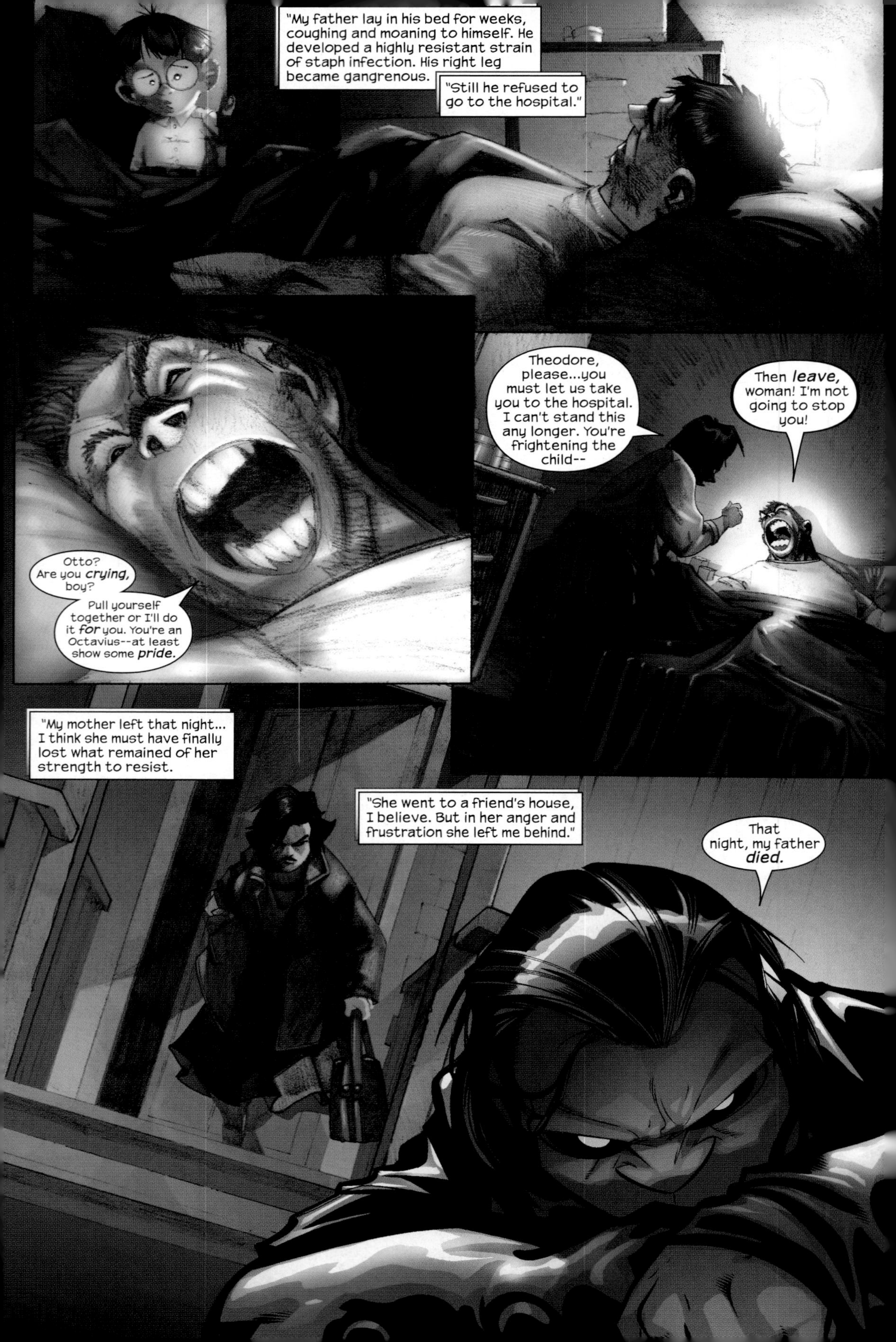
"My father lay in his bed for weeks, coughing and moaning to himself. He developed a highly resistant strain of staph infection. His right leg became gangrenous.
"Still he refused to go to the hospital."
Otto? Are you *crying,* boy?
Pull yourself together or I'll do it *for* you. You're an Octavius--at least show some *pride.*
Theodore, please...you must let us take you to the hospital. I can't stand this any longer. You're frightening the child--
Then *leave,* woman! I'm not going to stop you!
"My mother left that night... I think she must have finally lost what remained of her strength to resist.
"She went to a friend's house, I believe. But in her anger and frustration she left me behind."
That night, my father *died.*

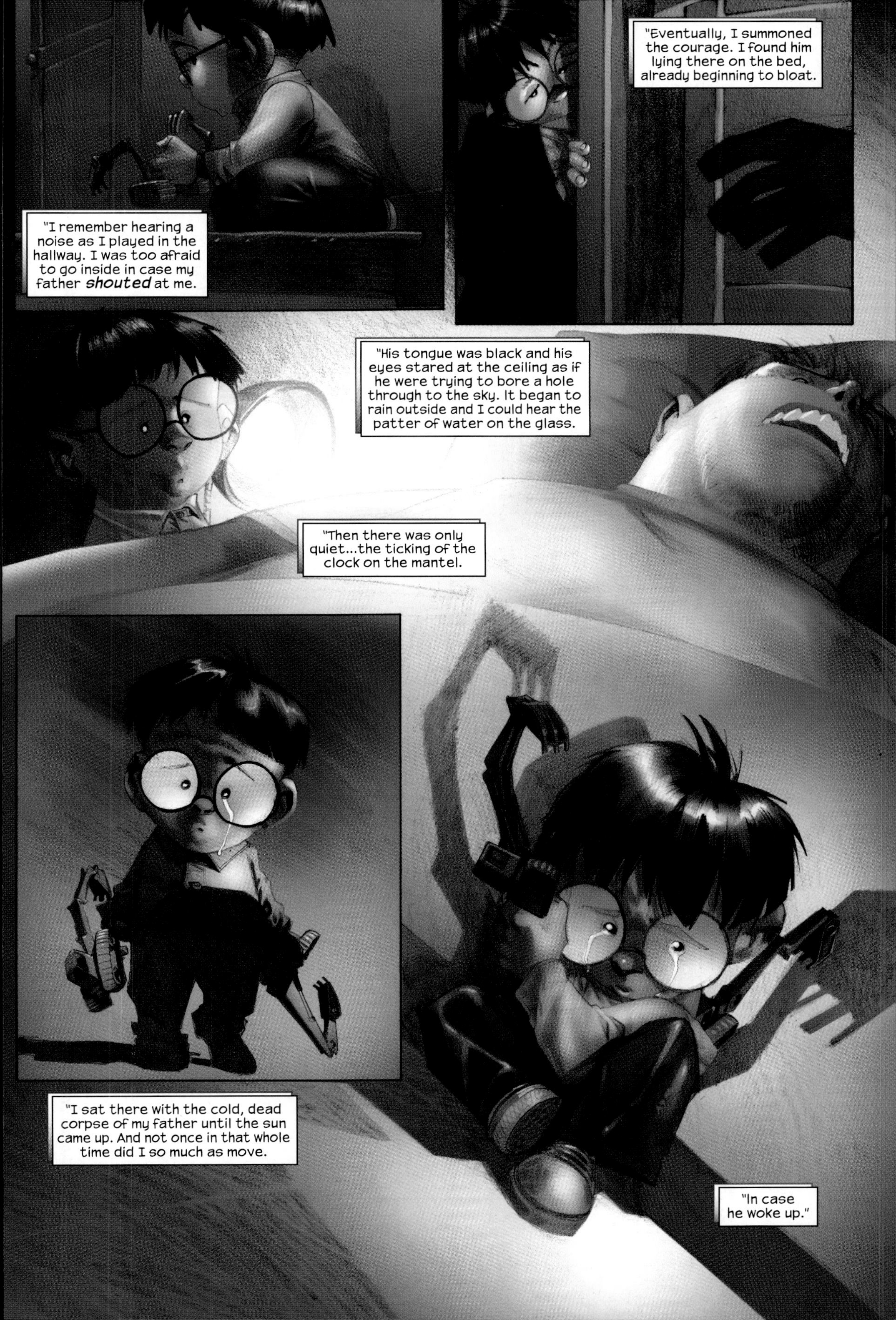
"I remember hearing a noise as I played in the hallway. I was too afraid to go inside in case my father *shouted* at me.
"Eventually, I summoned the courage. I found him lying there on the bed, already beginning to bloat.
"His tongue was black and his eyes stared at the ceiling as if he were trying to bore a hole through to the sky. It began to rain outside and I could hear the patter of water on the glass.
"Then there was only quiet...the ticking of the clock on the mantel.
"I sat there with the cold, dead corpse of my father until the sun came up. And not once in that whole time did I so much as move.
"In case he woke up."

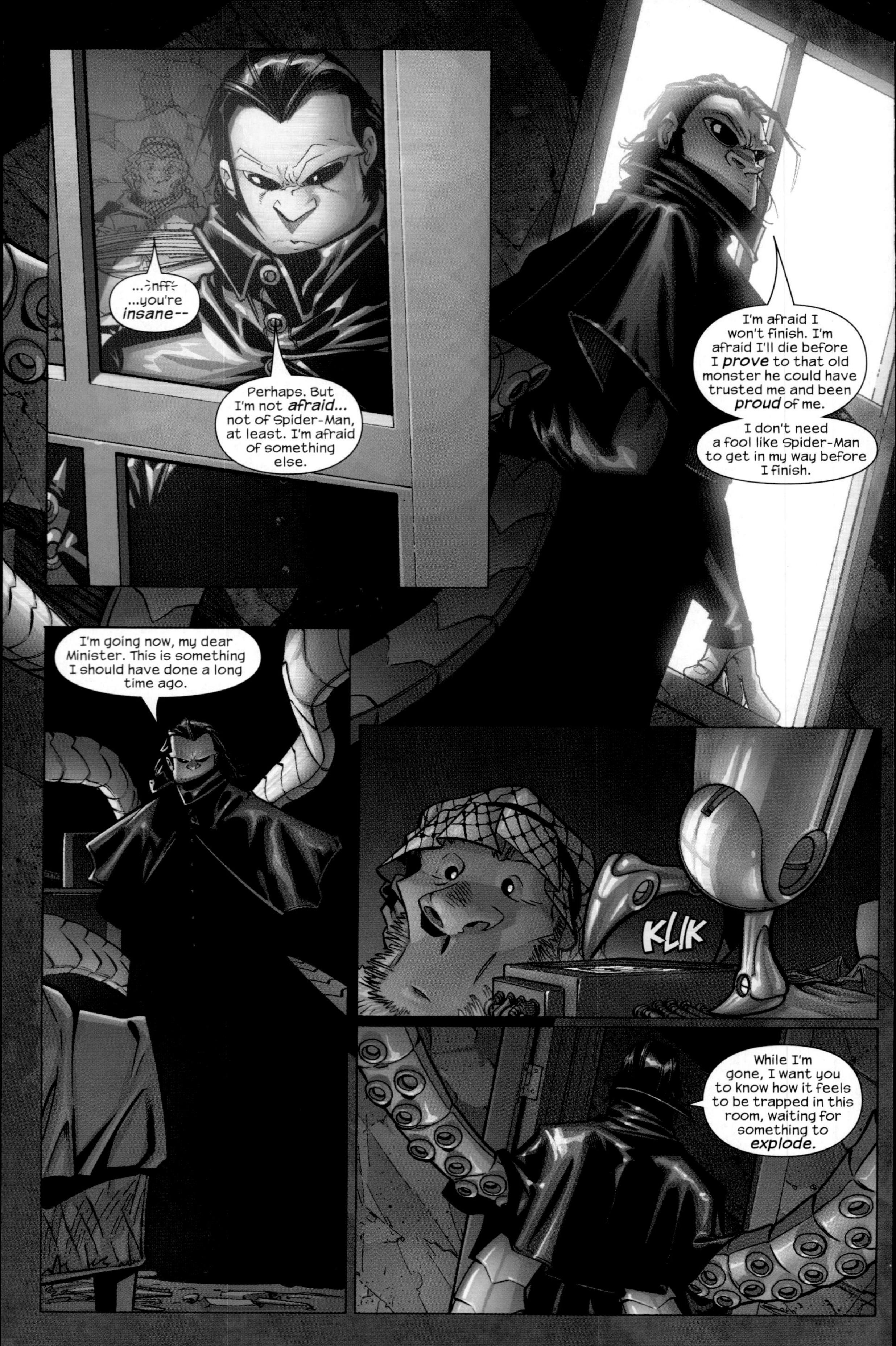

...snff
...you're *insane*--
Perhaps. But I'm not *afraid*... not of Spider-Man, at least. I'm afraid of something else.
I'm afraid I won't finish. I'm afraid I'll die before I *prove* to that old monster he could have trusted me and been *proud* of me.
I don't need a fool like Spider-Man to get in my way before I finish.
I'm going now, my dear Minister. This is something I should have done a long time ago.
KLIK
While I'm gone, I want you to know how it feels to be trapped in this room, waiting for something to *explode*.

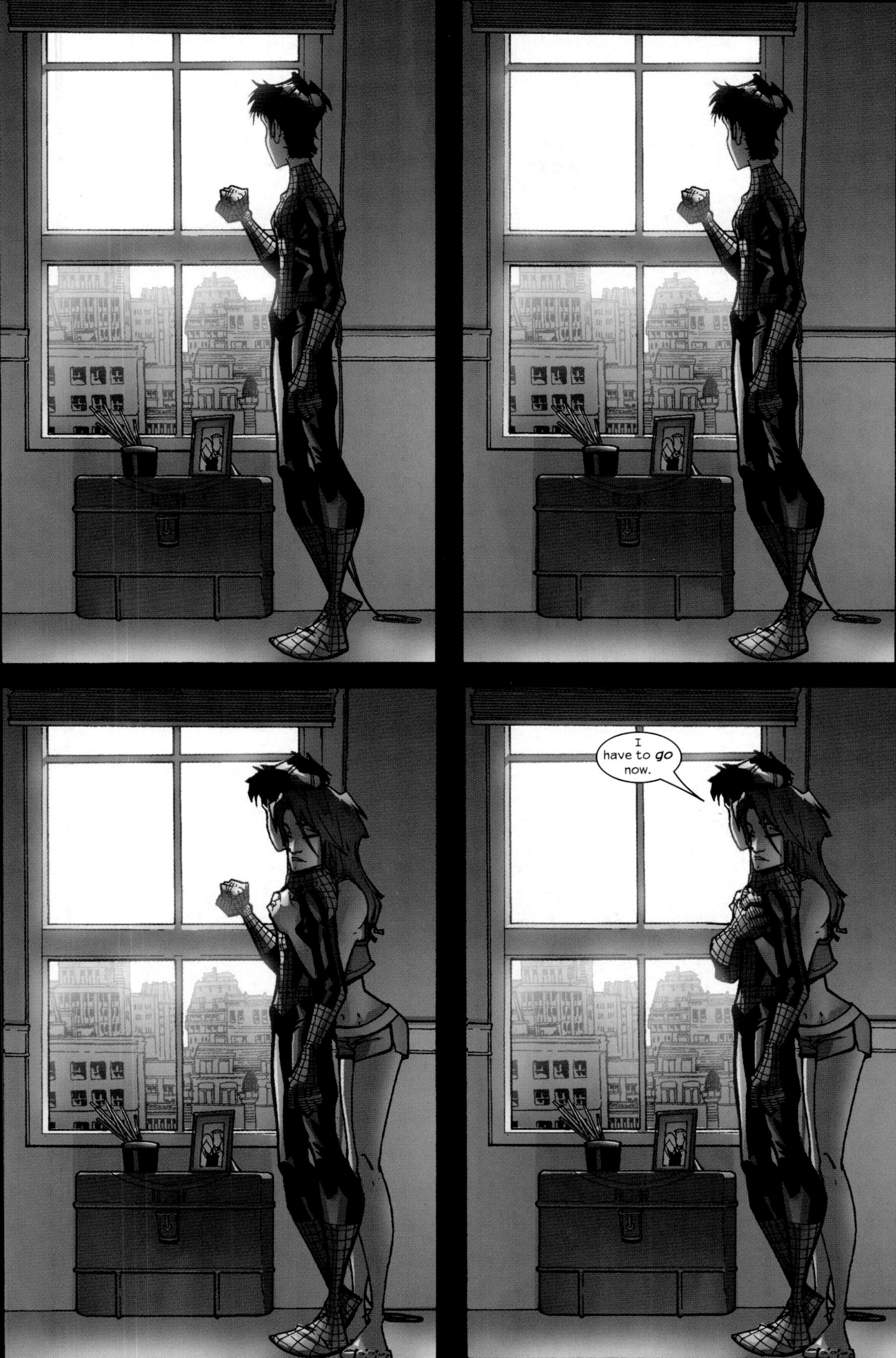
I have to *go* now.

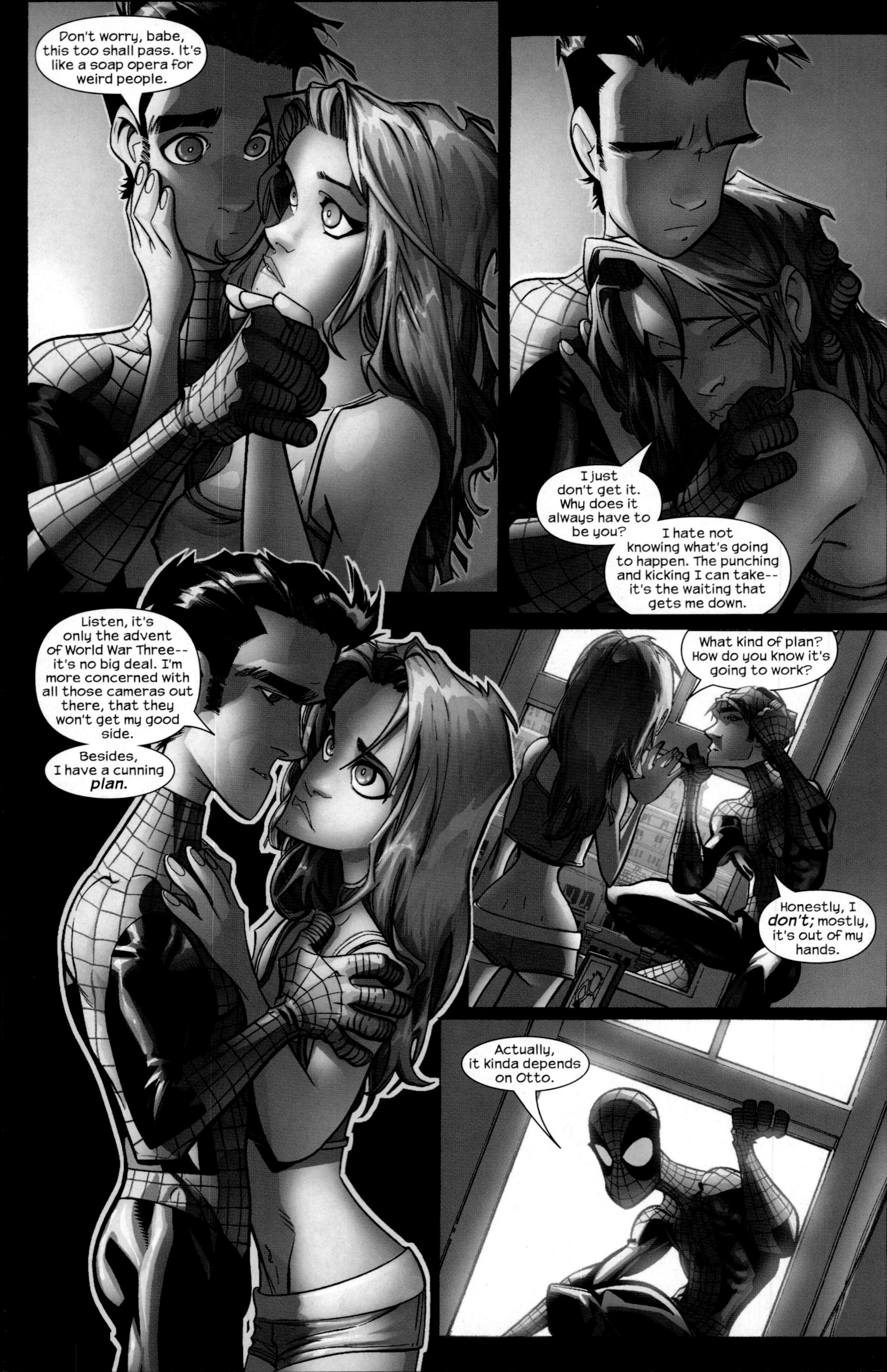

Don't worry, babe, this too shall pass. It's like a soap opera for weird people.
I just don't get it. Why does it always have to be you?
I hate not knowing what's going to happen. The punching and kicking I can take-- it's the waiting that gets me down.
Listen, it's only the advent of World War Three-- it's no big deal. I'm more concerned with all those cameras out there, that they won't get my good side.
Besides, I have a cunning *plan.*
What kind of plan? How do you know it's going to work?
Honestly, I *don't;* mostly, it's out of my hands.
Actually, it kinda depends on Otto.

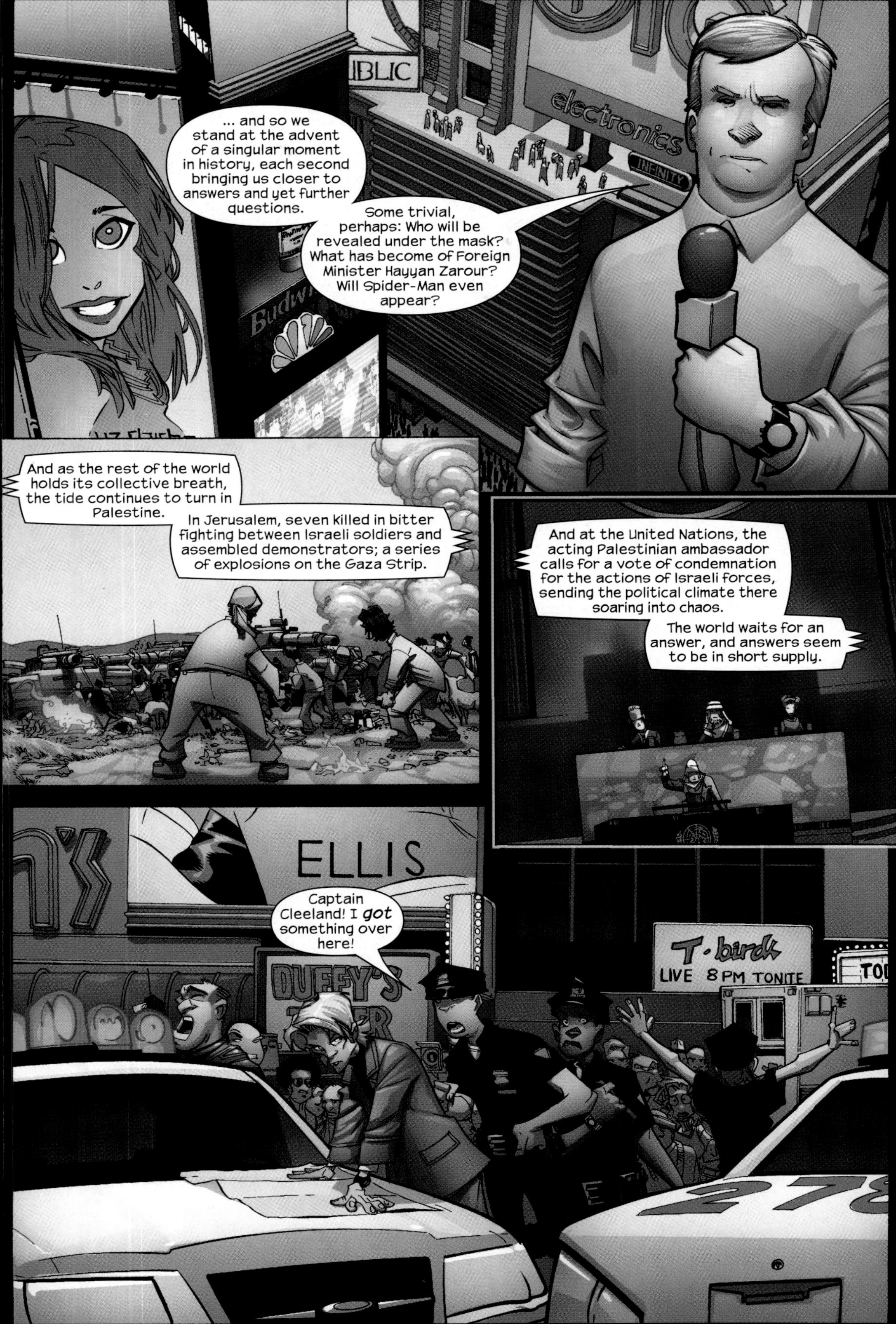
IBLIC
electronics
INFINITY
... and so we stand at the advent of a singular moment in history, each second bringing us closer to answers and yet further questions.
Some trivial, perhaps: Who will be revealed under the mask? What has become of Foreign Minister Hayyan Zarour? Will Spider-Man even appear?
And as the rest of the world holds its collective breath, the tide continues to turn in Palestine.
In Jerusalem, seven killed in bitter fighting between Israeli soldiers and assembled demonstrators; a series of explosions on the Gaza Strip.
And at the United Nations, the acting Palestinian ambassador calls for a vote of condemnation for the actions of Israeli forces, sending the political climate there soaring into chaos.
The world waits for an answer, and answers seem to be in short supply.
ELLIS
Captain Cleeland! I *got* something over here!
DUFFY'S
T·bird
LIVE 8 PM TONITE

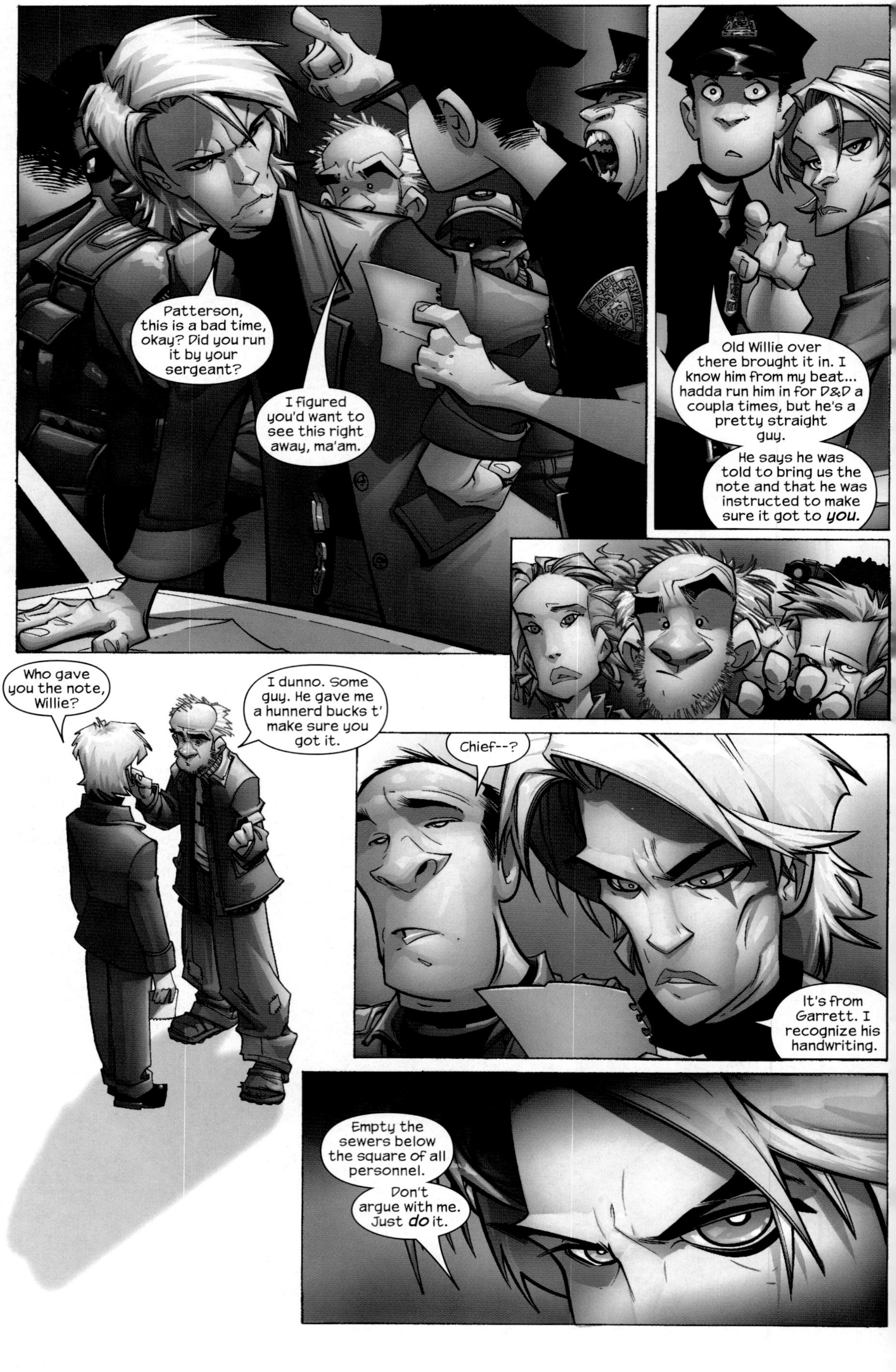
Patterson, this is a bad time, okay? Did you run it by your sergeant?
I figured you'd want to see this right away, ma'am.
Old Willie over there brought it in. I know him from my beat... hadda run him in for D&D a coupla times, but he's a pretty straight guy.
He says he was told to bring us the note and that he was instructed to make sure it got to *you.*
Who gave you the note, Willie?
I dunno. Some guy. He gave me a hunnerd bucks t' make sure you got it.
Chief--?
It's from Garrett. I recognize his handwriting.
Empty the sewers below the square of all personnel.
Don't argue with me. Just *do* it.

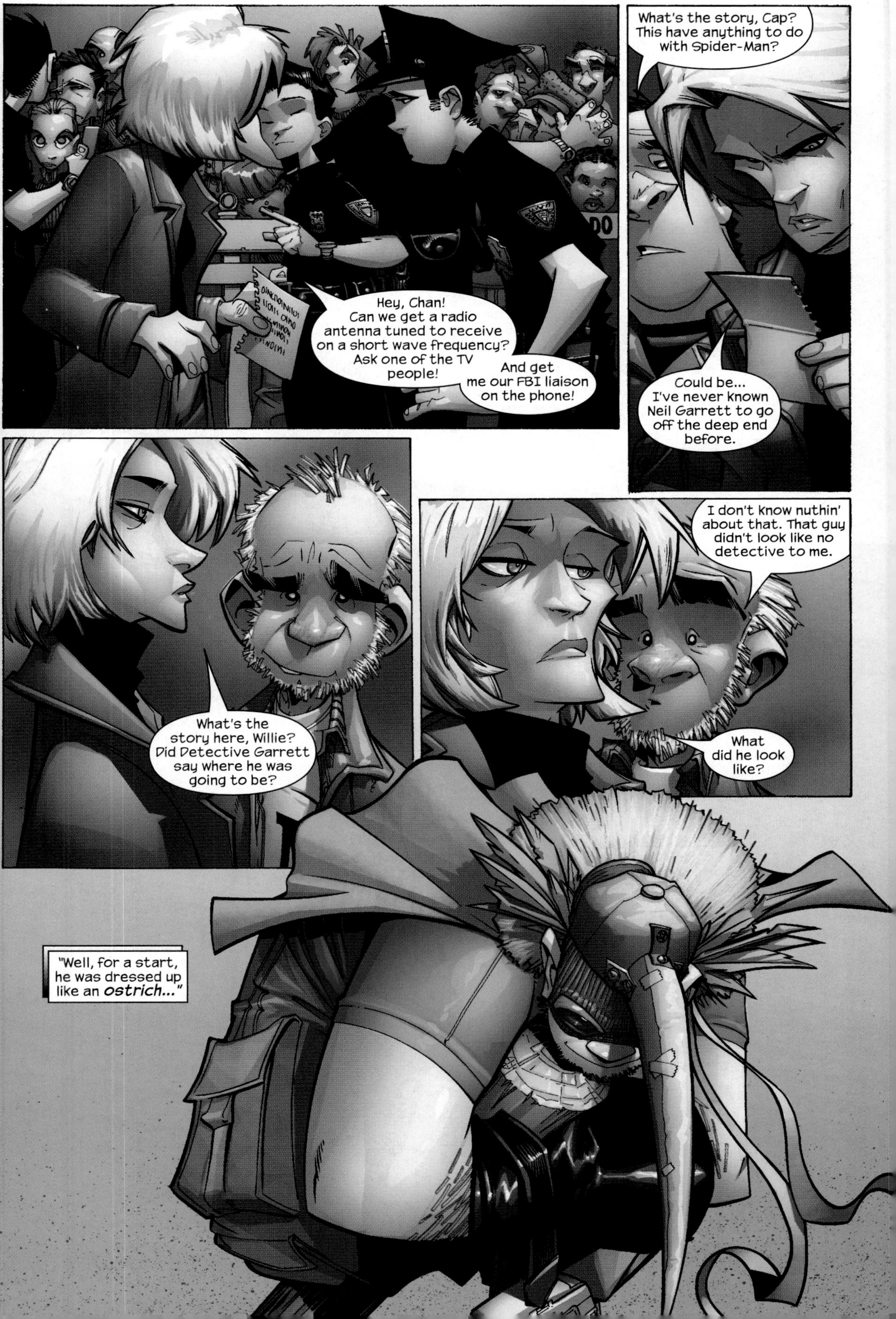
Hey, Chan! Can we get a radio antenna tuned to receive on a short wave frequency? Ask one of the TV people!
And get me our FBI liaison on the phone!
What's the story, Cap? This have anything to do with Spider-Man?
Could be... I've never known Neil Garrett to go off the deep end before.
What's the story here, Willie? Did Detective Garrett say where he was going to be?
I don't know nuthin' about that. That guy didn't look like no detective to me.
What did he look like?
"Well, for a start, he was dressed up like an ostrich..."

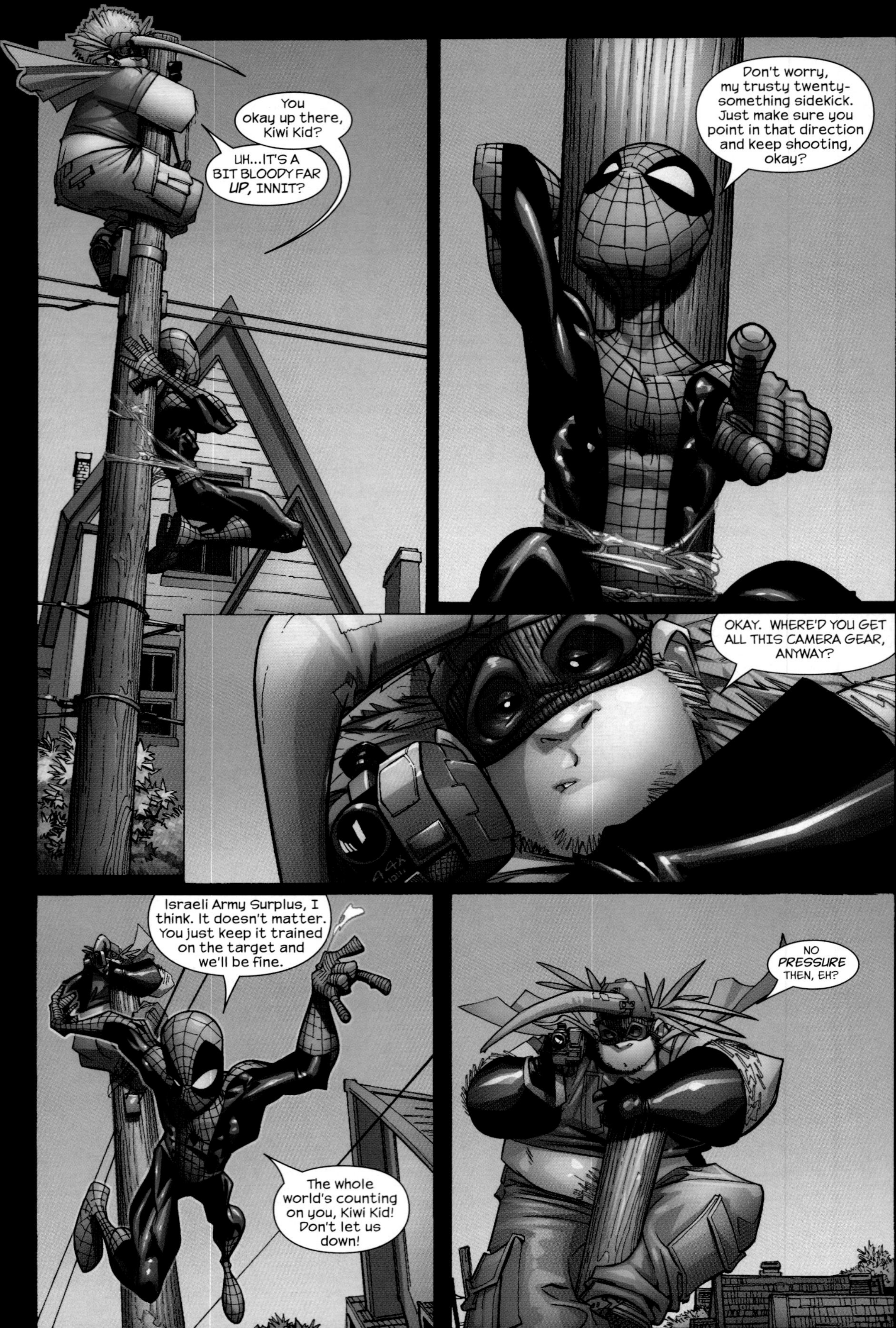
You okay up there, Kiwi Kid?
UH...IT'S A BIT BLOODY FAR UP, INNIT?
Don't worry, my trusty twenty-something sidekick. Just make sure you point in that direction and keep shooting, okay?
OKAY. WHERE'D YOU GET ALL THIS CAMERA GEAR, ANYWAY?
Israeli Army Surplus, I think. It doesn't matter. You just keep it trained on the target and we'll be fine.
The whole world's counting on you, Kiwi Kid! Don't let us down!
NO PRESSURE THEN, EH?

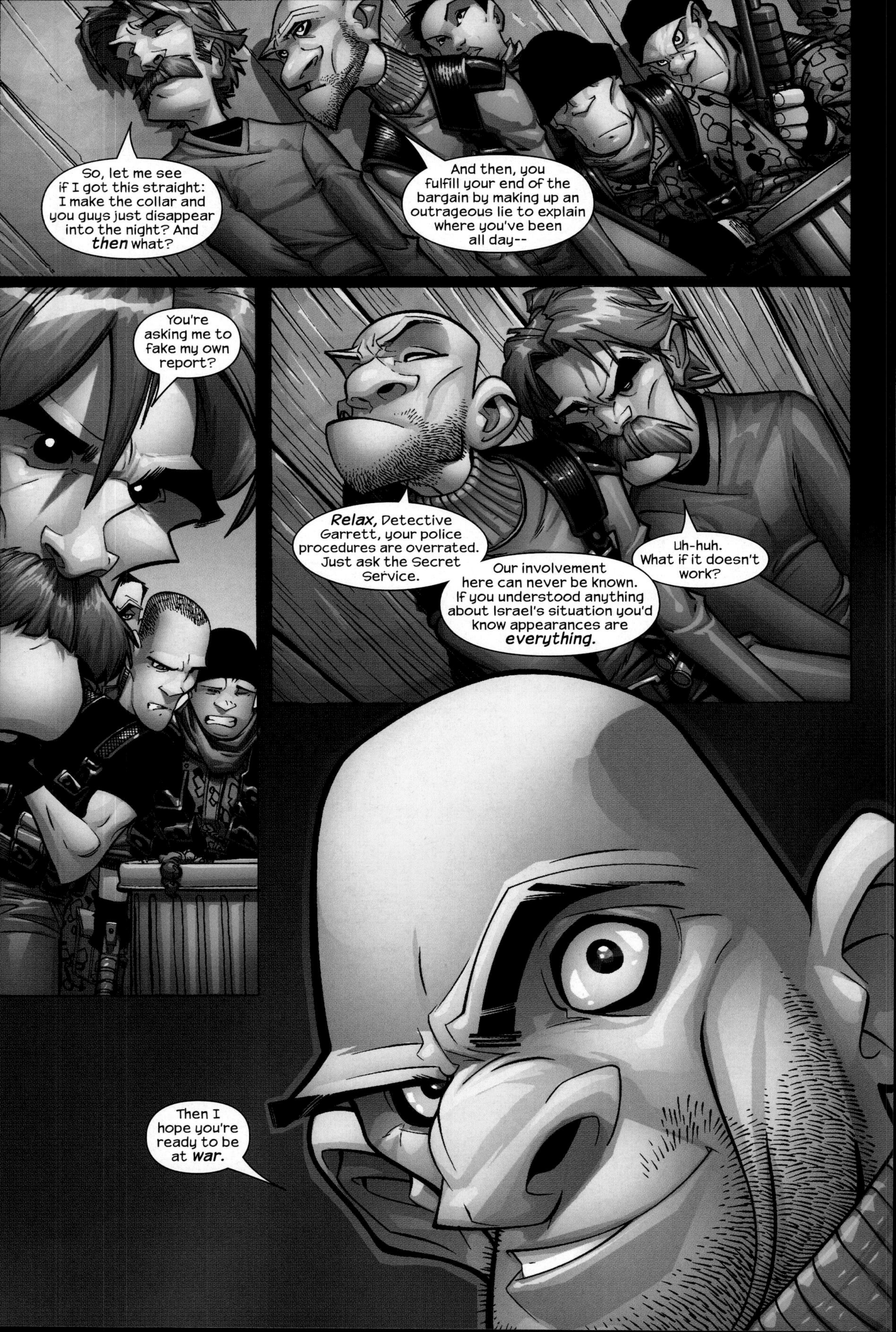

So, let me see if I got this straight: I make the collar and you guys just disappear into the night? And *then* what?
And then, you fulfill your end of the bargain by making up an outrageous lie to explain where you've been all day--
You're asking me to fake my own report?
Relax, Detective Garrett, your police procedures are overrated. Just ask the Secret Service.
Our involvement here can never be known. If you understood anything about Israel's situation you'd know appearances are *everything.*
Uh-huh. What if it doesn't work?
Then I hope you're ready to be at *war.*

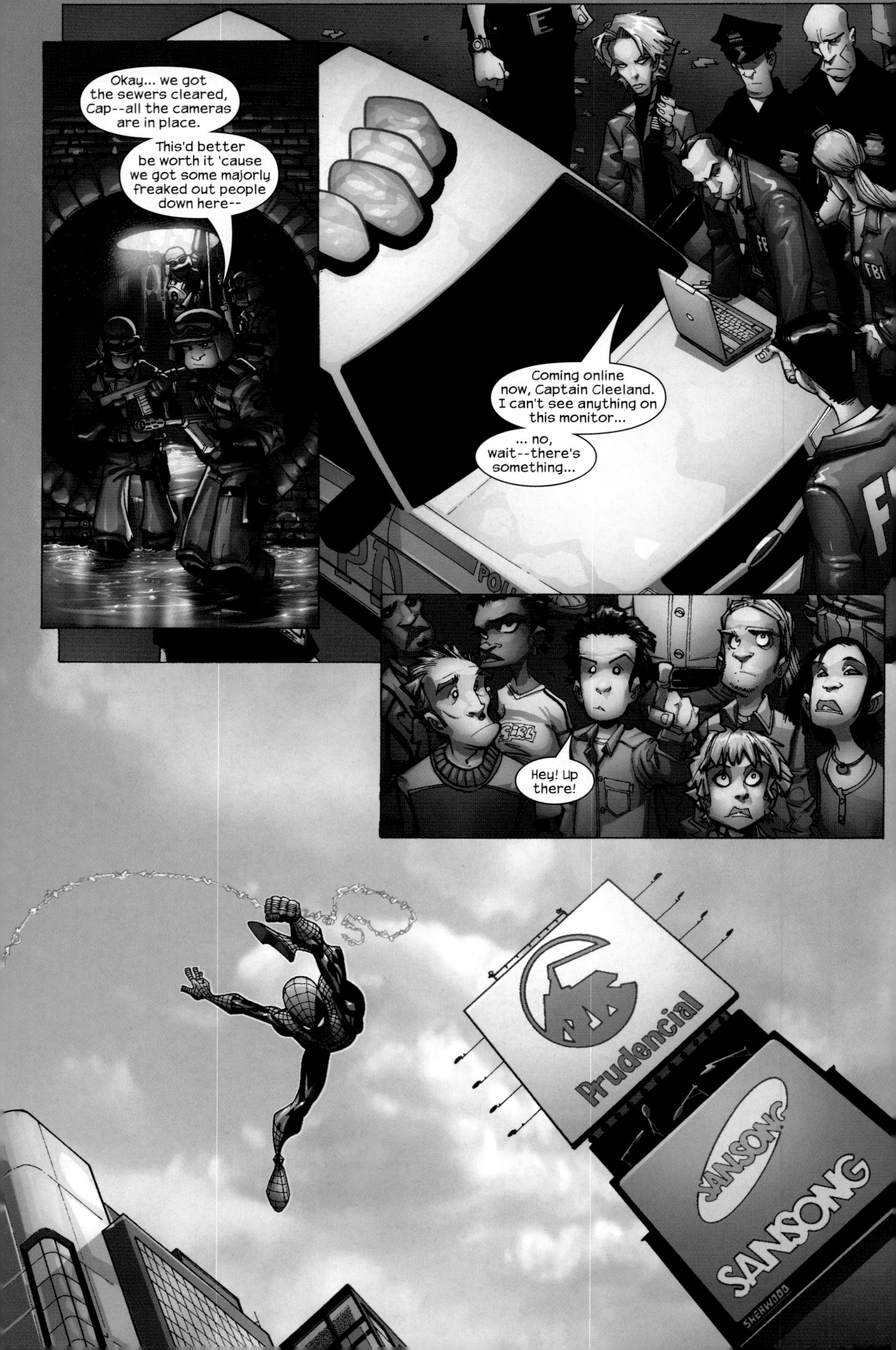
Okay... we got the sewers cleared, Cap--all the cameras are in place.
This'd better be worth it 'cause we got some majorly freaked out people down here--
Coming online now, Captain Cleeland. I can't see anything on this monitor...
... no, wait--there's something...
FBI
POLICE
GIRL
Hey! Up there!
Prudencial
SANSONG
SANSONG
SHERWOOD

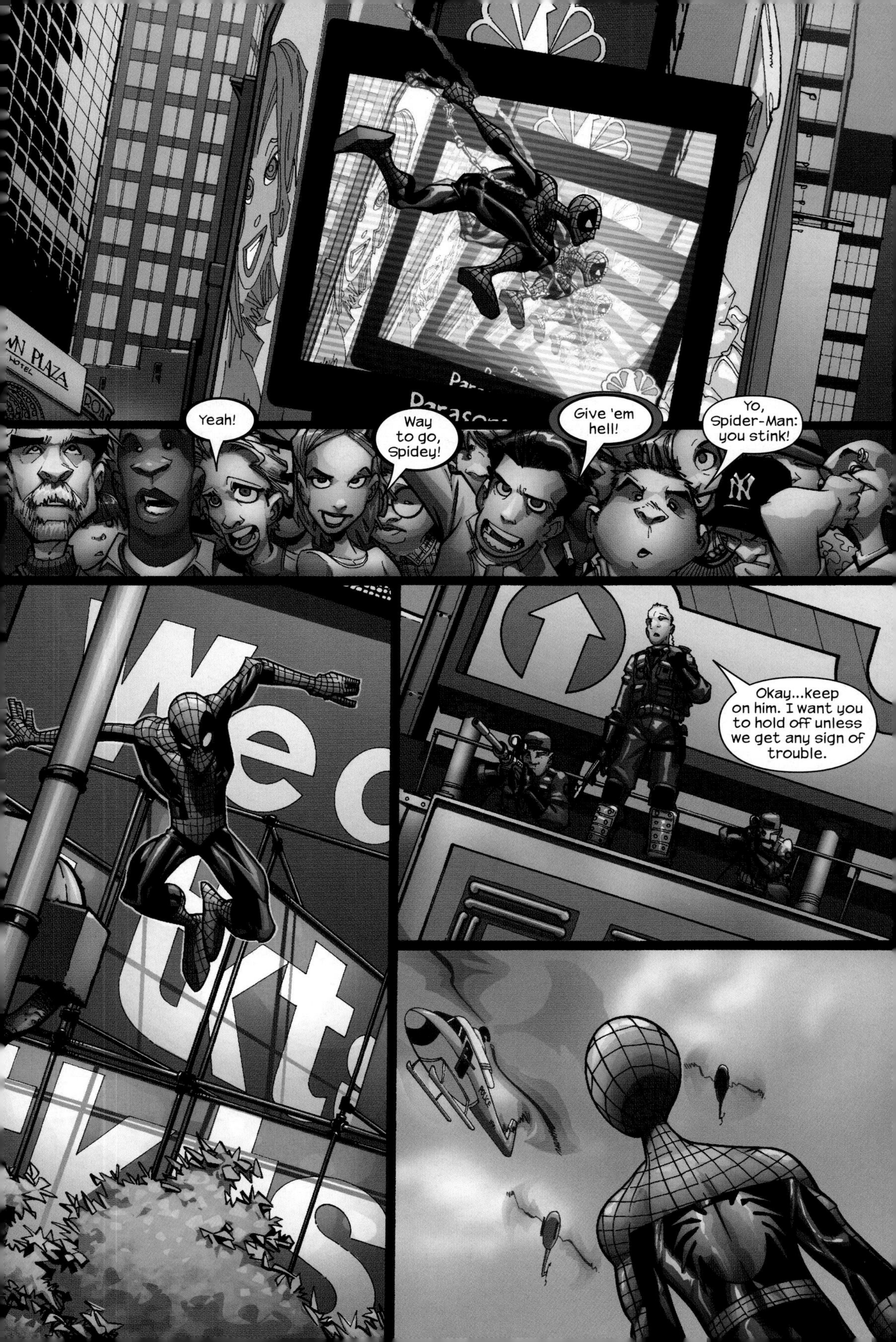

Yeah!
Way to go, Spidey!
Give 'em hell!
Yo, Spider-Man: you stink!
Okay...keep on him. I want you to hold off unless we get any sign of trouble.

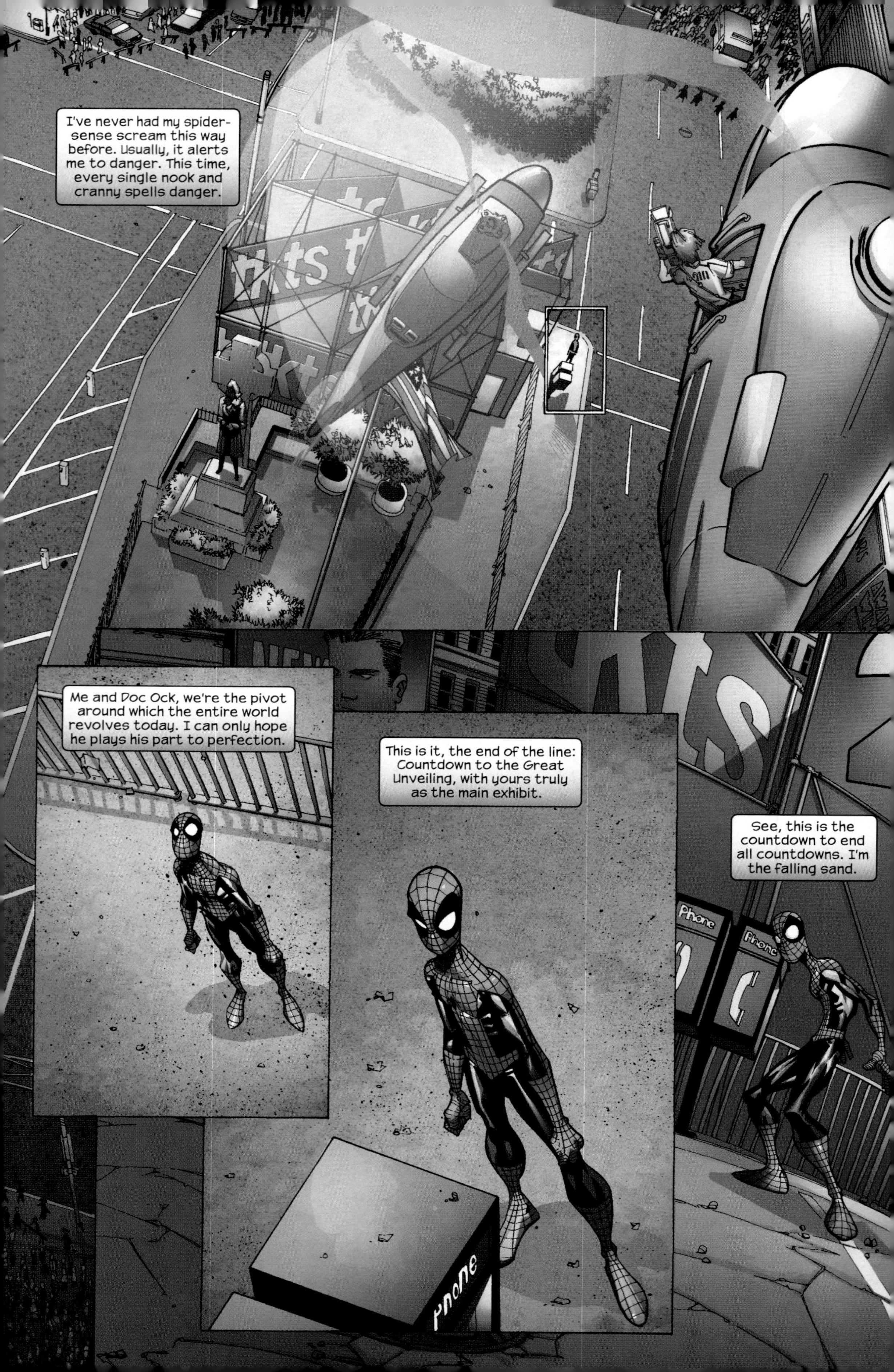
I've never had my spider-sense scream this way before. Usually, it alerts me to danger. This time, every single nook and cranny spells danger.
Me and Doc Ock, we're the pivot around which the entire world revolves today. I can only hope he plays his part to perfection.
This is it, the end of the line: Countdown to the Great Unveiling, with yours truly as the main exhibit.
See, this is the countdown to end all countdowns. I'm the falling sand.

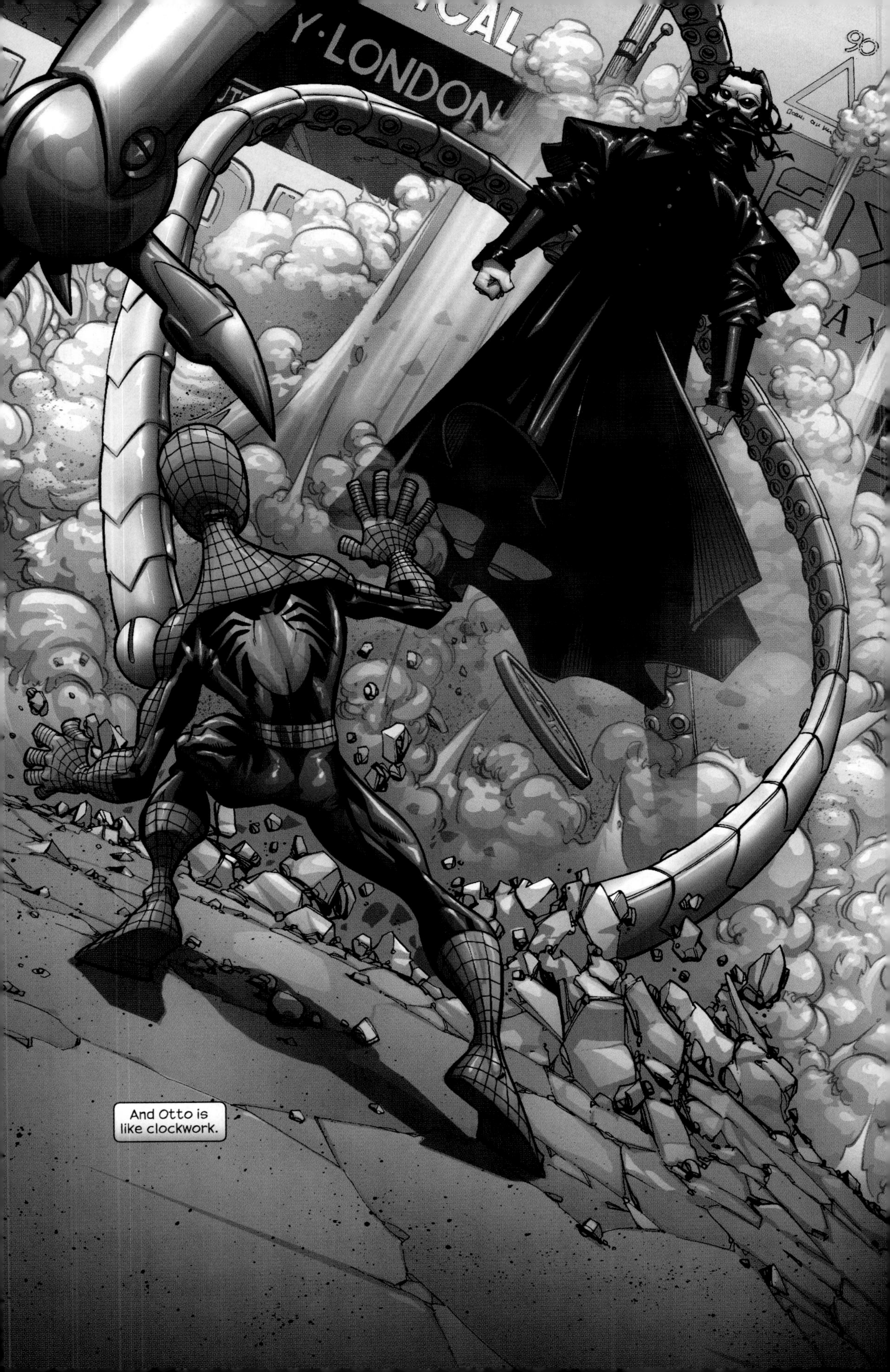
Y·LONDON
And Otto is like clockwork.

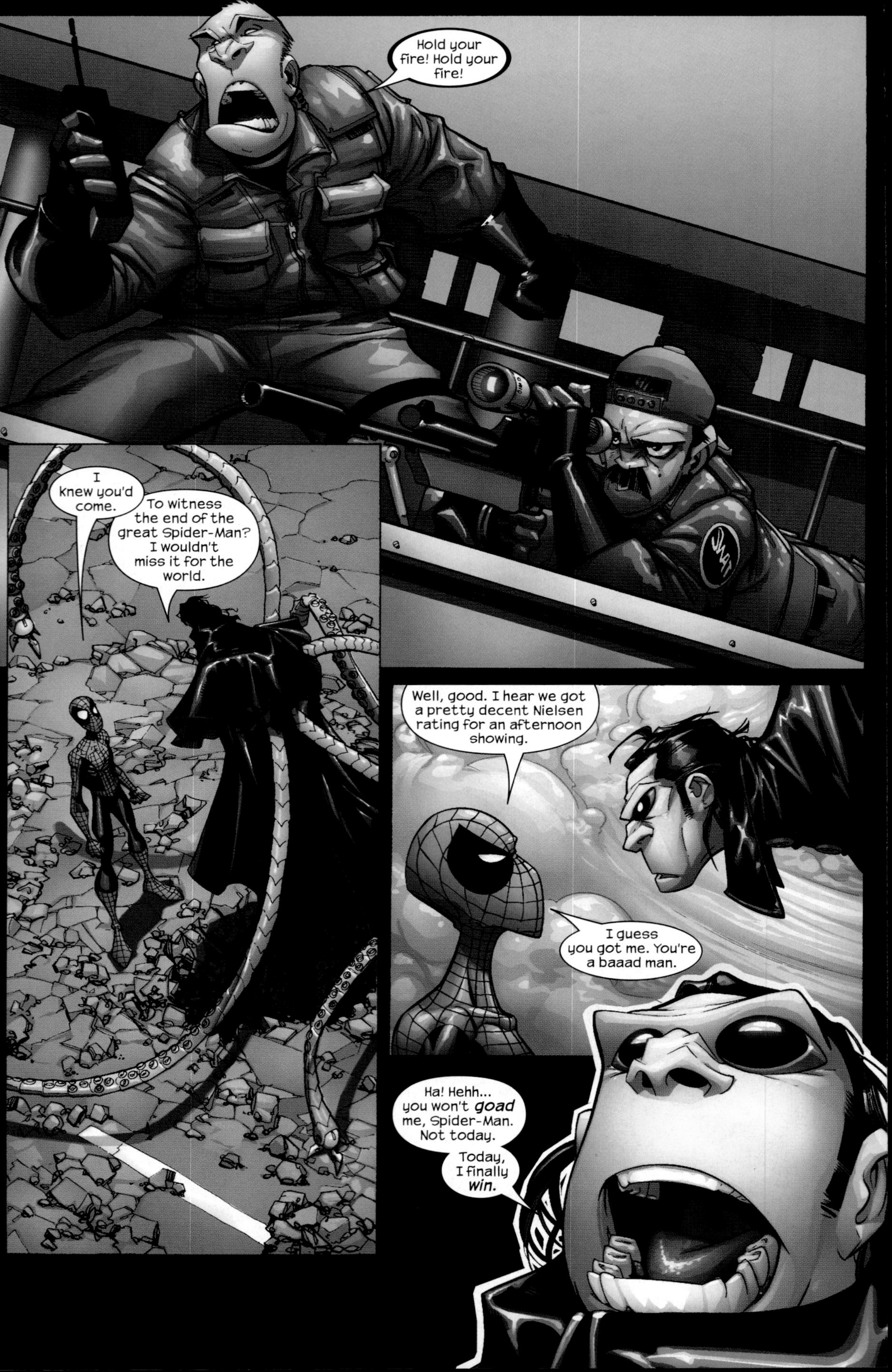
Hold your fire! Hold your fire!
I knew you'd come.
To witness the end of the great Spider-Man? I wouldn't miss it for the world.
Well, good. I hear we got a pretty decent Nielsen rating for an afternoon showing.
I guess you got me. You're a baaad man.
Ha! Hehh... you won't *goad* me, Spider-Man. Not today.
Today, I finally ***win.***

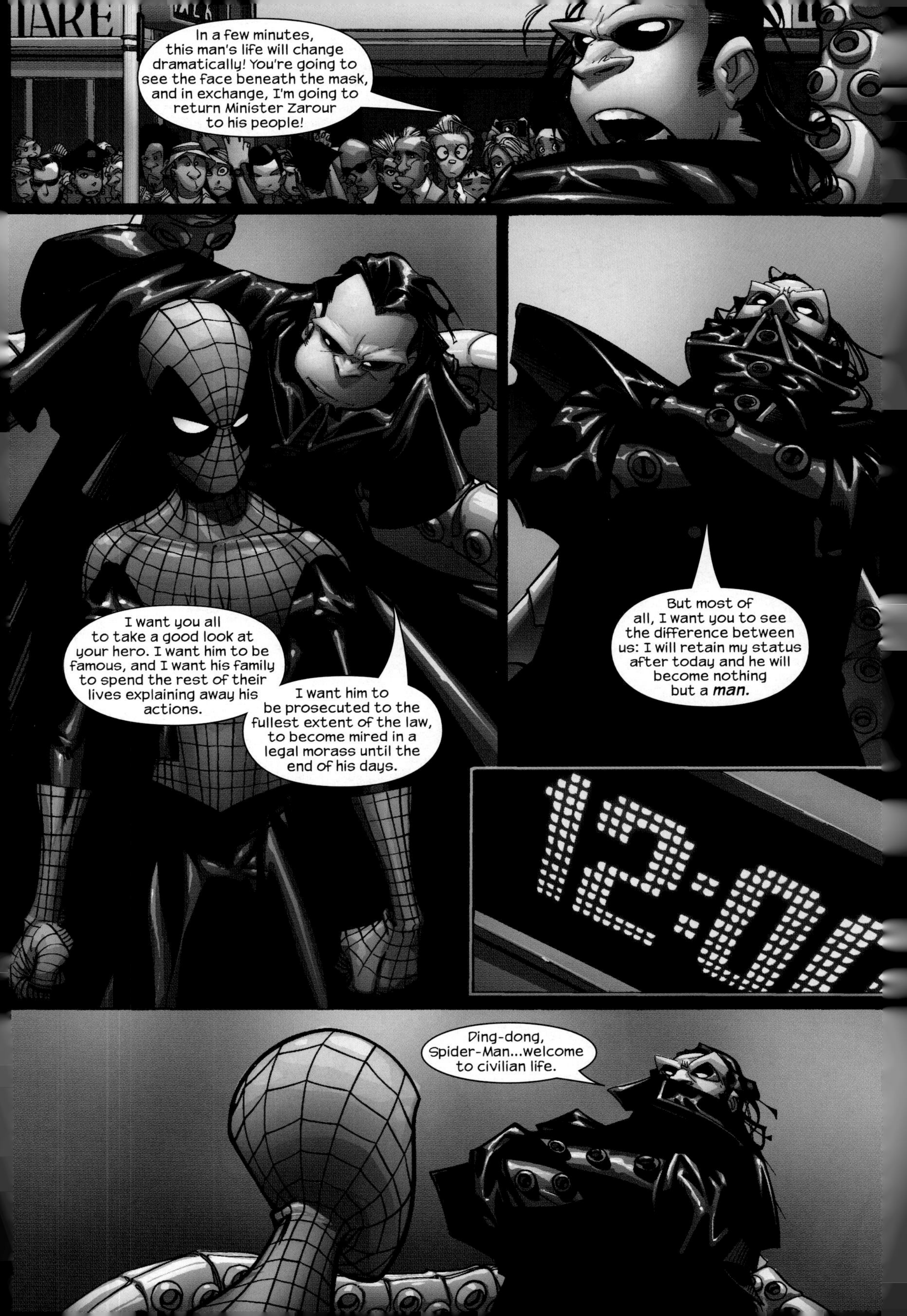
In a few minutes, this man's life will change dramatically! You're going to see the face beneath the mask, and in exchange, I'm going to return Minister Zarour to his people!
I want you all to take a good look at your hero. I want him to be famous, and I want his family to spend the rest of their lives explaining away his actions.
I want him to be prosecuted to the fullest extent of the law, to become mired in a legal morass until the end of his days.
But most of all, I want you to see the difference between us: I will retain my status after today and he will become nothing but a *man.*
12:0
Ding-dong, Spider-Man...welcome to civilian life.

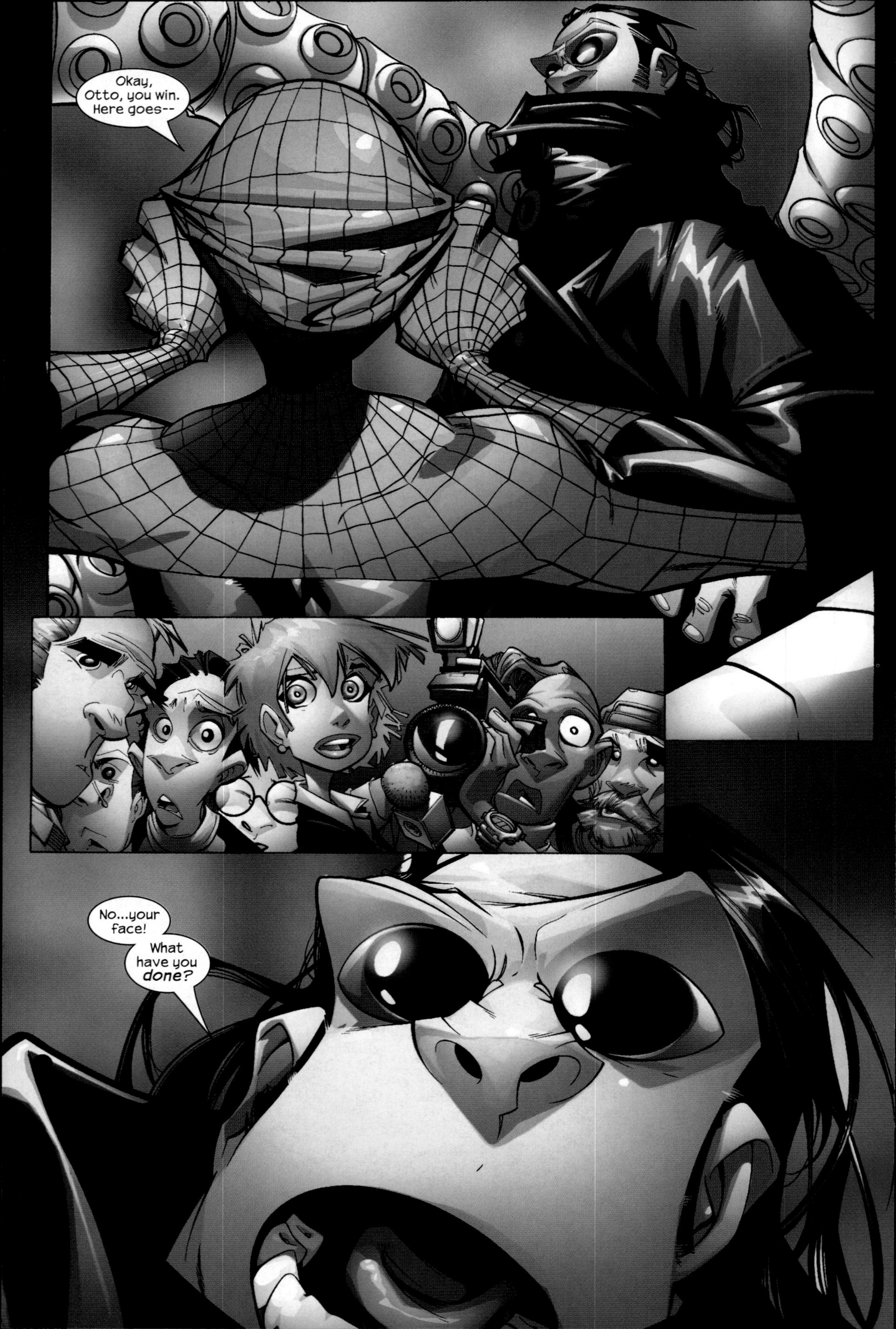
Okay, Otto, you win. Here goes--
No...your face! What have you *done*?

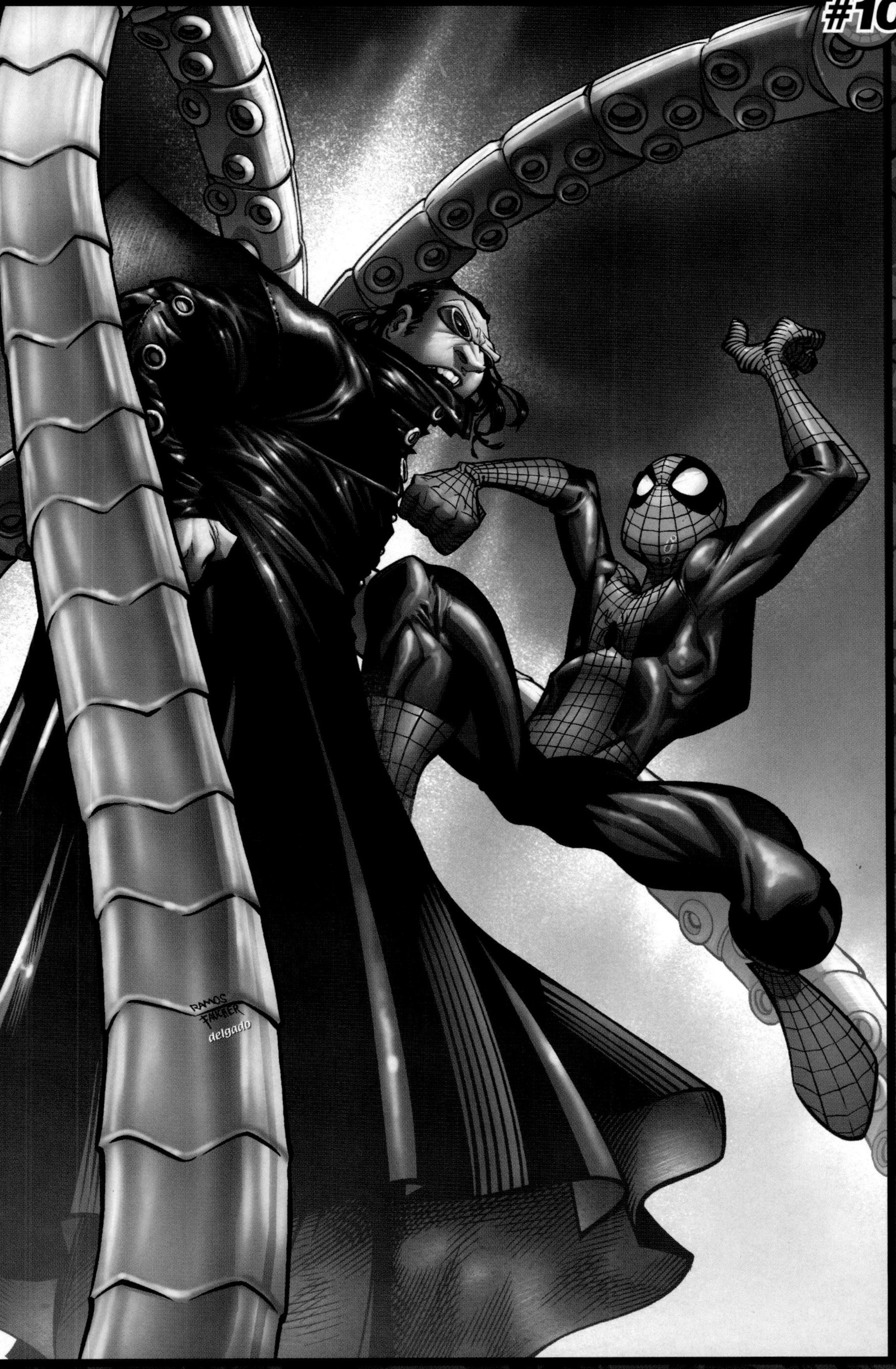
#10
RAMOS
FAKHER
delgado

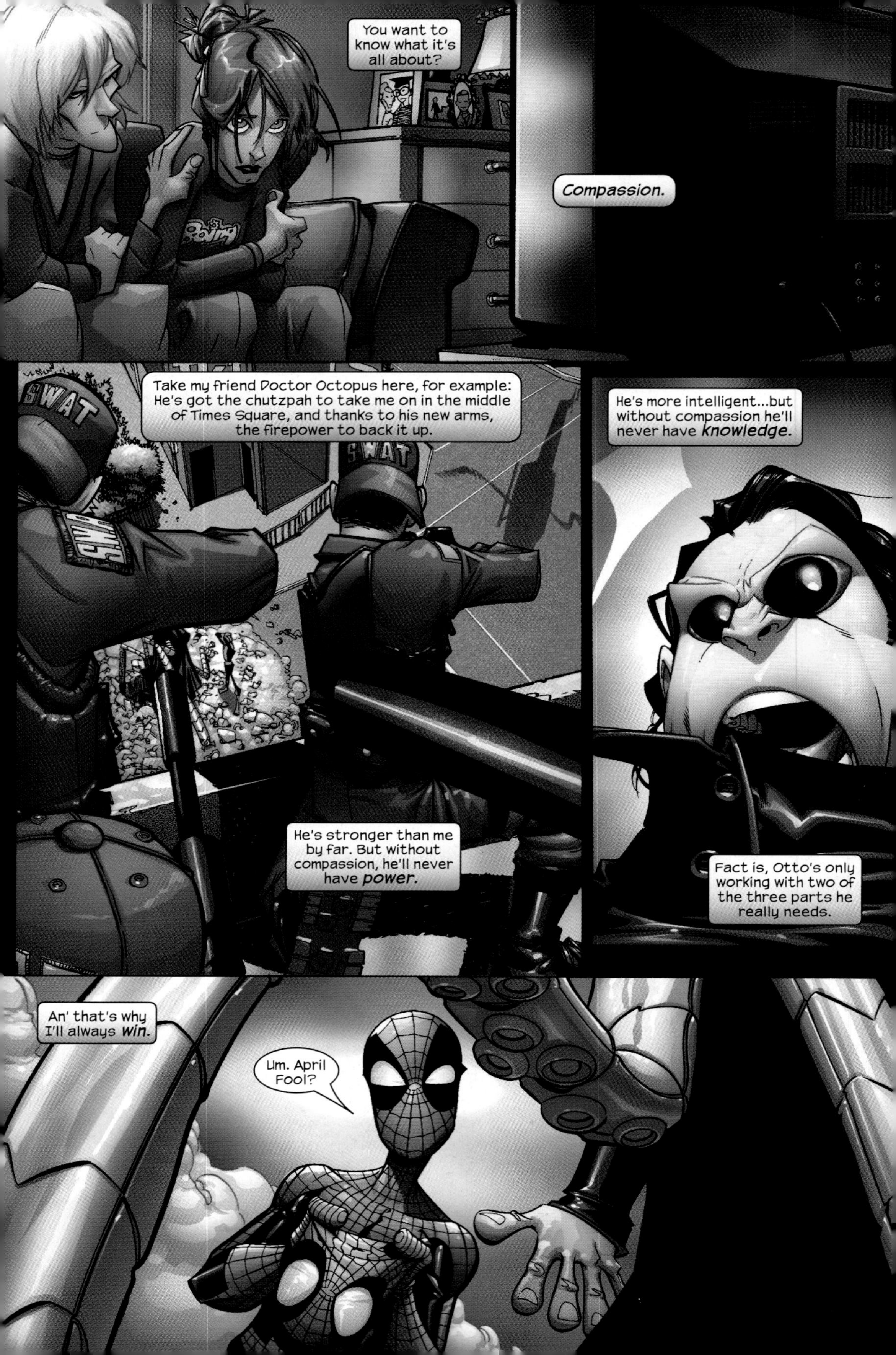
You want to know what it's all about?
Compassion.
Take my friend Doctor Octopus here, for example: He's got the chutzpah to take me on in the middle of Times Square, and thanks to his new arms, the firepower to back it up.
He's stronger than me by far. But without compassion, he'll never have *power.*
He's more intelligent...but without compassion he'll never have *knowledge.*
Fact is, Otto's only working with two of the three parts he really needs.
An' that's why I'll always *win.*
Um. April Fool?

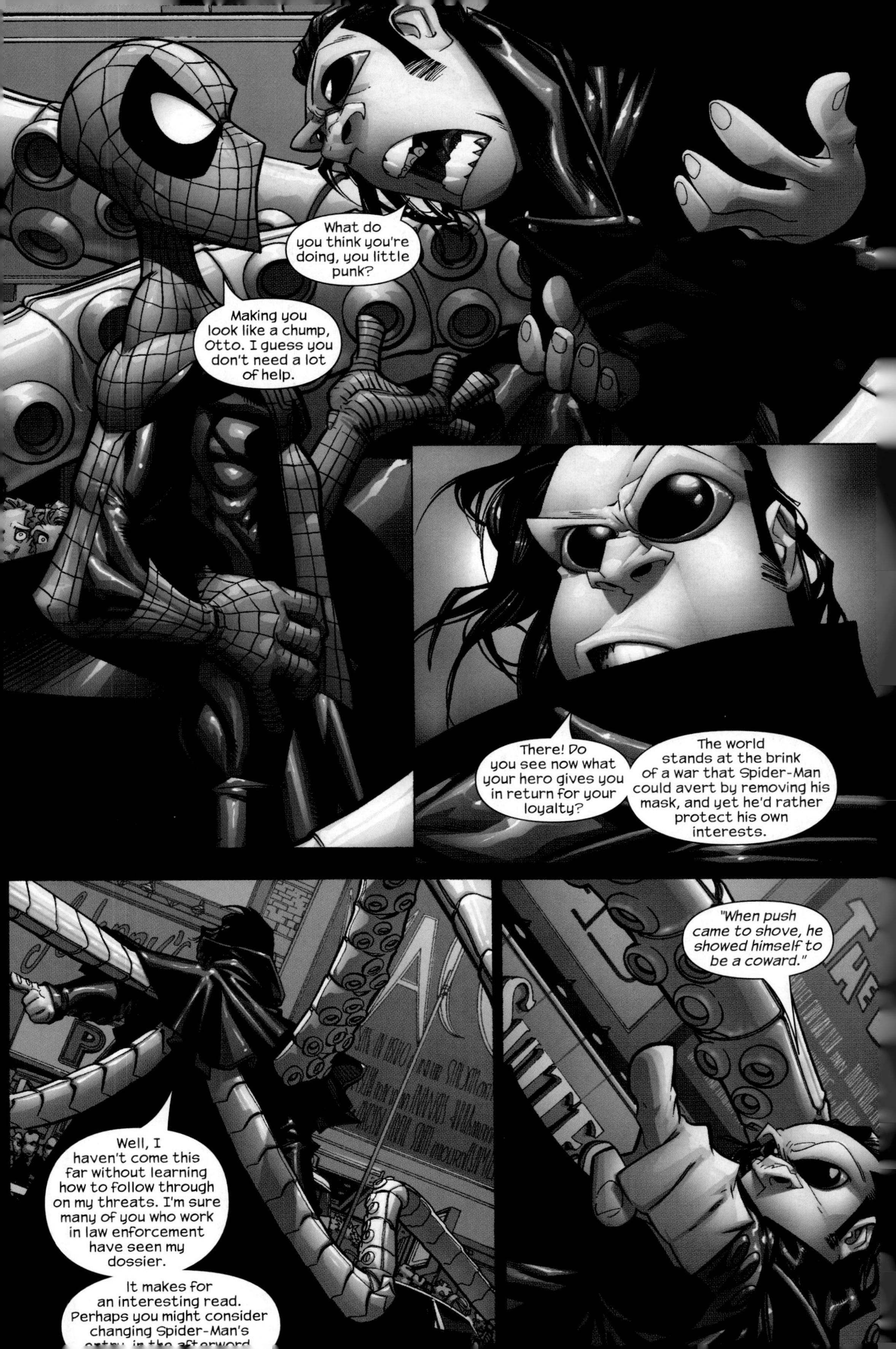
What do you think you're doing, you little punk?
Making you look like a chump, Otto. I guess you don't need a lot of help.
There! Do you see now what your hero gives you in return for your loyalty?
The world stands at the brink of a war that Spider-Man could avert by removing his mask, and yet he'd rather protect his own interests.
Well, I haven't come this far without learning how to follow through on my threats. I'm sure many of you who work in law enforcement have seen my dossier.
It makes for an interesting read. Perhaps you might consider changing Spider-Man's
"When push came to shove, he showed himself to be a coward."

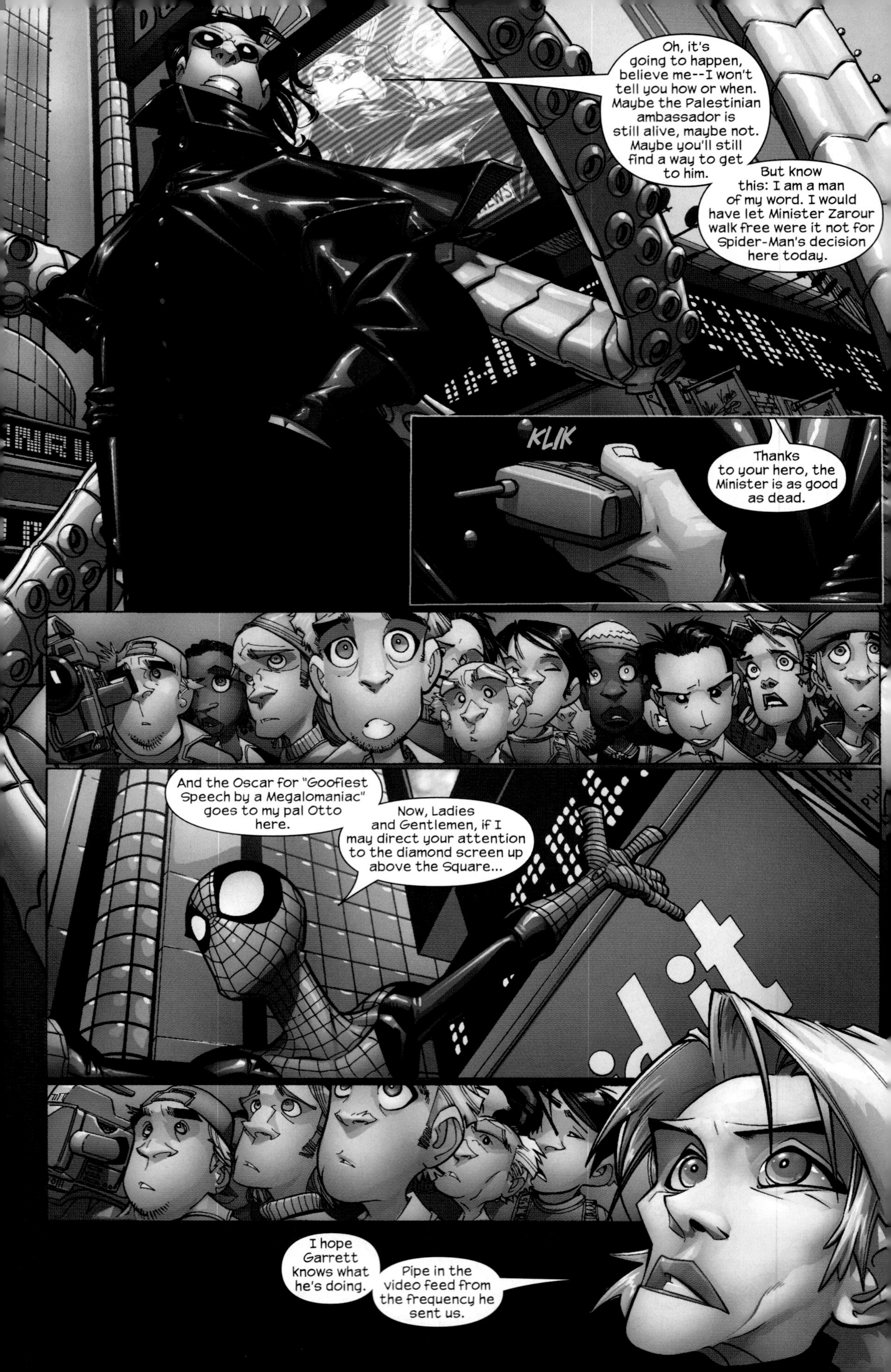
Oh, it's going to happen, believe me--I won't tell you how or when. Maybe the Palestinian ambassador is still alive, maybe not. Maybe you'll still find a way to get to him.
But know this: I am a man of my word. I would have let Minister Zarour walk free were it not for Spider-Man's decision here today.
KLIK
Thanks to your hero, the Minister is as good as dead.
And the Oscar for "Goofiest Speech by a Megalomaniac" goes to my pal Otto here.
Now, Ladies and Gentlemen, if I may direct your attention to the diamond screen up above the Square...
I hope Garrett knows what he's doing.
Pipe in the video feed from the frequency he sent us.

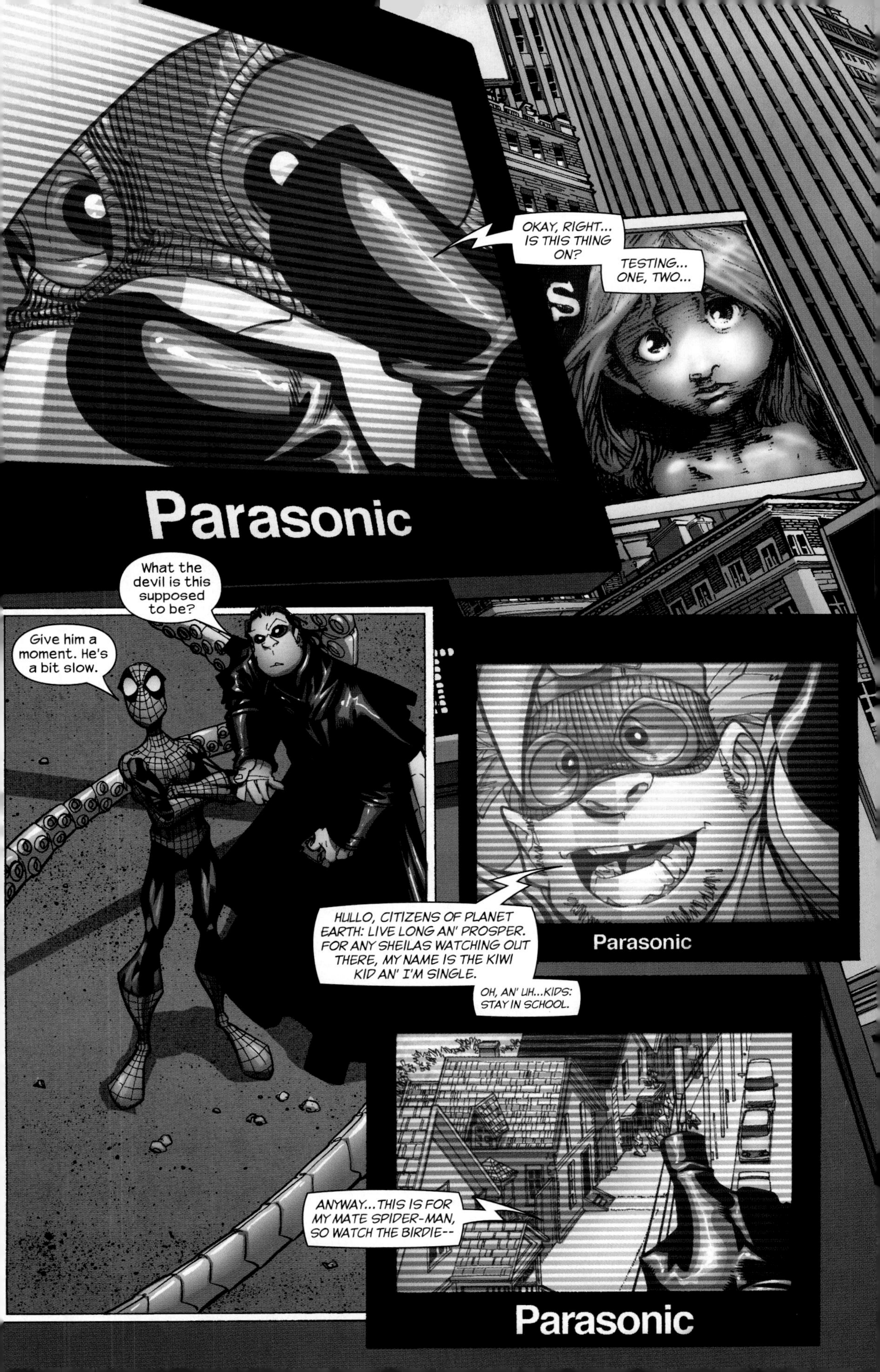
Parasonic
OKAY, RIGHT... IS THIS THING ON?
TESTING... ONE, TWO...
What the devil is this supposed to be?
Give him a moment. He's a bit slow.
HULLO, CITIZENS OF PLANET EARTH: LIVE LONG AN' PROSPER. FOR ANY SHEILAS WATCHING OUT THERE, MY NAME IS THE KIWI KID AN' I'M SINGLE.
OH, AN' UH...KIDS: STAY IN SCHOOL.
Parasonic
ANYWAY... THIS IS FOR MY MATE SPIDER-MAN, SO WATCH THE BIRDIE--
Parasonic

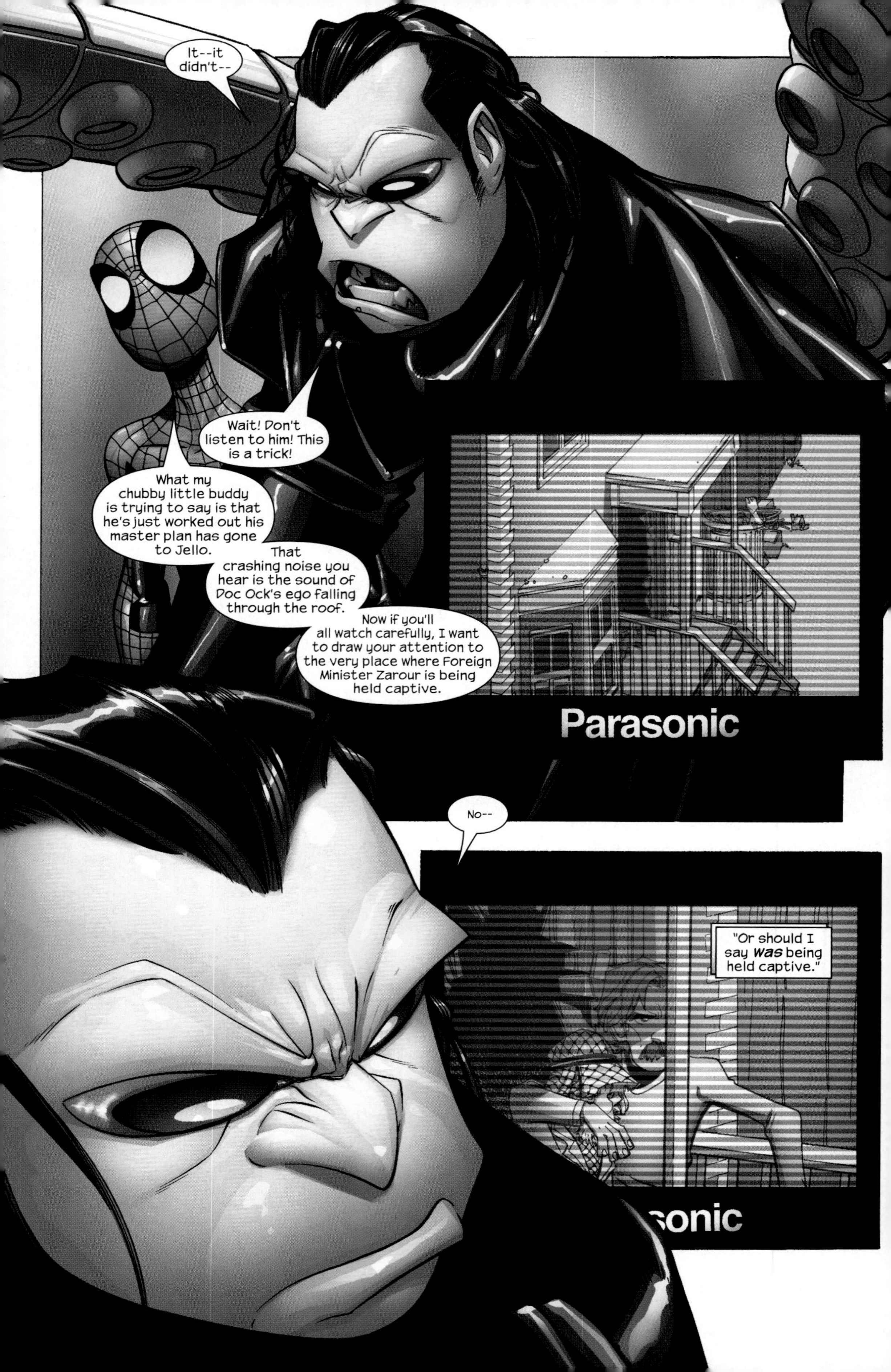
It--it didn't--
Wait! Don't listen to him! This is a trick!
What my chubby little buddy is trying to say is that he's just worked out his master plan has gone to Jello.
That crashing noise you hear is the sound of Doc Ock's ego falling through the roof.
Now if you'll all watch carefully, I want to draw your attention to the very place where Foreign Minister Zarour is being held captive.
Parasonic
No--
"Or should I say *was* being held captive."
sonic

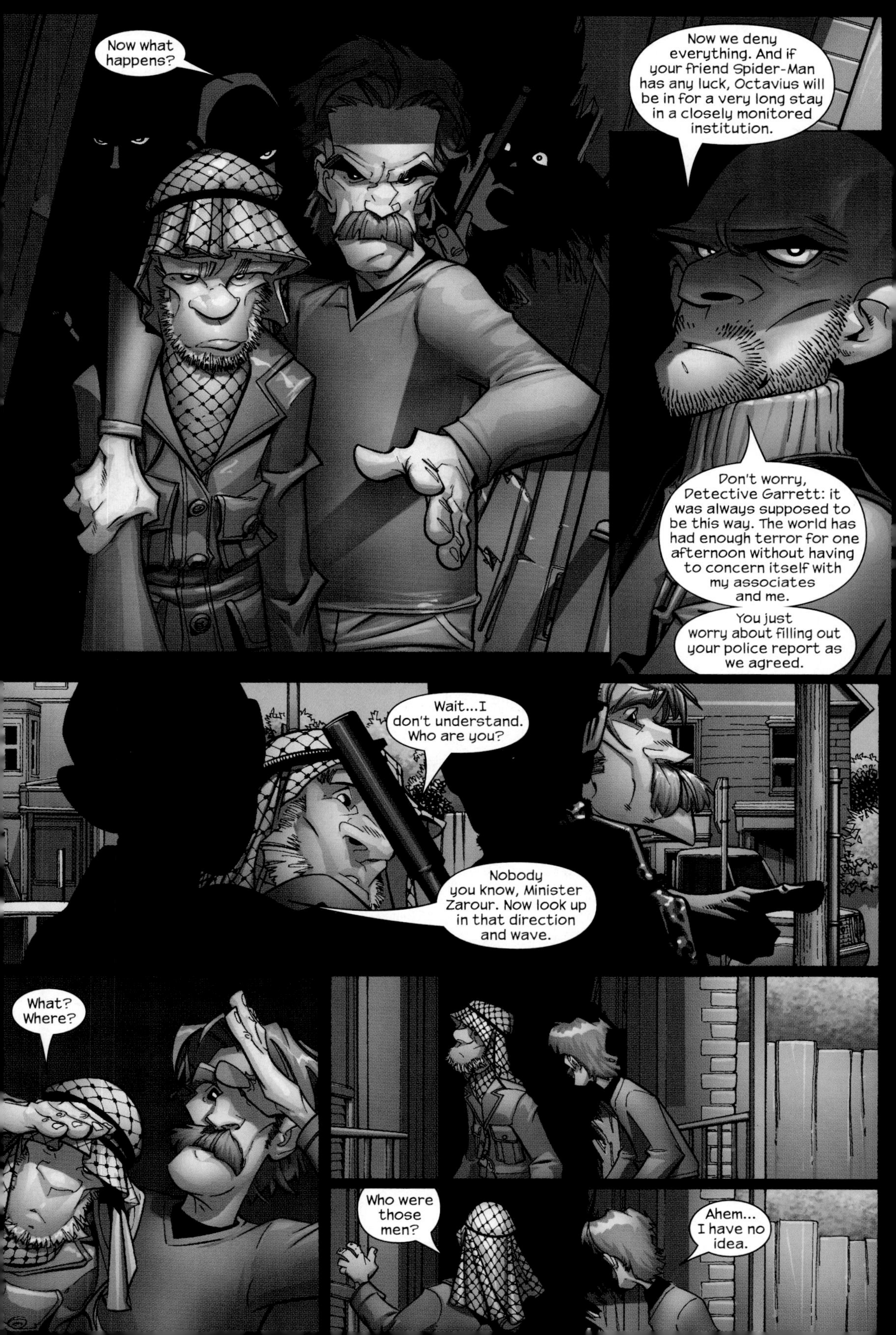
Now what happens?
Now we deny everything. And if your friend Spider-Man has any luck, Octavius will be in for a very long stay in a closely monitored institution.
Don't worry, Detective Garrett: it was always supposed to be this way. The world has had enough terror for one afternoon without having to concern itself with my associates and me.
You just worry about filling out your police report as we agreed.
Wait...I don't understand. Who are you?
Nobody you know, Minister Zarour. Now look up in that direction and wave.
What? Where?
Who were those men?
Ahem... I have no idea.

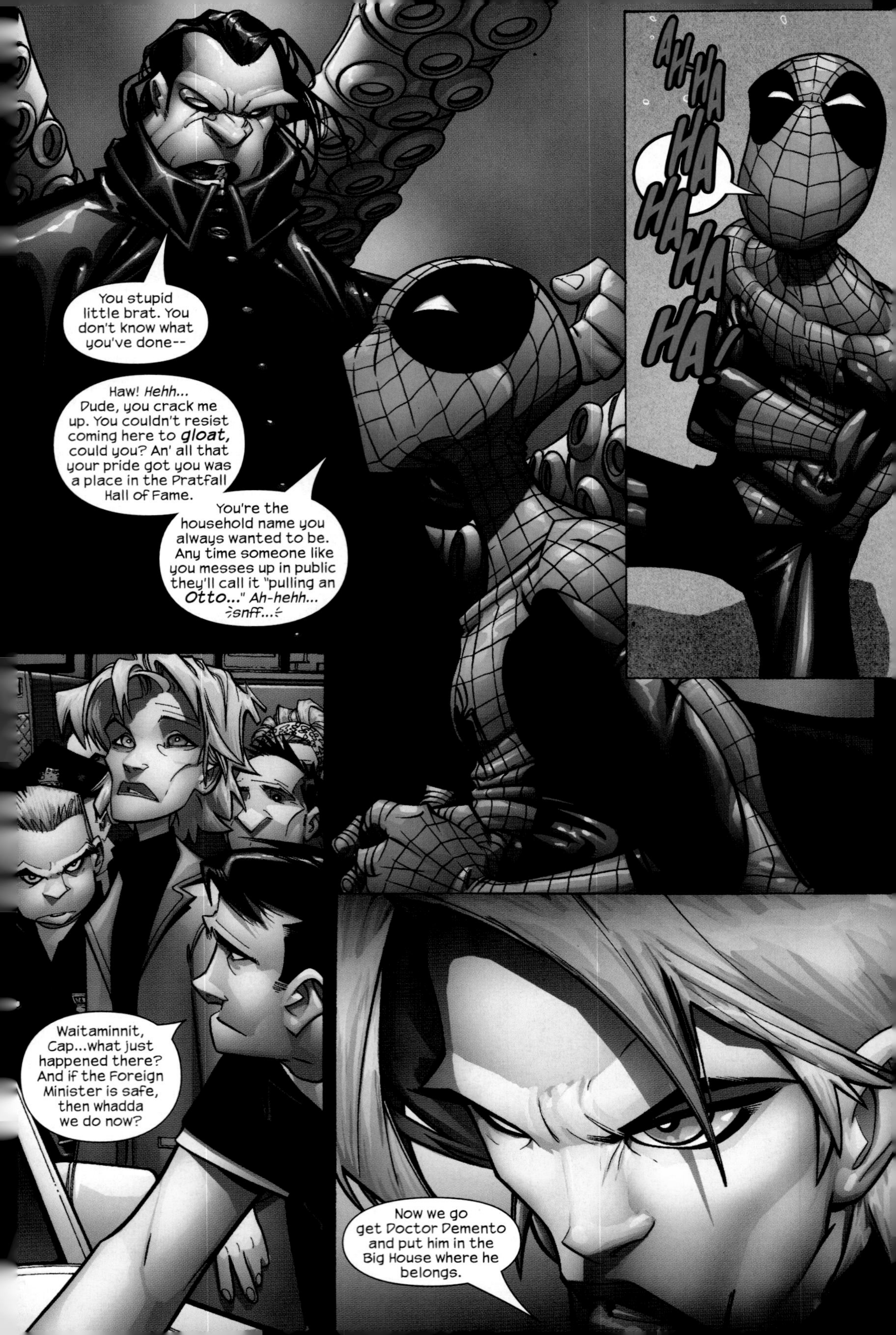
You stupid little brat. You don't know what you've done--
Haw! *Hehh...* Dude, you crack me up. You couldn't resist coming here to ***gloat,*** could you? An' all that your pride got you was a place in the Pratfall Hall of Fame.
You're the household name you always wanted to be. Any time someone like you messes up in public they'll call it "pulling an ***Otto...***" *Ah-hehh... snff...*
AH-HA HA HA HA HA HA HA!
Waitaminnit, Cap...what just happened there? And if the Foreign Minister is safe, then whadda we do now?
Now we go get Doctor Demento and put him in the Big House where he belongs.

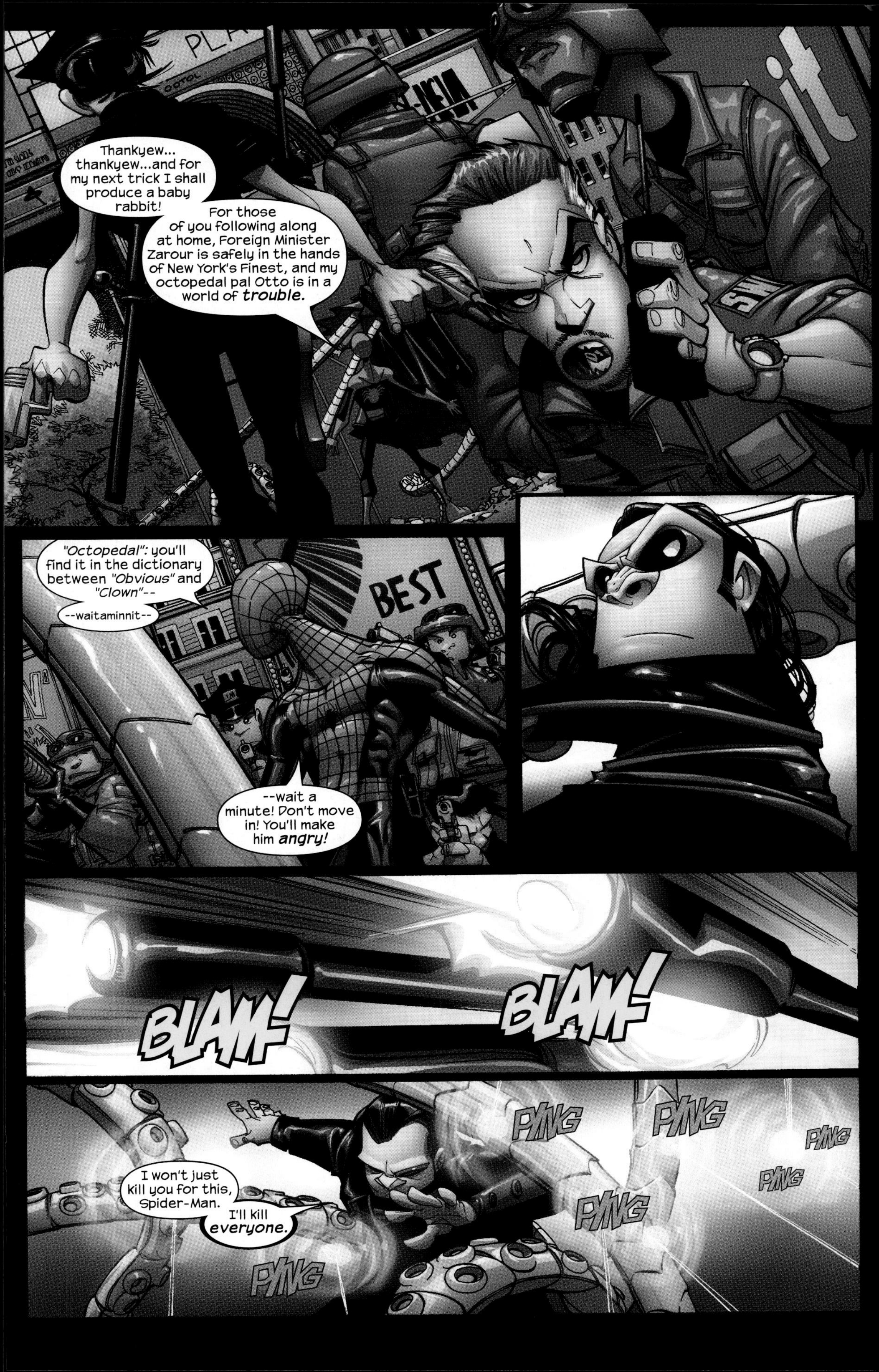
Thankyew... thankyew...and for my next trick I shall produce a baby rabbit!
For those of you following along at home, Foreign Minister Zarour is safely in the hands of New York's Finest, and my octopedal pal Otto is in a world of *trouble.*
BEST
"Octopedal": you'll find it in the dictionary between *"Obvious"* and *"Clown"*--
--waitaminnit--
--wait a minute! Don't move in! You'll make him *angry!*
BLAM!
BLAM!
PYING
PYING
PYING
PYING
PYING
PYING
I won't just kill you for this, Spider-Man.
I'll kill *everyone.*

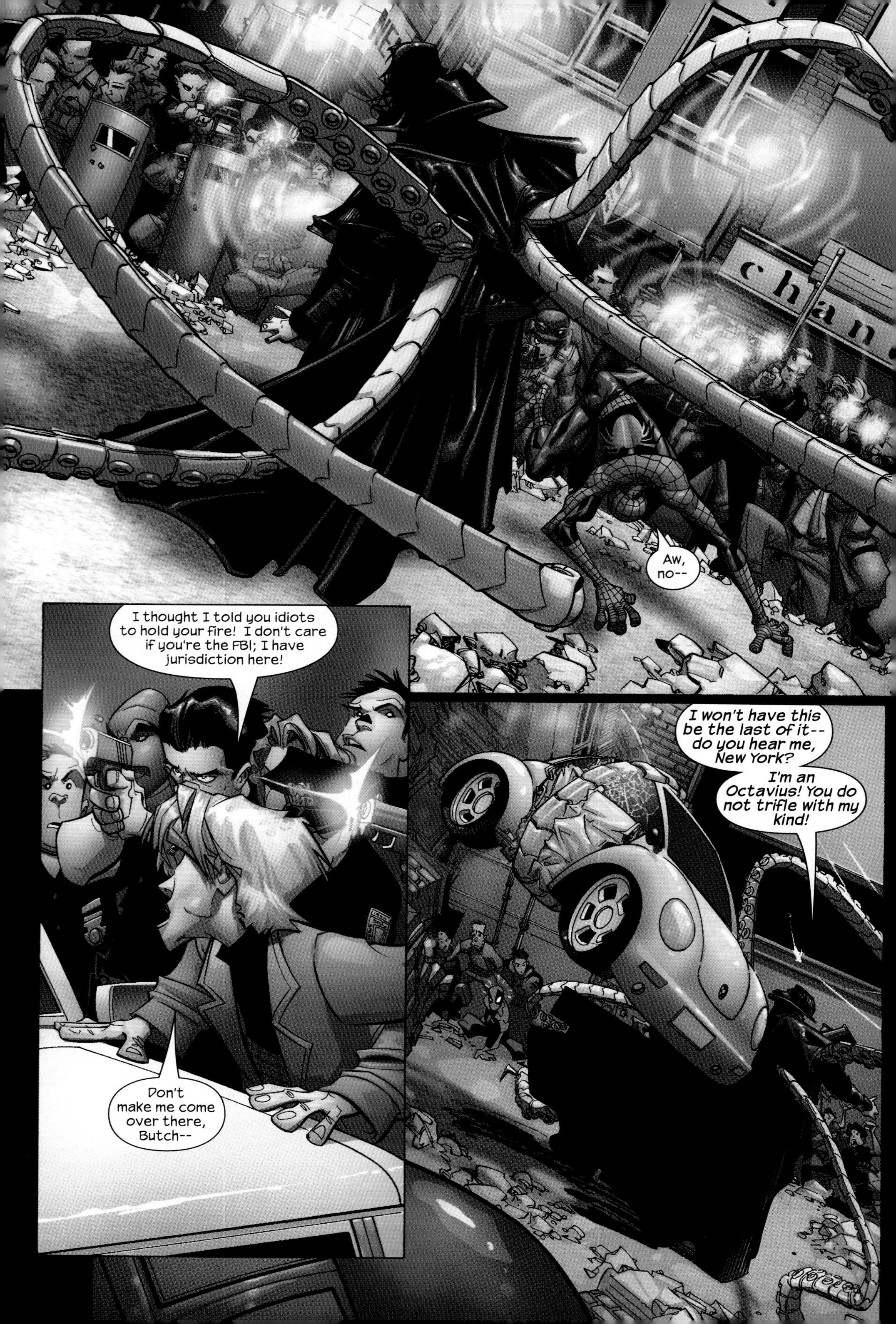
Aw, no--
I thought I told you idiots to hold your fire! I don't care if you're the FBI; I have jurisdiction here!
Don't make me come over there, Butch--
I won't have this be the last of it-- do you hear me, New York?
I'm an Octavius! You do not trifle with my kind!

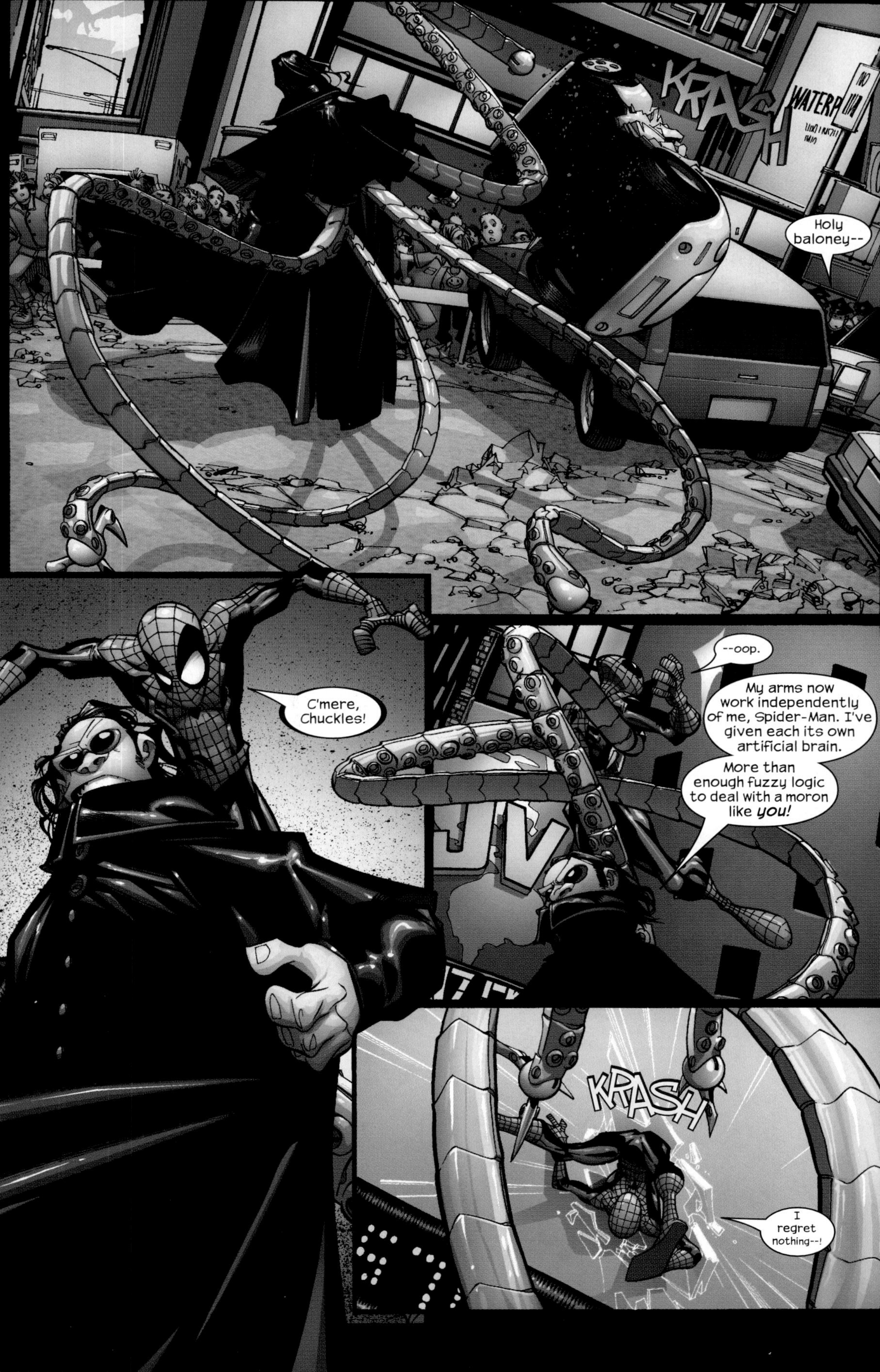
KRASH
WATERP
NO
Holy baloney--
C'mere, Chuckles!
--oop.
My arms now work independently of me, Spider-Man. I've given each its own artificial brain.
More than enough fuzzy logic to deal with a moron like *you!*
KRASH
I regret nothing--!

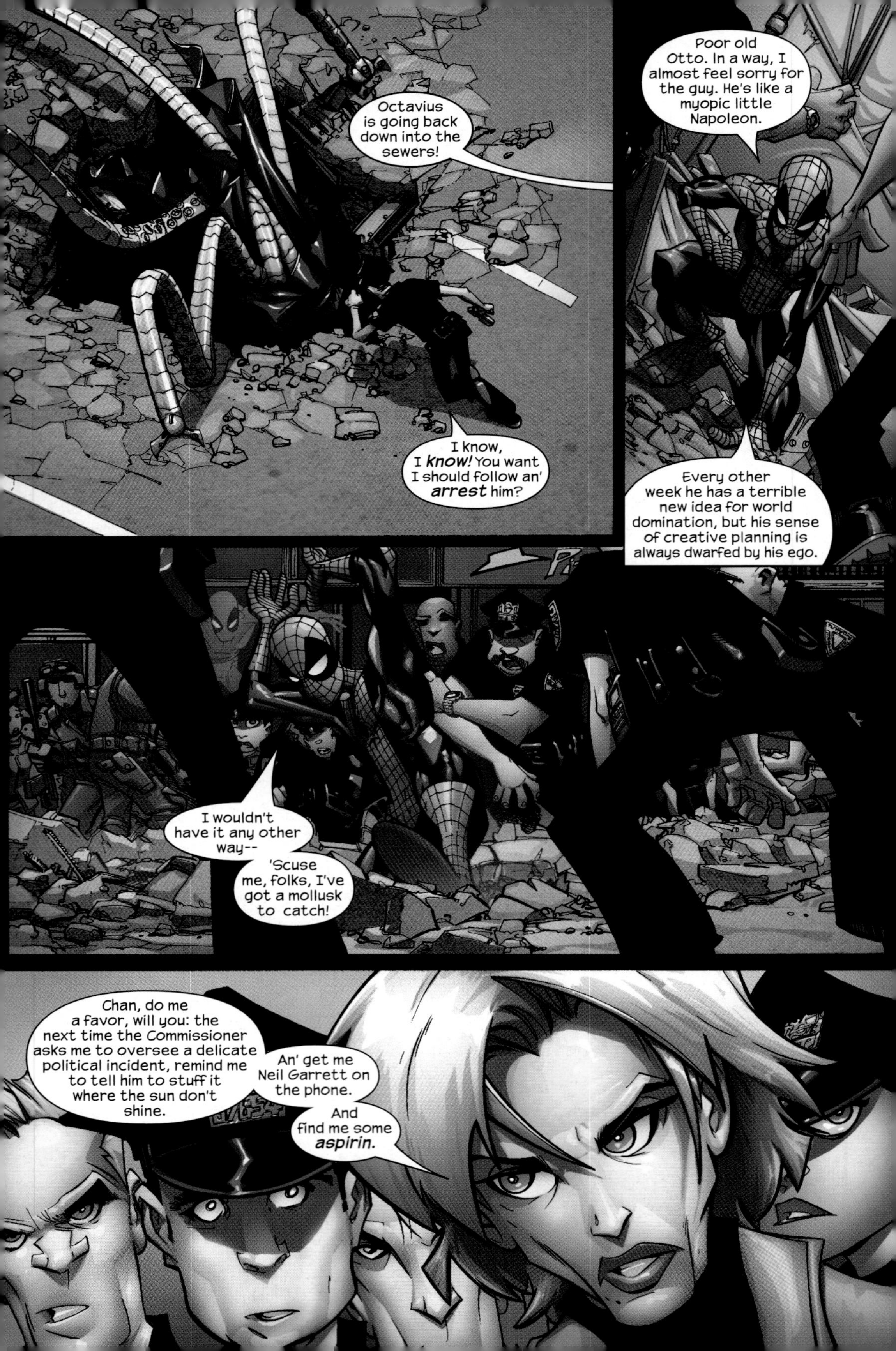
Octavius is going back down into the sewers!
I know, I *know!* You want I should follow an' *arrest* him?
Poor old Otto. In a way, I almost feel sorry for the guy. He's like a myopic little Napoleon.
Every other week he has a terrible new idea for world domination, but his sense of creative planning is always dwarfed by his ego.
I wouldn't have it any other way--
'Scuse me, folks, I've got a mollusk to catch!
Chan, do me a favor, will you: the next time the Commissioner asks me to oversee a delicate political incident, remind me to tell him to stuff it where the sun don't shine.
An' get me Neil Garrett on the phone.
And find me some *aspirin.*

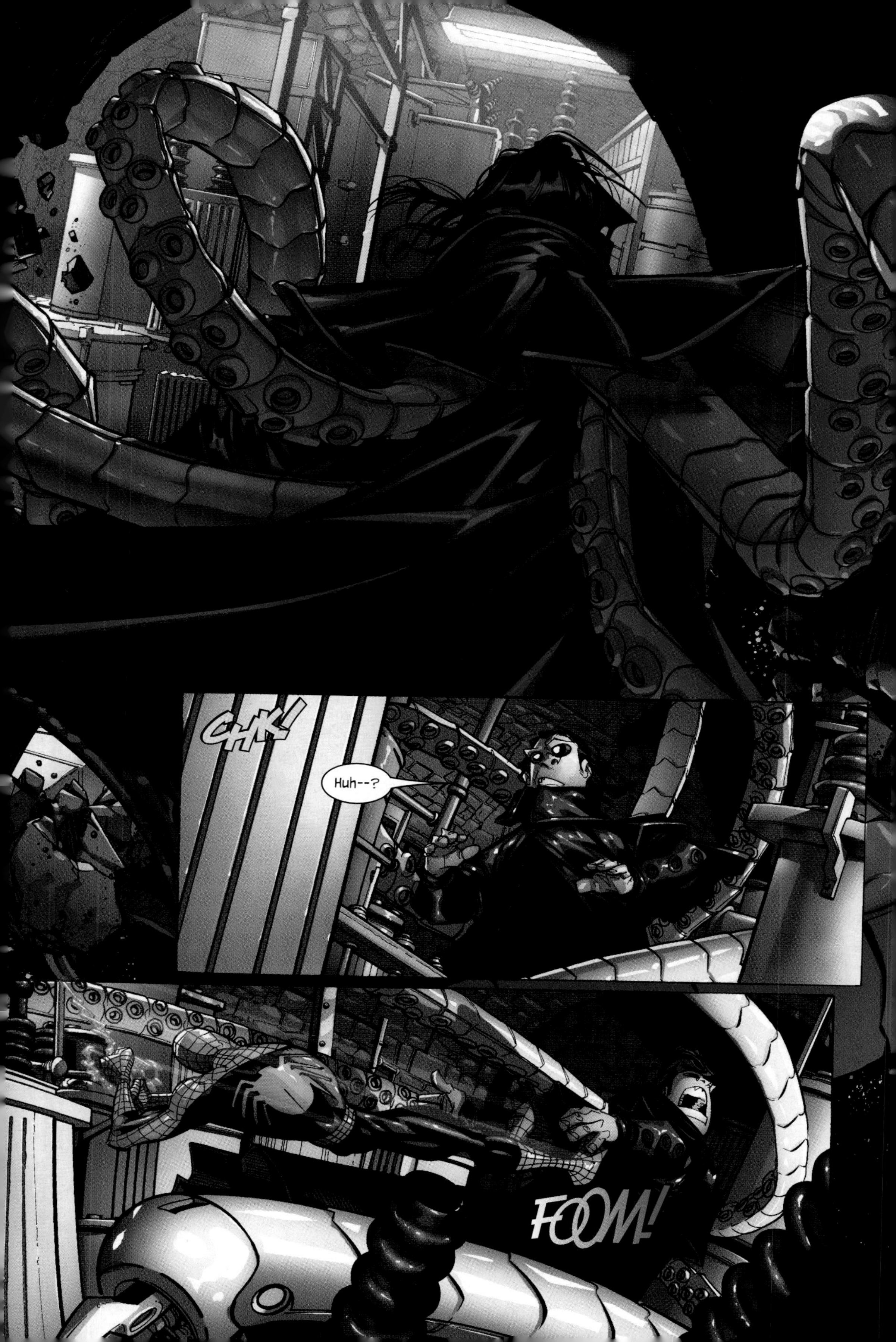
CHK!
Huh--?
FOOM!

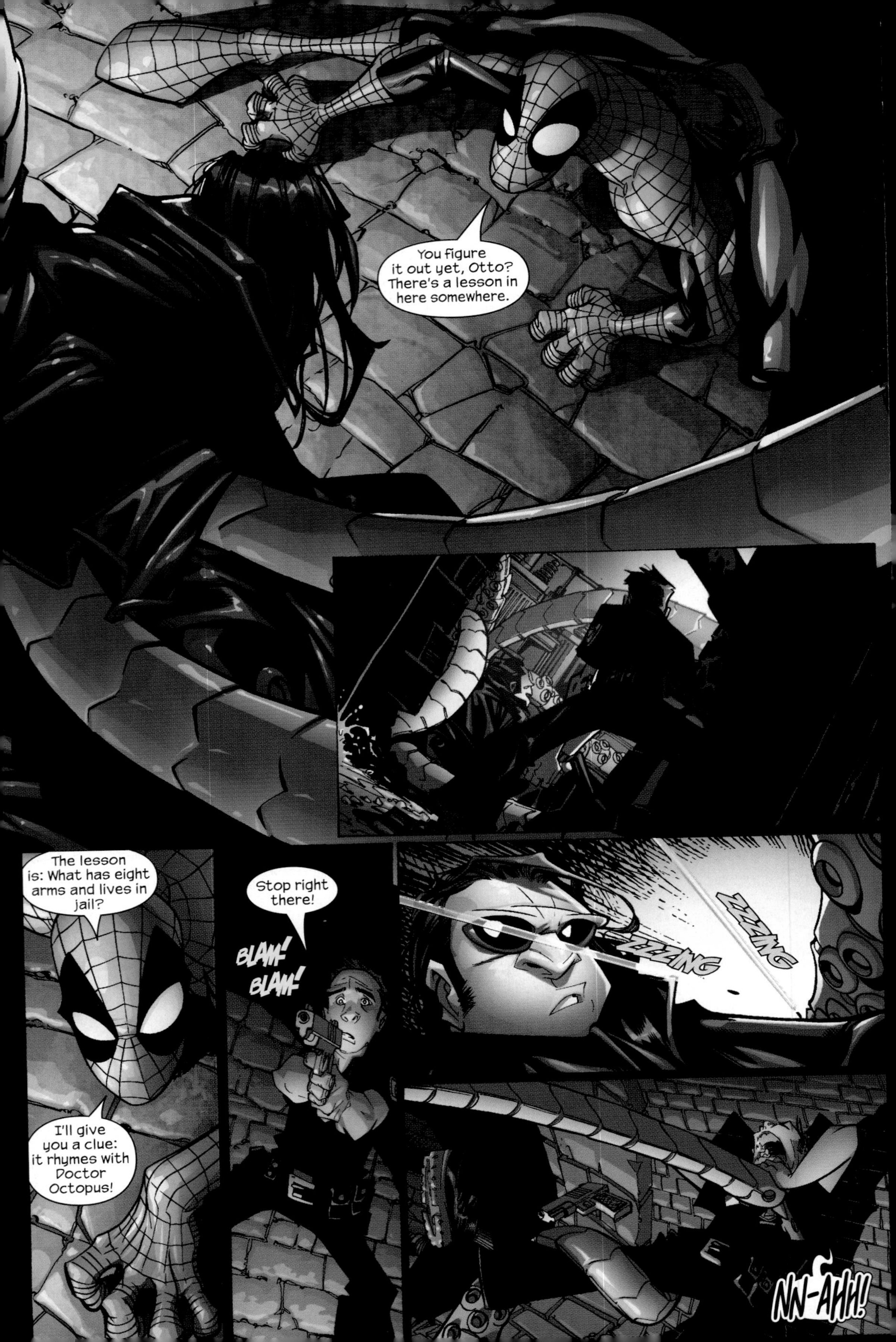
You figure it out yet, Otto? There's a lesson in here somewhere.
The lesson is: What has eight arms and lives in jail?
I'll give you a clue: it rhymes with Doctor Octopus!
Stop right there!
BLAM! BLAM!
ZZZING
ZZZING
NN-AHH!

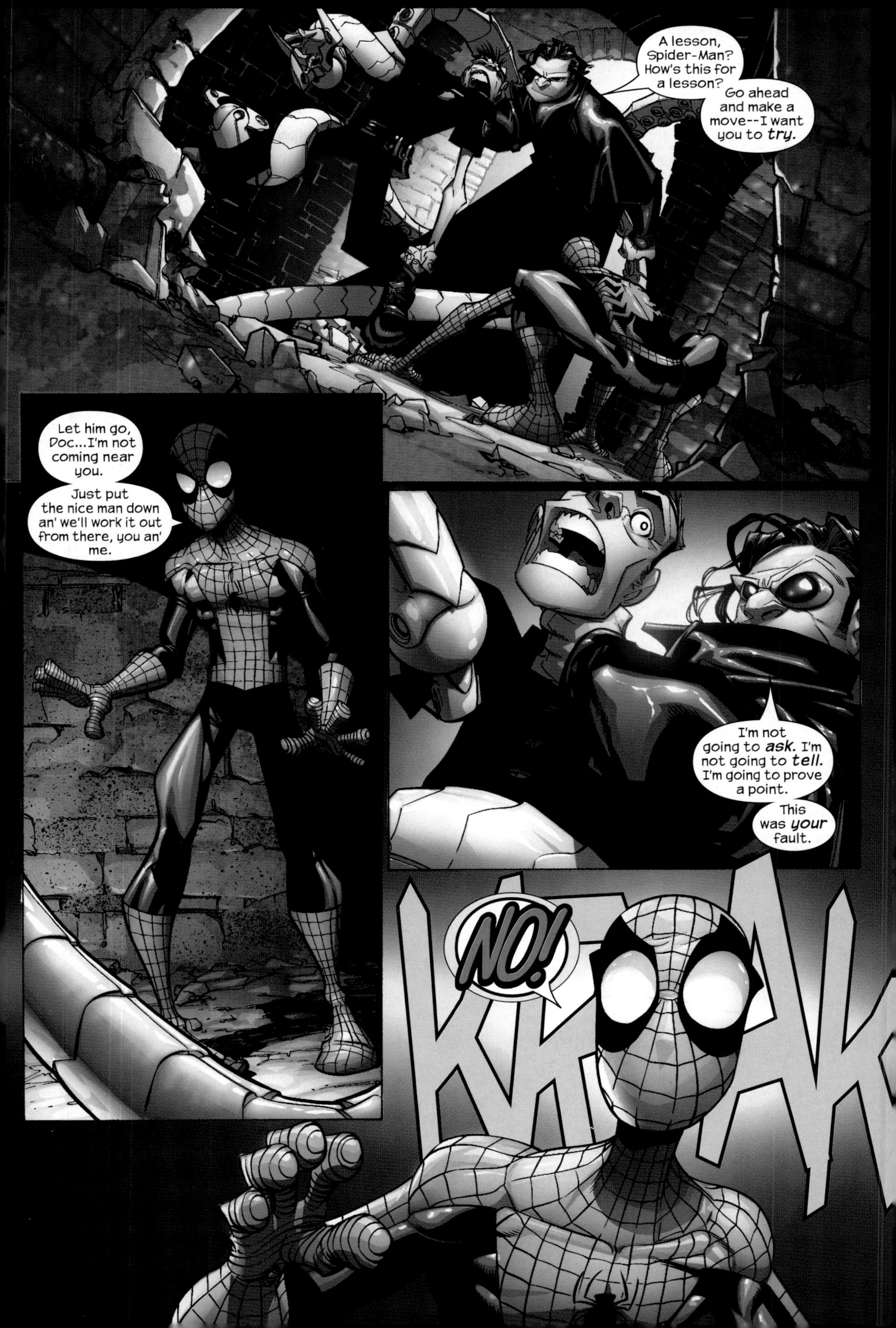
A lesson, Spider-Man? How's this for a lesson?
Go ahead and make a move--I want you to *try.*
Let him go, Doc...I'm not coming near you.
Just put the nice man down an' we'll work it out from there, you an' me.
I'm not going to *ask.* I'm not going to *tell.* I'm going to prove a point.
This was *your* fault.
NO!

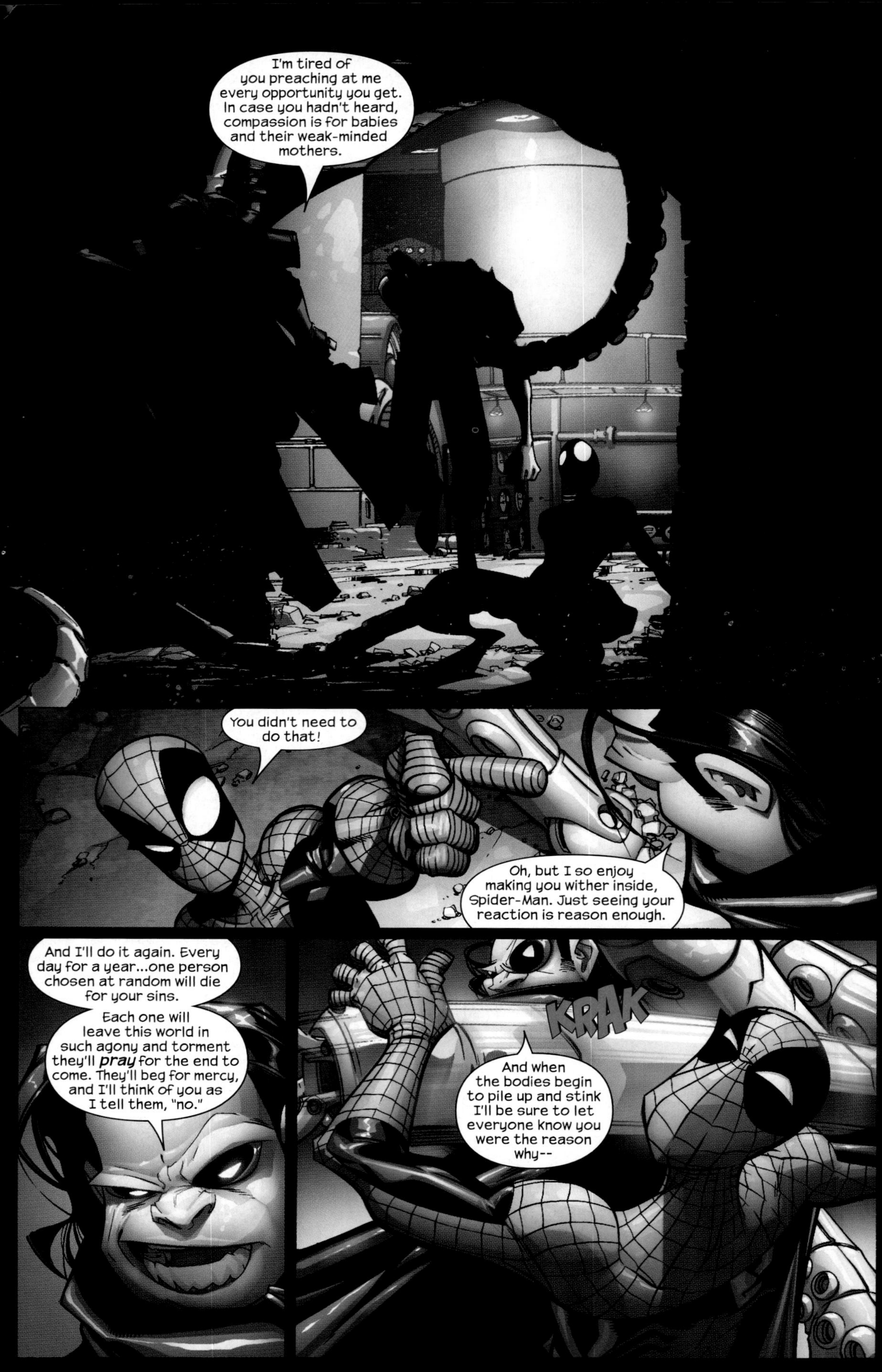
I'm tired of you preaching at me every opportunity you get. In case you hadn't heard, compassion is for babies and their weak-minded mothers.
You didn't need to do that!
Oh, but I so enjoy making you wither inside, Spider-Man. Just seeing your reaction is reason enough.
And I'll do it again. Every day for a year...one person chosen at random will die for your sins.
Each one will leave this world in such agony and torment they'll *pray* for the end to come. They'll beg for mercy, and I'll think of you as I tell them, "no."
KRAK
And when the bodies begin to pile up and stink I'll be sure to let everyone know you were the reason why--

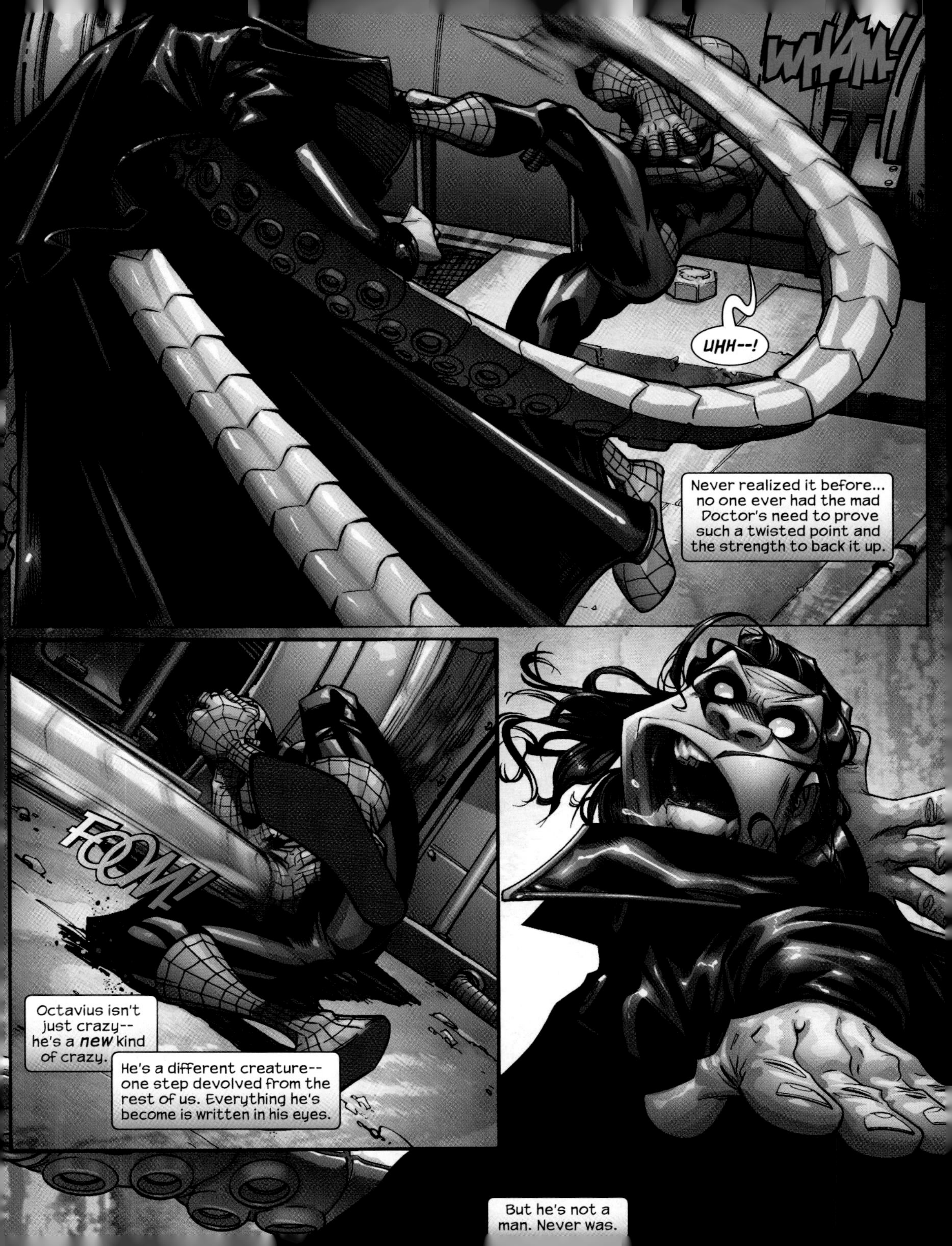

WHAM!
UHH--!
Never realized it before... no one ever had the mad Doctor's need to prove such a twisted point and the strength to back it up.
FOOM!
Octavius isn't just crazy-- he's a *new* kind of crazy.
He's a different creature-- one step devolved from the rest of us. Everything he's become is written in his eyes.
But he's not a man. Never was.

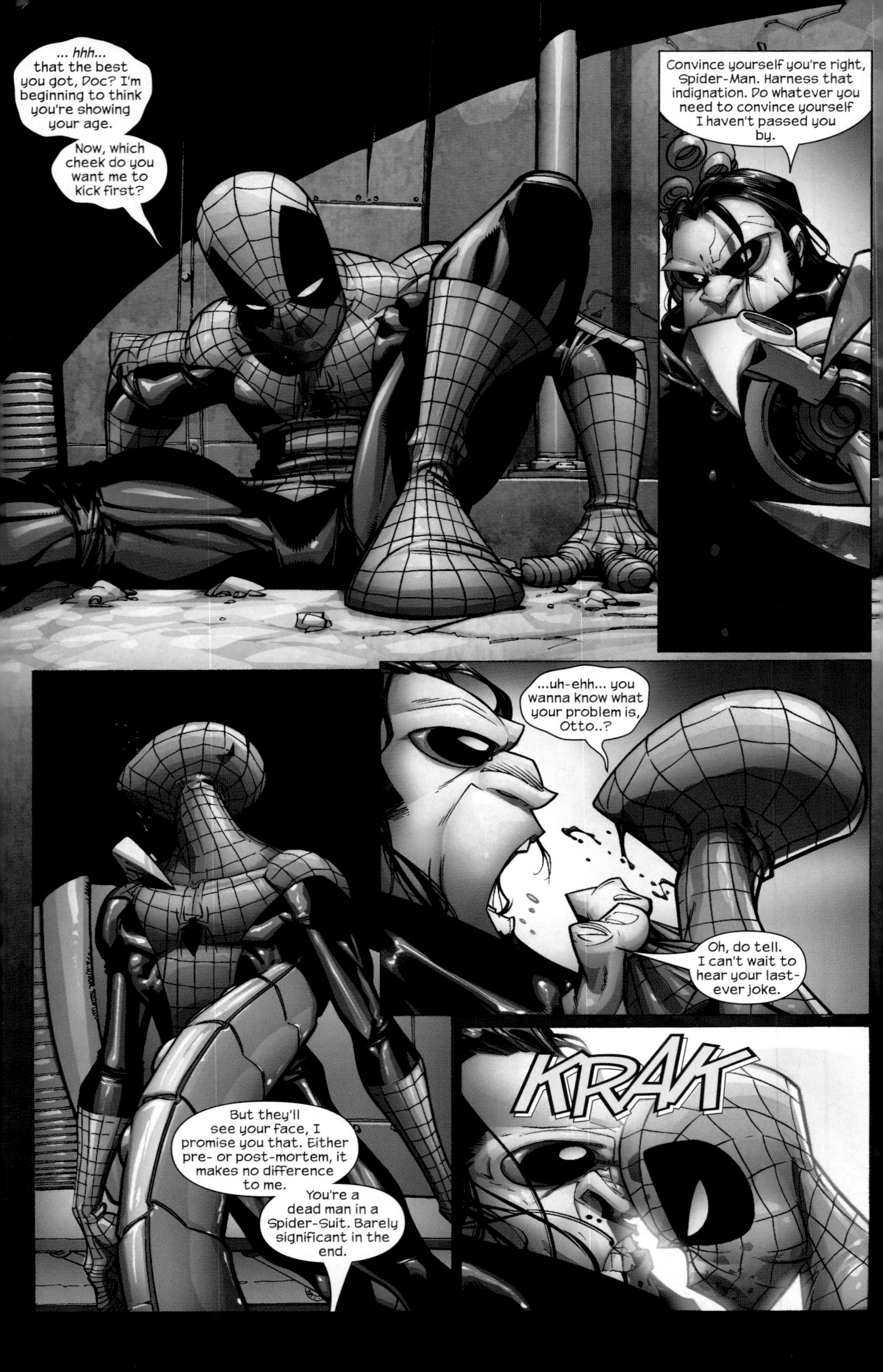
... hhh... that the best you got, Doc? I'm beginning to think you're showing your age.
Now, which cheek do you want me to kick first?
Convince yourself you're right, Spider-Man. Harness that indignation. Do whatever you need to convince yourself I haven't passed you by.
...uh-ehh... you wanna know what your problem is, Otto..?
Oh, do tell. I can't wait to hear your last-ever joke.
But they'll see your face, I promise you that. Either pre- or post-mortem, it makes no difference to me.
You're a dead man in a Spider-Suit. Barely significant in the end.
KRAK

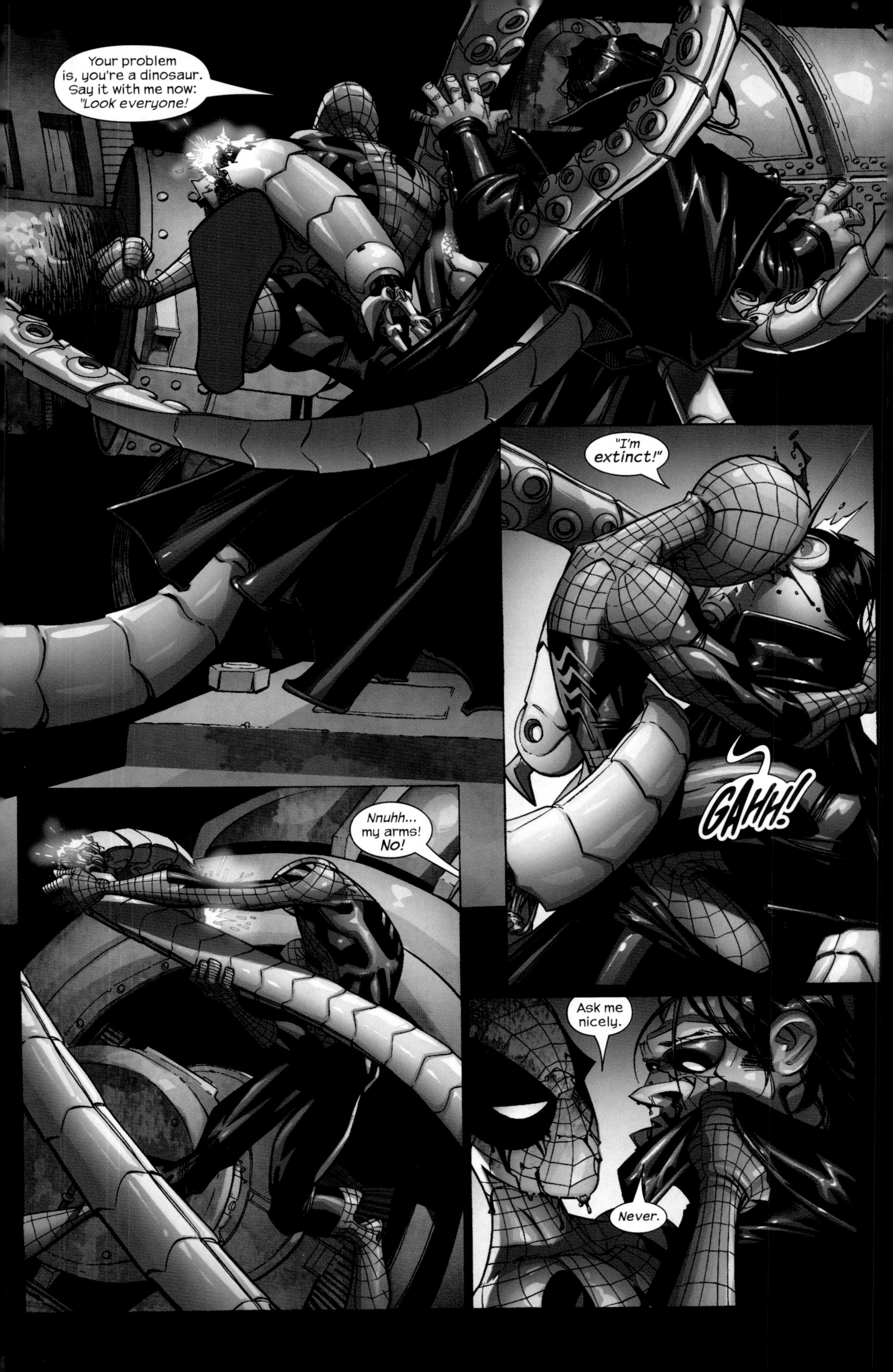
Your problem is, you're a dinosaur. Say it with me now: "Look everyone!
"I'm extinct!"
GAHH!
Nnuhh... my arms! NO!
Ask me nicely.
Never.

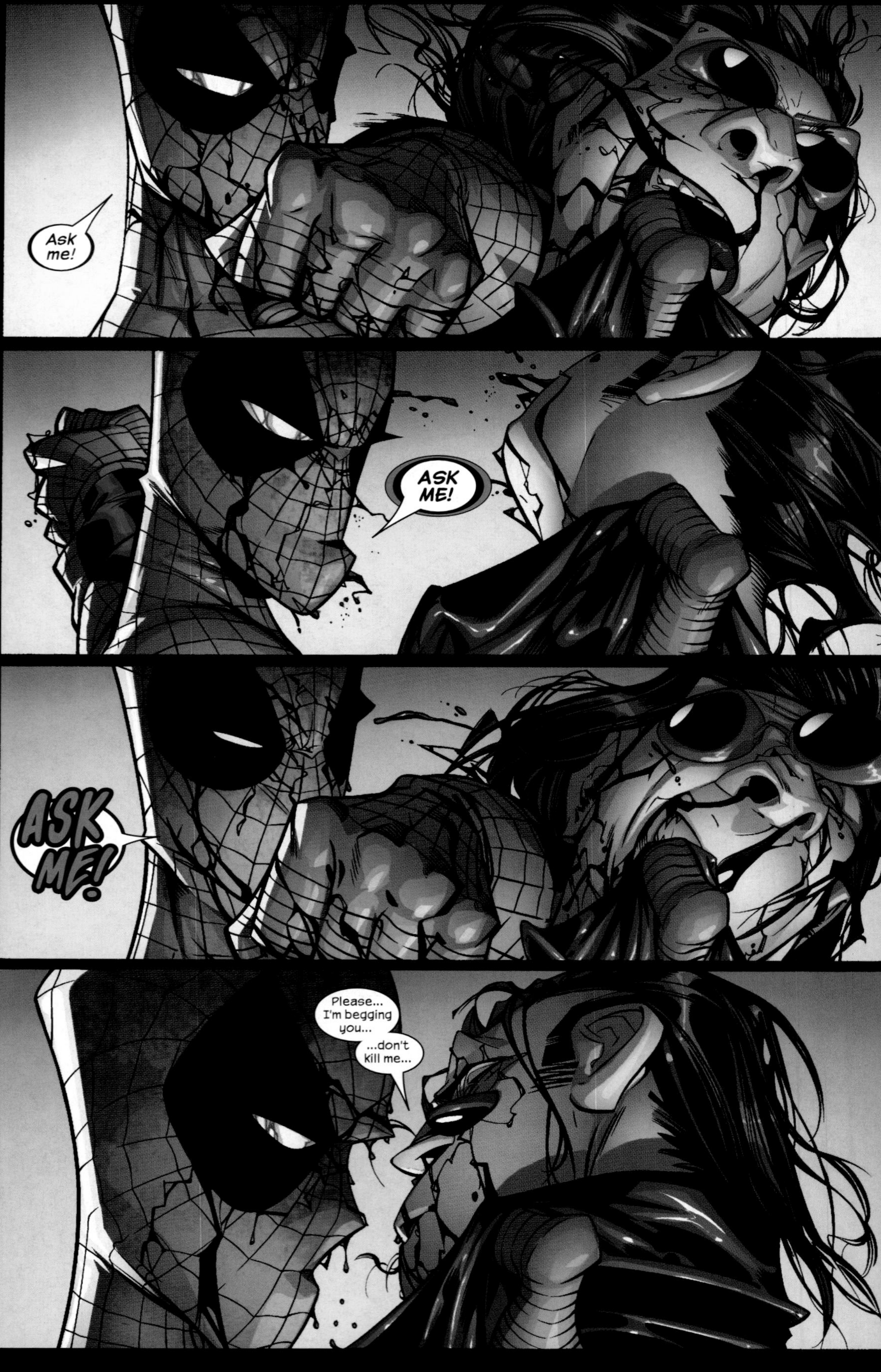
Ask me!
ASK ME!
ASK ME!
Please... I'm begging you...
...don't kill me...

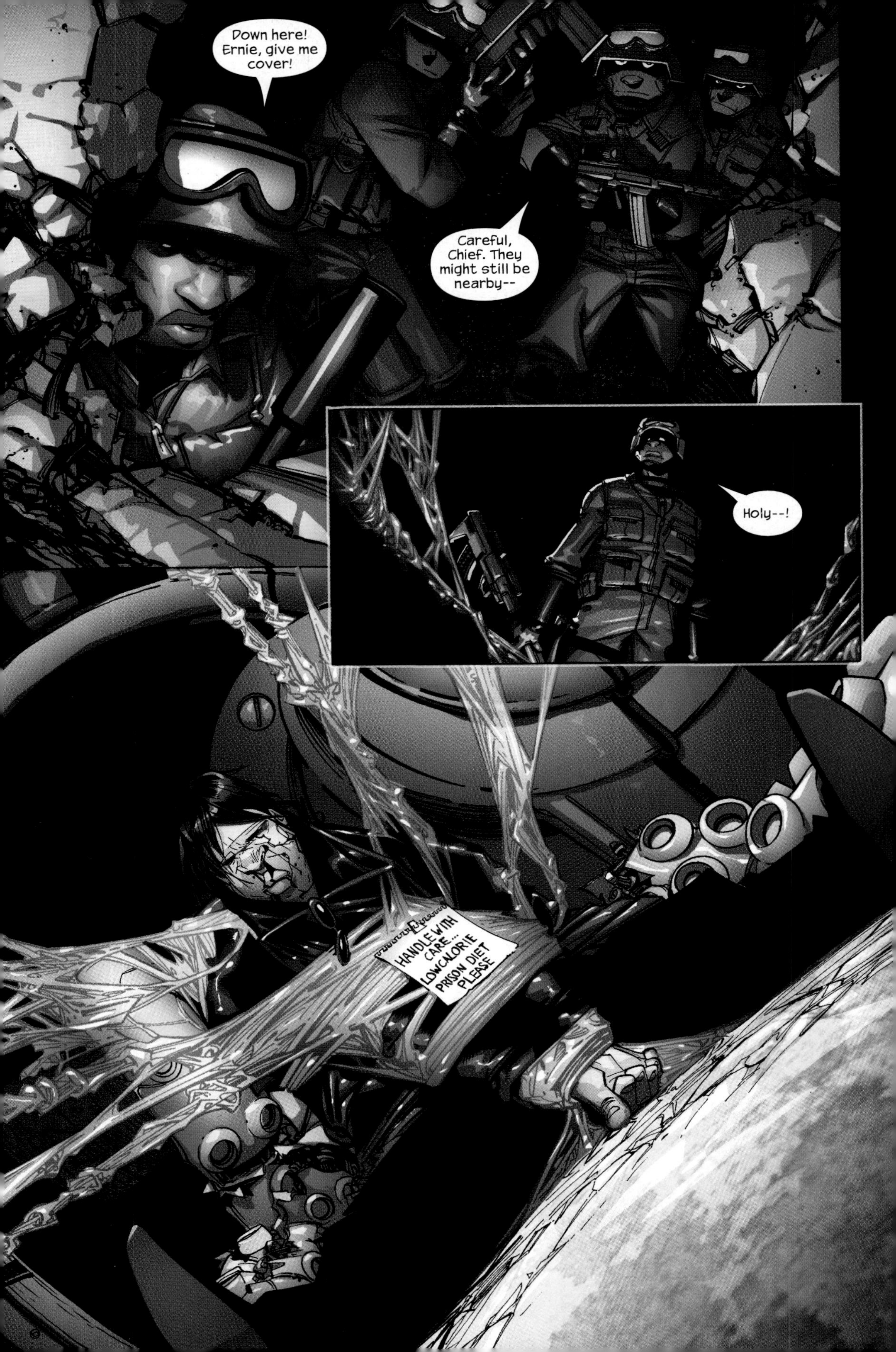
Down here! Ernie, give me cover!
Careful, Chief. They might still be nearby--
Holy--!
HANDLE WITH CARE... LOWCALORIE PRISON DIET PLEASE

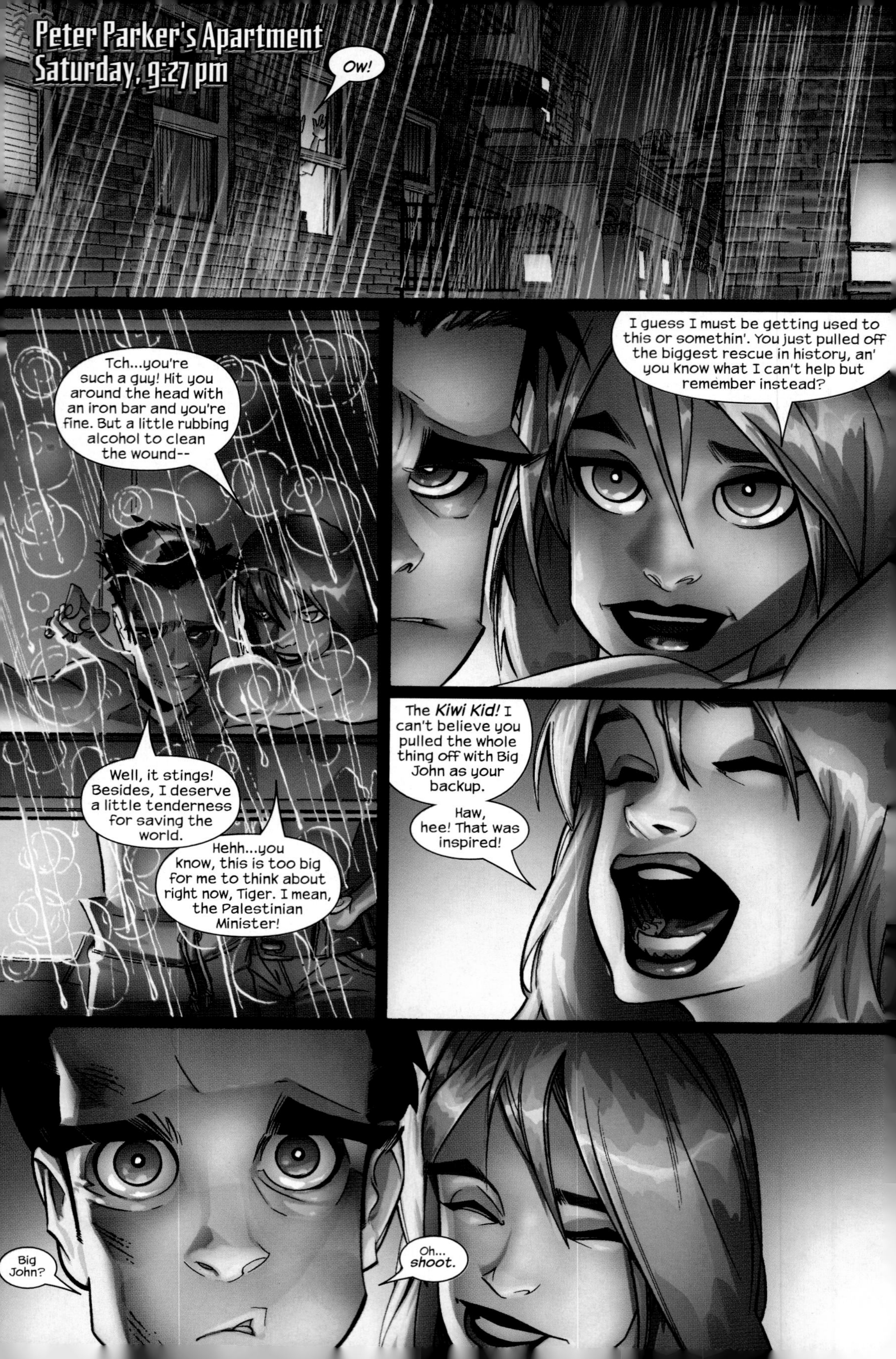
Peter Parker's Apartment
Saturday, 9:27 pm
Ow!
Tch...you're such a guy! Hit you around the head with an iron bar and you're fine. But a little rubbing alcohol to clean the wound--
Well, it stings! Besides, I deserve a little tenderness for saving the world.
Hehh...you know, this is too big for me to think about right now, Tiger. I mean, the Palestinian Minister!
I guess I must be getting used to this or somethin'. You just pulled off the biggest rescue in history, an' you know what I can't help but remember instead?
The *Kiwi Kid!* I can't believe you pulled the whole thing off with Big John as your backup.
Haw, hee! That was inspired!
Big John?
Oh... **shoot.**

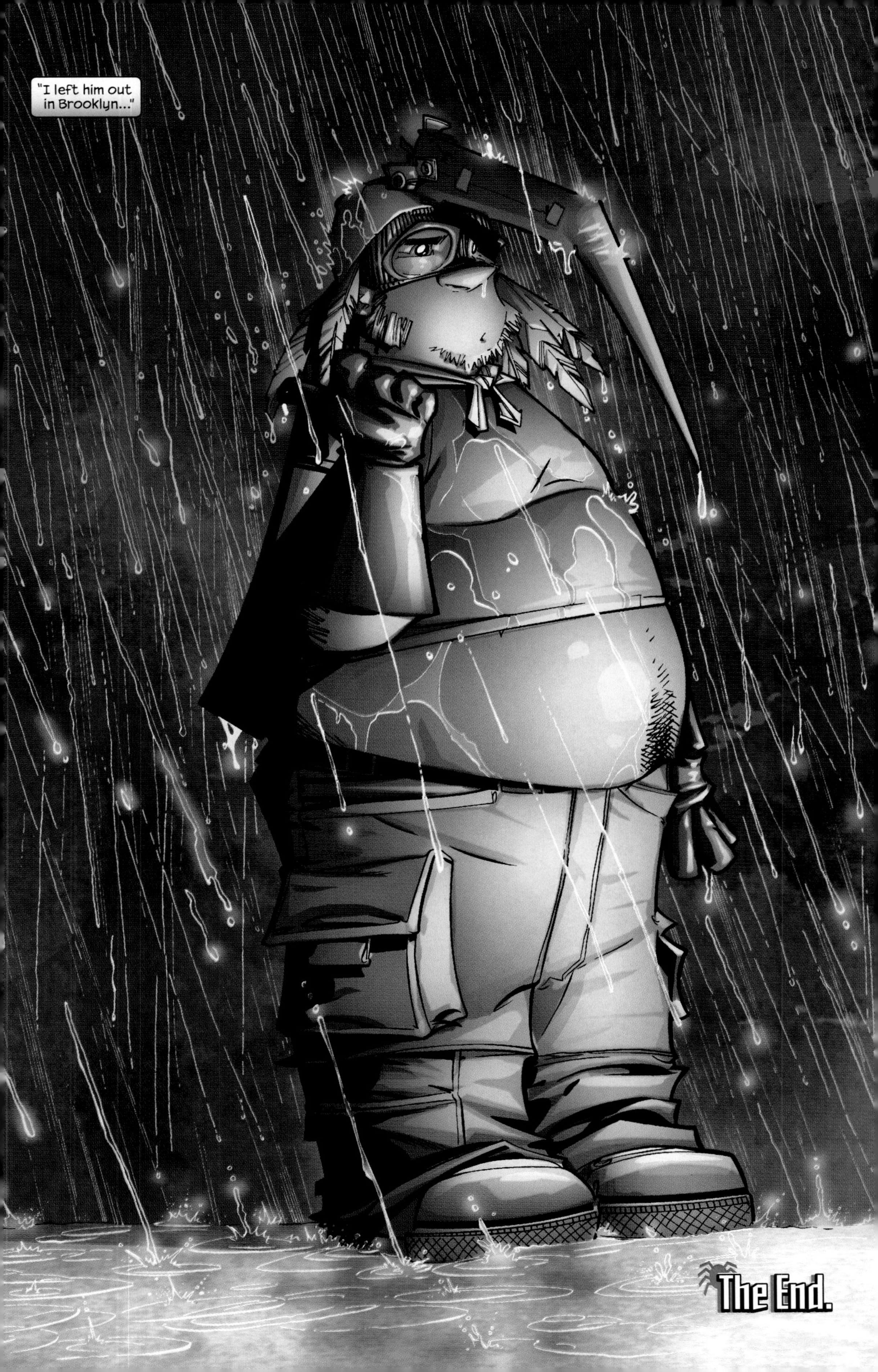
"I left him out
in Brooklyn..."
The End.

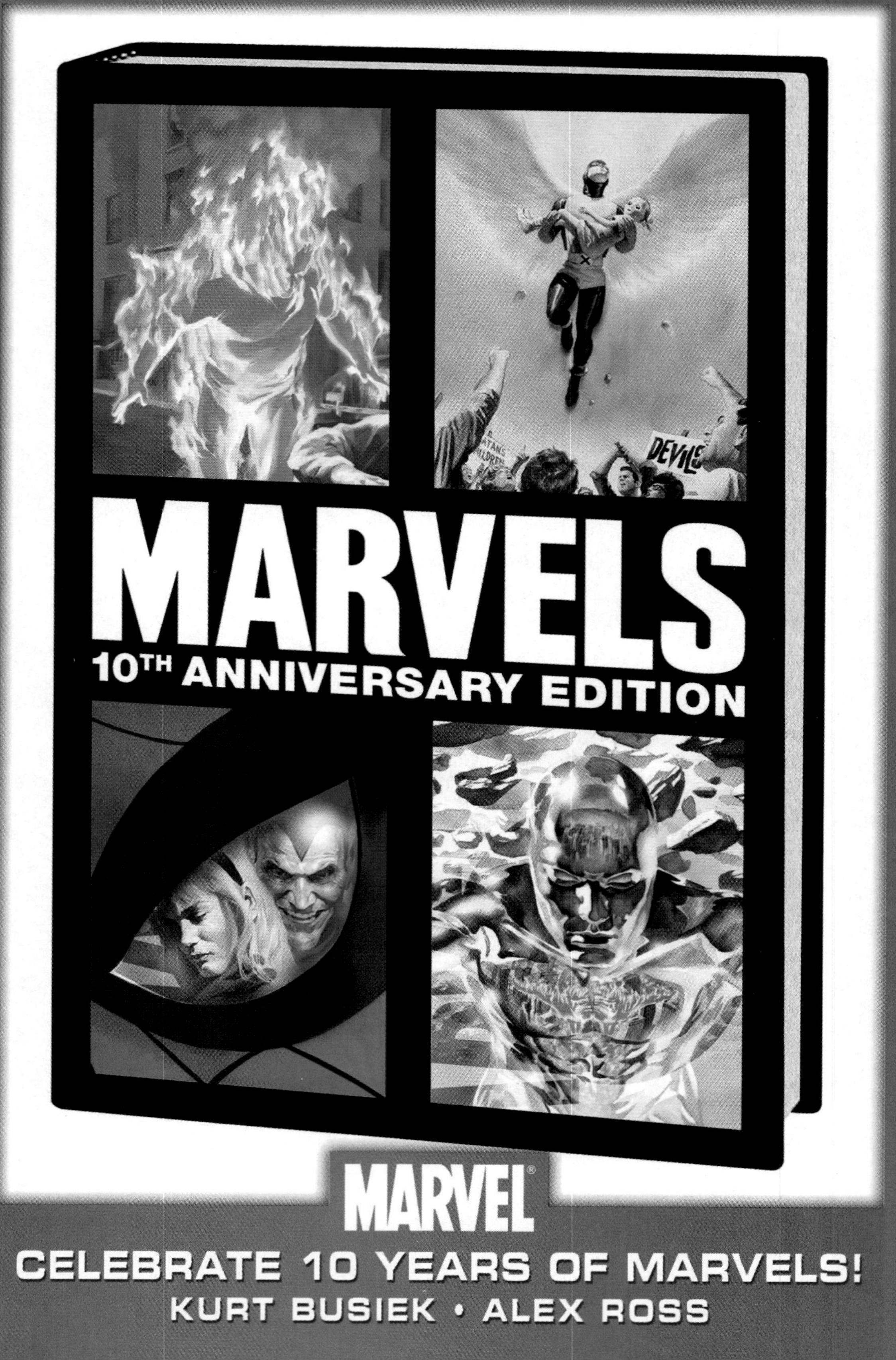
MARVELS
10TH ANNIVERSARY EDITION
MARVEL
CELEBRATE 10 YEARS OF MARVELS!
KURT BUSIEK • ALEX ROSS

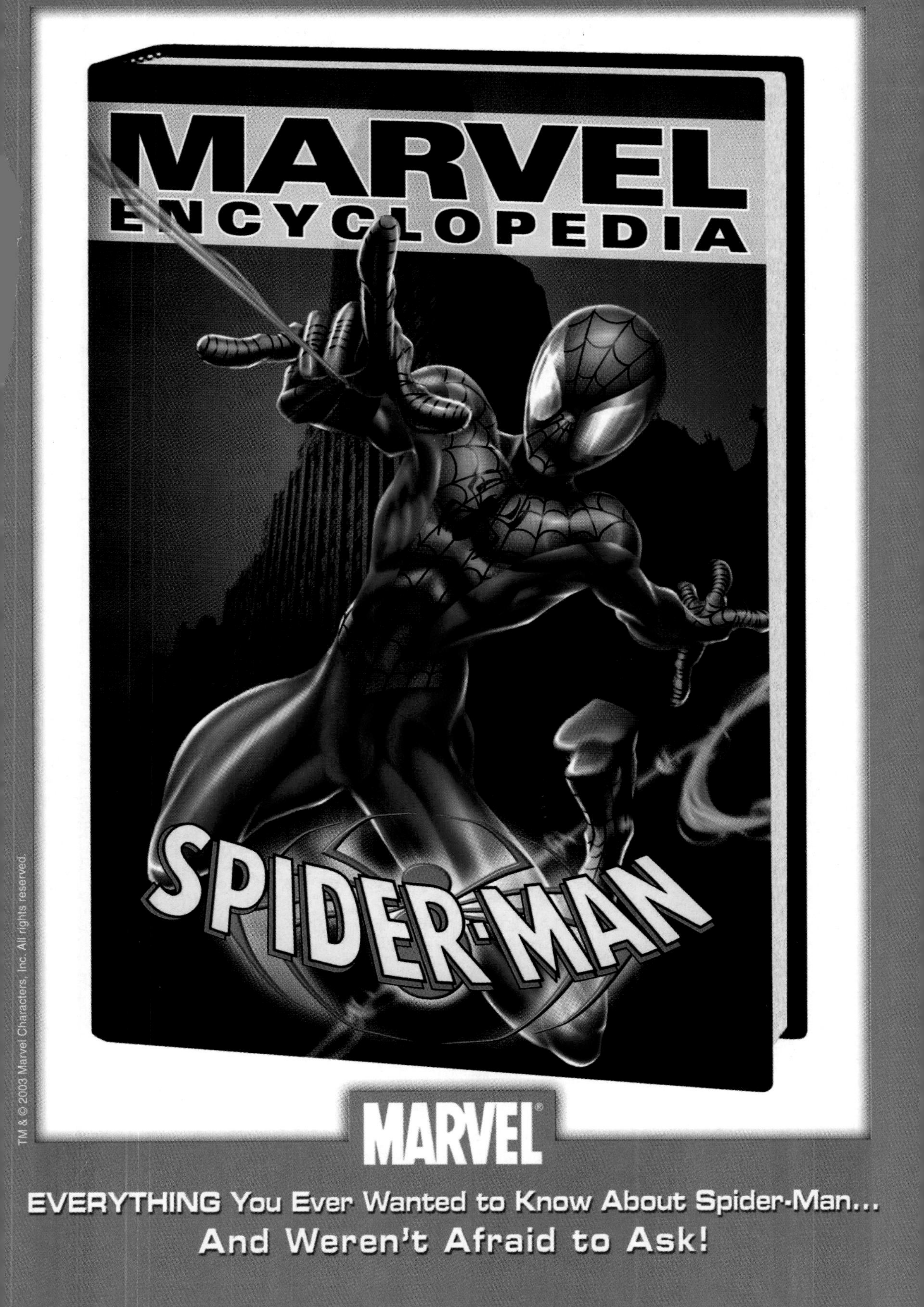
MARVEL ENCYCLOPEDIA
SPIDER-MAN
MARVEL
EVERYTHING You Ever Wanted to Know About Spider-Man...
And Weren't Afraid to Ask!

Mary Jane

A novel by Judith O'Brien

MARVEL®

Marvel's First Young Adult Prose Novel In Hardcover!

Written by Popular Romance Writer Judith O'Brien with Illustrations by Mike Mayhew